Teaching
Physical Education 5–11

Edited by Richard Bailey and Tony Macfadyen

continuum
LONDON • NEW YORK

Continuum

The Tower Building	80 Maiden Lane
11 York Road	Suite 704
London SE1 7NX	New York, NY 10038

Reprinted 2001, 2003, 2004, 2005, 2006

British Library Cataloguing-in-Publication Data
A catalogue record for this book is available from the British Library

ISBN 0–8264–4842–9

Typeset by Kenneth Burnley, Wirral, Cheshire
Printed on acid-free paper in Great Britain by
Antony Rowe Ltd, Chippenham, Wiltshire

Children, Teachers and Learning Series
General Editor: Cedric Cullingford

TEACHING PHYSICAL EDUCATION 5–11

Also available:

Peter Arnold: *Sport, Ethics and Education*

Asher Cashdan and Lynn Overall (eds): *Teaching in Primary Schools*

Nicholas Gair: *Outdoor Education*

Leo Hendry, Janet Shucksmith and Kate Philip: *Educating for Health: School and Community Approaches with Adolescents*

Berry Mayall: *Negotiating Health*

Contents

Part II   Content of Primary Physical Education

Author Information

EDITORS

Dr Richard Bailey is Lecturer in Physical Education and Child Development in the School of Education, University of Reading. His teaching and research focus upon child development, special needs and philosophy relating to physical education and exercise science. He has taught at primary and secondary schools, and was most recently a Senior Lecturer at Canterbury Christ Church University College.

Tony Macfadyen is Lecturer in Physical Education and Leadership in Sport at the School of Education, University of Reading. His research interests focus upon physical activity promotion, giftedness and leadership in sport. He was previously Head of Physical Education at the Garden International School, Kuala Lumpur.

CONTRIBUTORS

Len Almond is a Senior Lecturer in the Department of Physical Education, Sport Science and Recreational Management at the University of Loughborough.

Ann Davies is Curriculum Adviser for Dance in Northamptonshire.

Dr Colin Hardy is a Senior Lecturer in the Department of Physical Education, Sport Science and Recreational Management at the University of Loughborough.

Dr Jo Harris is a Lecturer in the Department of Physical Education, Sport Science and Recreational Management at the University of Loughborough.

Brin Martin is General Adviser for Physical Education for West Sussex Advisory and Inspection Service.

Jean O'Keeffe studied Physical Education at the University of Reading, and is now teaching at Our Lady of Grace RC Primary School, London.

Mike Osborne is a Lecturer and PGCE Tutor in Physical Education and Sport at the University of Reading.

Dr Susan Piotrowski is Principal Lecturer in Education and Dean of Students at Canterbury Christ Church University College.

Tony Reynolds is County Inspector for Physical Education in Hampshire.

Christopher Robertson is a Lecturer in Special Educational Needs at the University of Birmingham.

Foreword

The books in this series stem from the conviction that all those who are concerned with education should have a deep interest in the nature of children's learning. Teaching and policy decisions ultimately depend on an understanding of individual personalities accumulated through experience, observation and research. Too often in recent years decisions on the management of education have had little to do with the realities of children's lives, and too often the interest shown in the performance of teachers, or in the content of the curriculum, has not been balanced by an interest in how children respond to either. The books in this series are based on the conviction that children are not fundamentally different from adults, and that we understand ourselves better by our insight into the nature of children.

The books are designed to appeal to *all* those who are interested in education and who take it as axiomatic that anyone concerned with human nature, culture or the future of civilization is interested in education – in the individual process of learning, as well as what can be done to help it. While each book draws on recent findings in research and is aware of the latest developments in policy, each is written in a style that is clear, readable and free from the jargon that has undermined much scholarly writing, especially in such a relatively new field of study.

Although the audience to be addressed includes all those concerned with education, the most important section of the audience is made up of professional teachers, the teachers who continue to learn and grow and who need both support and stimulation. Teachers are very busy people, whose energies are taken up in coping with difficult circumstances. They deserve material that is stimulating, useful and free of jargon and is in tune with the practical realities of classrooms.

Each book is based on the principle that the study of education is a discipline in its own right. There was a time when the study of the principles of learning and the individual's response to his or her environment was a collection of parts of other disciplines – history, philosophy, linguistics, sociology and psychology. That time is assumed to be over and the books address those who are interested in the study of children and how they respond to their environment.

Each book is written both to enlighten the readers and to offer practical help to develop their understanding. They therefore not only contain accounts of what we understand about children, but also illuminate these accounts by a series of examples, based on observation of practice. These examples are designed not as a series of rigid steps to be followed, but to show the realities on which the insights are based.

Most people, even educational researchers, agree that research on children's learning has been most disappointing, even when it has not been completely missing. Apart from the general lack of a 'scholarly' educational tradition, the inadequacies of such study come about because of the fear of approaching such a complex area as children's inner lives. Instead of answering curiosity with observation, much educational research has attempted to reduce the problem to simplistic solutions, by isolating a particular hypothesis and trying to improve it, or by trying to focus on what is easy and 'empirical'. These books try to clarify the real complexities of the problem, and are willing to be speculative.

The real disappointment with educational research, however, is that it is very rarely read or used. The people most at home with children are often unaware that helpful insights can be offered to them. The study of children and the understanding that comes from self-knowledge are too important to be left in obscurity. In the broad sense, real 'research' is carried out by all those engaged in the task of teaching or bringing up children.

All the books share a conviction that the inner worlds of children repay close attention, and that their subsequent behaviour and attitudes are strongly influenced by the early years. They also share the conviction that children's natures are not markedly different from those of adults, even if they are more honest about themselves. The process of learning is reviewed as the individual's close and idiosyncratic involvement in events, rather than the passive reception of, and processing of, information.

CEDRIC CULLINGFORD

Acknowledgements

As Editors, our first acknowledgement must be to the authors who have contributed to this book. We recognize the many pressures which educators face, and are grateful for their energy and enthusiasm in seeing their chapters through to the end.

We would like to express our warmest thanks to our families, friends and colleagues at the University of Reading for their support during the preparation of this book. We would like to thank the following people for taking the time to read and comment upon draft chapters: Joan Evans (University of Reading), Sarah Dean (Bohunt Community School, Hampshire), John Macfadyen (formerly University of Southampton) and Ian Stafford (University of Durham). We would like to give particular thanks to Russell Jago, researcher in physical education, for reading the manuscript and offering many valuable suggestions.

Preface

Teaching Physical Education 5–11 aims to assist the teacher in the successful delivery of physical education in the primary school. Drawing upon recent research and wide experience, it offers the reader guidance in a range of areas that relate to good practice in physical education teaching. As editors, we asked ourselves a simple question: What information, support and ideas would a teacher require in order to teach appropriately, effectively and safely? As such, Part I contains chapters considering key aspects of provision, such as planning, teaching methods, assessment and special educational needs. There are also chapters on areas that are not often included in general texts, but which we felt were of enormous importance, like the place of the subject within the wider curriculum, movement development and subject leadership. Part II contains chapters on different areas of the physical education curriculum, including games, gymnastics, dance, outdoor and adventurous activities, swimming, athletics and health-related exercise.

As teachers and teacher trainers, we are fully aware of the requirements of the National Curriculum in England and Wales. However, we are concerned that there can be a tendency to confuse *is* with *ought*. While many of us have to work with the National Curriculum, we should not assume that its content and processes always represent the best ways forward. Therefore, each author has been encouraged to challenge received wisdom and provide alternatives. We hope that the separate chapters each make some contribution to debates within physical education. Together, we would wish that they make up a book that helps, guides and stimulates the teacher.

A brief word on style. In order to avoid the use of the awkward s/he or he/she, we have opted to refer to the child as 'she' and the teacher as 'he'. We trust this act of convenience does not cause offence.

RICHARD BAILEY AND TONY MACFADYEN
University of Reading
September 1999

Part I

Good Practice in Primary Physical Education

Chapter 1

Physical Education and Primary Schools

LEN ALMOND

INTRODUCTION

For many people, physical education represents an amalgam of different activity areas such as gymnastics, games, dance, track and field athletics, outdoor and adventurous activities and swimming. There may well be cultural differences in some countries but in essence this list tends to represent a broad spectrum of what the content of physical education looks like. These activity areas represent a view of a certain sort of curriculum in which each activity area is seen as almost identical in significance. However, is gymnastics better than athletics or outdoor pursuits? Games represent an enormous field of activity which contains a substantial number of very influential activities. Is it equal to swimming? The basis of this framework is not obvious but it probably represents a traditional view of physical education, a view which has hardly been challenged; it therefore becomes a part of received knowledge.

There is a sense in which we believe that because we have always taught gymnastics, it must be OK. I believe gymnastics can play an important part in many people's lives. I have chosen it simply because it serves a very distinctive purpose. Gymnastics should be chosen because its value has been recognized and it is part of a clearly chosen range of activities for young people.

My criticisms of the current physical education curriculum need to be balanced with a proposal about how we can reconstruct a physical education curriculum and meet my reservations. This represents my starting point for this chapter. I propose to re-create a vision of physical education for primary schools and to outline a rationale to inform a framework that guides practice. In many respects this is rather a tall order, and therefore I am proposing a heuristic that could stimulate debate and discussion about how best to inform the practice of teachers and generate a curriculum that really does make a difference.

WHY IS PHYSICAL EDUCATION IMPORTANT?

I do not want to disappoint those readers who would like to follow a detailed analysis or a philosophical statement on the value of physical education. There are a number of distinguished contemporary papers (Arnold, 1997; Carr, 1997; McNamee, 1998; Parry, 1998; Reid, 1997) that provide ample opportunities for the interested reader to peruse such detailed arguments for physical education. In this chapter I shall draw on their inspirations but I shall put forward a more sharply focused framework, a framework that goes beyond the impoverished and narrow vision of physical education as skills, fitness and enjoyment.

Physical education represents an umbrella term for a wide range of purposeful physical pursuits that can enrich lives and improve the quality of living. The purposeful activities of physical education provide the means by which we can initiate young people into the richness and potential of a wide range of cultural practices of significance. These human practices are of great significance because people all over the world prize them and spend a great deal of time and effort pursuing them due to the values they generate. As a result they have become a fundamental and important part of human heritage and cultural life. Such activities have the power to enrich and transform lives, provide the opportunity for the enhancement of human capacities and qualities and become absorbing interests which reward and fulfil. These activities generate a great deal of media attention with the result that they can enter the lives of many people, especially when international festivals of sporting excellence can so easily be made accessible. These purposeful physical activities represent a significant feature of our cultural wealth which contains rich traditions and exemplifies the very best of human endeavour.

If the very best of our culture is to be made accessible to all young people, we need to ensure that we provide the means for engagement in such cultural activities so that young people can come to understand the scope of human endeavour and learn to recognize their significance. It would be an impoverished curriculum if the purposeful physical activities of physical education in schools were not made accessible.

The cultural practices associated with physical education are dance and sport, which represent two quite unique and different forms. Dance is an 'art-form' which demands a very distinctive approach to physical activity and focuses upon the body's expressiveness together with its capacity to employ aesthetic qualities in the exploration and presentation of symbolic meanings, moods and emotions. As an artistic experience, dance has the capacity to stimulate imagination, sensitivity and the appreciation of movement. On the other hand, sport (e.g. a game of football) is a competitive activity in which a person strives to win. In striving to win, a competitor presents his/her opponent with difficult problems in order to maximize his or her own chances of winning. In the same way, one's opponent does exactly the same. When each person or team strives to win by creating different problems for his/her opponent(s) to solve, they are mutually striving to play a good game. It is this striving to play well that generates the satisfactions of the activity (it generates value for the individual) and provides the means for playing a good game. Thus dance and sport offer very different experiences and satisfactions.

Nevertheless, there are other forms of activity that are neither competitive nor expressive/artistic. There is a sense in which people need to seek out and face personal challenges where they can extend themselves, push back personal limits, overcome fears, barriers or difficult odds or test their mastery of some complex task. I am suggesting that many people like to face challenges at a personal level; they simply wish to extend their physical capacities and powers into new dimensions, not in competition with others. Of course, not everybody falls into this category, but it is a realm of human endeavour that attracts some people.

Finally, sport, dance and adventure pursuits can promote the corporate life of a school by stimulating morale and providing opportunities for teachers, pupils and ancillary staff to find mutual satisfaction in individual and team successes. When schools place a high value on these activities they can promote further participation beyond the school.

In the same way that purposeful physical activities have the capacity to enrich lives and enhance the quality of living, we need to recognize the importance of promoting active living. There is so much recent evidence (Armstrong and Welsman, 1997; HEA, 1998; US Department of Health and Human Services, 1996) to support the promotion of regular physical activity: exercise is simply good for your health. It has been recognized that most diseases (such as coronary heart disease, hypertension, obesity and osteoporosis) are a result of lifelong habits and processes, yet exercise can have a powerful impact for the good on these conditions. Nevertheless, there needs to be some caution here. In recognizing the value of physical activity to the health of adults, it is important to acknowledge that young people are the healthiest segment of society, relatively free from medical impairments and the fittest in terms of functional capacity. They do not see illness or disease in the same way that adults do, because they believe that adult-onset diseases are reversible, irrelevant to them and far too distant in the future. Thus it does not make sense to promote physical activity as a way of combating disease. We need a different model to that of disease prevention.

However, lifelong processes start in childhood, and if we are to make any changes in reversing the trends of lifestyle-related diseases we need to recognize the importance of promoting exercise habits in children and adolescents that can persist into adulthood. Such exercise habits need to become a commitment stimulated and reinforced by young people finding success and continued satisfaction in purposeful physical activities. In learning to love being active, young people will hopefully recognize the value of regular physical activity in their lifestyle and acquire a commitment to a process of active living. In this way, we may be able to persuade many young people that active living generates its own rewards here and now, and that such a commitment brings further benefits in the future.

It is important to recognize the limitations of current prescriptions for promoting health-enhancing physical activity and to ensure that the experience of physical activity in a school setting is positive and rewarding. This is the very essence of physical activity and its association with health. One reminder needs to be emphasized: the promotion of health-related exercises has led many primary schoolteachers to see them as warming up and cooling down together with some reference to exercise having an effect on the body. Unfortunately this minimalist approach has deterred teachers from recognizing that we tend to value that which we do well and enjoy; it is this that promotes active living and generates further participation.

In the above discussion the main focus has been on what Strike (quoted in Almond, 1997) called 'the goods of accomplishment', but he went on to propose that these activities are also the context for friendships and community. Even though Strike was not speaking about physical education, his point is very important. Physical education should not be merely concerned with its content – the goods of accomplishment – but also a neglected (forgotten or perhaps ignored) feature of learning is the context in which there are opportunities for interpersonal competences to be acquired and shaped. As a result of interactions with others, the context of teaching physical education can be used to promote important educational values, the 'goods of relationships'. These values are associated with social, moral and emotional dispositions. In the first instance, interpersonal competences are associated with two aspects: interactions *to* others and *with* others.

To others:

- respect others and their need for privacy;
- show others they are valued: reciprocity; resolving disputes;
- care about others: be considerate, show loyalty, trust and sensitivity to needs;
- conduct: the central feature of conduct is the need to promote fairness and tolerance. This entails helping pupils refrain from:
  - breaking rules deliberately;
  - seeking to gain unfair advantages;
  - exploiting situations for one's own selfish desire;
  - taking unacceptable actions such as intimidation, direct aggression, verbal abuse or disagreements with officials.

With others:

- learning with and from others;
- working productively with others, learning to co-operate, to share and to plan together;
- sense of belonging: affiliation and loyalty to a group or team.

All these competences are important learning outcomes with which physical education should be associated, because they can provide significant opportunities for getting to know oneself as a person through individual encounters with the 'goods of accomplishment', as well as 'goods' that can be generated in interaction with others – 'the goods of relationships'.

There is a further consideration that we need to account for. In one sense there are also intrapersonal competences which represent emotional reactions to situations in physical education. Thus pupils have to learn to cope with:

- frustration in their attempts in practising or rehearsing a dance;
- success, disappointment or losing in a competition;
- tension in a competition or presenting a performance;
- the pressure of preparing well or meeting expectations;
- fear in gymnastics or adventure activities, or in failure to reach a certain standard.

Just as teachers construct action plans to establish continuity, development and coherence across a whole key stage in terms of the 'goods of accomplishment', I would argue also that they need to plan in the same way and consider how they can create a suitable school structure to realize the 'goods of relationships'.

This makes the process of planning and mapping opportunities for young people to encounter the goods of accomplishment and also the goods of relationships, worthy of our best deliberations and the need for informed debate. It is important to recognize how the context of physical education is a powerful medium for promoting interpersonal competence. Without such careful planning and recognition of the value of interpersonal competences our teaching would be based on an impoverished curriculum.

At some stage one has to move beyond a statement of purposes and outline a framework that can guide practice and help teachers move towards more informed practice. In order to do this I shall propose that we identify two key phases in the primary school curriculum:

- Phase one: early years 5–7.
- Phase two: transition into the middle years 7–11.

TRANSLATING ASPIRATIONS INTO PRACTICE

The main focus during phase one is the promotion of play forms to generate movement capabilities. This needs to be explained more clearly. In 1993 Daryl Siedentop, speaking at the 36th ICHPER World Congress in Japan, made the point that physical activity is most meaningful and therefore much more likely to be valued when it is playful. He went on to propose that play is a fundamental form of human behaviour and also to make the further point that it is very different from adult play which is characterized by competence, ritual, a taste for imposed difficulties and organization; it is a disciplined form of play. The play of young people is very different.

This is my starting point because I believe that we have gradually eroded the opportunity for play within young people's lives. We have begun to regiment their lives and to organize their activities to fit into adult time-scales and the need to co-ordinate transport. A concern for road safety and the fear of attacks on children have compounded the problem. As a result we have removed from children's lives the opportunity for independence, exploration and relative freedom. Many teachers, parents and students report that young people do not appear to have a rich fund of practical games to play; they appear to have lost the art of physical play. Observations over many years would support this subjective impression but it is not an observation that can be supported in the research literature. Newspapers, radio and television programmes consistently report that young people are drawn to passive forms of play such as computers and game consoles, where it is more safe and young people can be monitored.

It is time to restore play forms that promote physical activity and enable young people to acquire competence in basic fundamental movement patterns and promote optimal physical development – the biological functioning components (the organs and systems of the body). Young people take delight in the opportunity to be active and respond to a whole range of physical challenges. Rowland (1991) speaks of this keenness to be active as a central drive mechanism that wanes with age. Therefore, we need to capitalize on this motivation to provide a wide experience of activity in a range of different environments – water, gymnasia, playgrounds, playing fields and other terrains – because they provide a rich source of possibilities. Young people can learn to manage, co-ordinate and control their bodies in purposeful physical activities so that they can acquire a range of motor competences and extend their physical capacities. In exploring and experimenting with different movement patterns they learn how to practise in order to improve and make progress, to refine their movements, to control and acquire mastery as they enlarge their experiences.

In this way, play forms become the foundation on which movement capability is built and the physical well-being of young people is promoted. It is important to point out that physical well-being entails a concern for aerobic capacity and stamina-building activities. Primary school physical education, especially in the early years, is often too heavily focused on gymnastic-style activities at the expense of stamina and aerobic capacity. The play forms should emphasize being playful in which there are opportunities to explore a whole range of activities, to face challenges like 'Can you do this or that?' or to be creative and make something of their own, as well as to practise and do something that is absorbing. The notion of challenges is crucial here because this is where teachers' skills are so vital; they need access to a whole range of challenges so that they can make them readily available and provide variety and developmental challenges that can capture a child's imagination, interest and attention.

The real challenge for teachers is to acquire the skills of creating environments and challenges that enable young people to develop their play. At the same time teachers need the skills to allow choice, the development of responsibility and independent action. It is this climate that is missing in young people's lives. At the same time teachers need the skill to enable young people to love being active so that they learn to value physical activity sufficiently to make decisions about their participation. Play forms can be promoted through games and expressive movement such as dance, two very distinct forms of movement.

The play of children is my starting point, but we need to educate and socialize in a developmentally appropriate format the basic play forms so that we can move our young people towards adult forms. This takes me on to my next phase which I see as a transitional context in which we use play as a tool. We need to look very differently at physical education because play forms are important, but we need to recognize the need for more disciplined forms of activity which have distinctive features. Play forms represent the roots for the development of disciplined forms of purposeful physical activity but both forms need to operate side by side during this new phase. Hence the difficulty for teachers.

The disciplined forms of purposeful physical activity that I propose are sport (competition) and dance (artistic expressive movement). I am using the expression 'disciplined forms' because they require learning a sense of dedication and a need to practise, striving to acquire complex skills and movement patterns, thorough preparation for competitions, festivals or performances before an audience or an expedition in an outdoor learning environment. All these capacities need sensitive handling in a developmentally appropriate, progressive programme, a programme that needs careful thought to promote continuity, coherence and consistency together with a basic common experience for all children. In addition, the link and transition between phases one and two can be enhanced by promoting and developing the notion of a challenge curriculum (non-competitive, purposeful physical activity). We also need to recognize the role that purposeful physical activity can play in providing opportunities that are recreative and relaxing, where there can be solitude and calmness and an opportunity to engage in an absorbing interest with no pressure.

By emphasizing only three components of a primary school curriculum for 8–11 year olds, namely,

- sport programme;
- artistic programme (dance);
- challenge programme,

I have made decisions about what to choose easier and allowed teachers the freedom to select activities which represent characteristics of the three components. Nevertheless, this apparent simplicity entails the need to develop a comprehensive and coherent repertoire of progressive practices. It is here that teachers will need considerable help and support. Current resources available to teachers represent a good starting point, but they need to be reinforced and built into a progressive package or tool kit that enables teachers to match their pedagogical skills of the classroom with informed content that is both progressive and developmental.

At the same time that we are concerned with developing the *content* which young people will experience, we need to build on *processes* from the early-years curriculum that accompany promoting play and to encourage dispositions such as sharing in the learning process, self-management skills, involvement in their own learning, learning from doing, and stimulating independent action.

Pedagogical skills represent a missing ingredient in transforming physical education. For too long we have emphasized content at the expense of how we present a range of tasks that young people will encounter. It is here that we need to highlight the key features of pedagogical principles. For me it is important to recognize the every-child principle as an important commitment for all teachers. In such a commitment, the teacher stresses that every child:

- is important;
- can learn;
- can achieve success and make progress;
- can achieve satisfaction;
- can acquire confidence;
- can gain self-respect;

and their practice needs to match this commitment. In acknowledging this commitment teachers also need to recognize that:

1. physical activity needs to be fun, challenging, exciting and purposeful (it has a point, it leads somewhere);
2. young people need to experience challenges with real mastery possibilities. They also need to work productively within a clear structure that is consistent, supportive and provides constant encouragement and justified praise;
3. purposeful physical activity needs to be personalized and accommodate differentiation principles. This means that provision has to be made for different:

   - starting points;
   - rates of progress;
   - routes;
   - outcomes;
   - motivations within a class;

   so that tasks can be matched with different capabilities, abilities, needs and interests;
4. pupils need to obtain positive and supportive feedback from both teachers and their peers;

5. relationships which are based on mutuality, respect, relatedness, receptivity and trust need to be promoted. This also involves learning to value others and treat them accordingly and, in sport and competitions, to respect others as worthy individuals and opponents.

However, a caring pedagogy that I have outlined needs a school reward structure together with motivation schemes (personal and social) and a recognition system (by the whole school, individual teachers, peers) that is transparent and supports the educational needs of all young people.

ISSUES AND CONCERNS

Earlier I identified two important and, I would argue, significant notions. One concerned the *content* of the curriculum while the other focused on the *context* of learning. This was followed by an emphasis on play which generated opportunities for learners to be independent, to be involved in their own learning, to share in the learning process and to learn from doing. These represent processes in which learners move from dependence to independence and acquire a sense of autonomy. At the same time I have stressed the idea that mastery should be a central feature of engagement in disciplined forms of purposeful physical activity. If these notions are to be embedded within the physical education curriculum there needs to be some sort of procedure which focuses teachers' attention on the content of the curriculum and ensures that these are taken into account.

In order to achieve this, the content of a curriculum needs to have key strands that run through the whole process of translating content into practice. These strands would represent essential features of the whole curriculum. I would identify four such strands:

- autonomy and independence;
- mastery (or intelligent performance);
- intrapersonal competences;
- interpersonal competences.

In this way teachers can plan for both content and context. Unless we develop such procedures we are doomed to see moral and social education as add-on distractions which hinder the real education of young people. In the same way, we need to address how citizenship can become a feature of physical education as a central strand that permeates the essence of our teaching and generates learning that will make a difference.

In my discussions on health-related exercise I mentioned Rowland's (1991) idea that there is a central drive mechanism which declines with age, with the result that many young people simply reduce their activity levels as they move towards adolescence. In this case teachers need to recognize that if exercise is important for health and well-being, it is essential that we present physical education as a form of enrichment and an exciting, challenging experience. Without this the chance to promote active living is diminished. Added to this we need to create an atmosphere that is conducive to promoting enjoyment and mastery.

Furthermore, teachers in primary schools must look towards their commitment to extending opportunities beyond the curriculum. There is insufficient time within existing curriculum timetables; therefore opportunities at playtime and after school provide the only real chance of providing a reasonably comprehensive programme.

Playgrounds can be redesigned to permit a wider range of physical activities and encourage more purposeful play. If the opportunity is made available and we can teach young people games and physical pastimes there will be far more activity during the day, especially during inclement weather.

If we are serious about increasing the activity patterns of young people we need to expand our current provision in extra-curricular activities. However, we need to be cautious about the extent to what we can achieve realistically. In a school of 200, a 50 per cent involvement would mean that twenty different children on each day of the week would have to turn up for one practice each week. However, one opportunity for young people to practise is hardly likely to enhance the skill level and achievement of young people. Nor is it likely to promote active living. If we are to increase participation rates and also raise achievement levels we need to examine closely what needs to be done and to recognize the enormity of such a commitment. The implications of this commitment are considerable and would require a great effort on the part of teachers.

We would need to consider what range of activities to provide and the number of sessions that can be realistically provided without overburdening some teachers. What is a reasonable commitment to extra-curricular activities for primary teachers? This question will remain unanswered until there is a recognition by headteachers that the curriculum and extra-curricular provision go hand in hand if we are to maximize the role of schools in developing opportunities for all young people to make progress and achieve levels of success that stimulate further participation. At present there is an unequal structure that favours some pupils and excludes many others.

SUMMARY

I have tried to propose that the key features of physical education are:

- learning to play;
- moving beyond play into disciplined forms of physical activity such as sport (competitive activities) and dance (artistic expressive activities);
- ensuring that non-competitive forms of physical activity are available as challenges.

At the same time that we translate these key features into curricular content, we need to recognize the role of the context in which physical activity is made accessible to young people. It is this context that provides opportunities for important learning such as interpersonal competences of a social nature as well as conduct in competitions.

Nevertheless, we may well plan a whole range of activities that we wish young people to encounter but, unless we recognize the importance of pedagogy and how we teach, all our endeavours are likely to be unproductive. Pedagogy is important, yet it is often the last thing that we consider.

Chapter 2

Planning and Preparation for Effective Teaching

RICHARD BAILEY

'Fail to prepare, and prepare to fail.'
(Attributed to Abraham Lincoln)

INTRODUCTION

Effective teaching can be a challenging business. Teaching is a complex activity requiring teachers to make a continuous series of decisions based upon the curriculum, the pupils and the match between the two. Effective planning is one way of supporting such teaching and, significantly, it is a method that lies in the hands of the teacher.

There are different sorts of plans for different purposes. Plans can help the teacher prepare for the coming year, for the coming term or half-term, or for the coming lesson. In all cases, planning is an essential ingredient in successful and rewarding teaching.

WHAT IS THE POINT OF PLANNING?

Teaching is a professional 'thinking' activity and what is actually done is largely dependent upon the teacher's thought processes that have gone before the lesson. (Mawer, 1995, p. 54)

Trainee or inexperienced teachers sometimes bemoan the time and effort spent constructing their plans, pointing out more experienced colleagues who seem to manage to deliver high-quality lessons without detailed plans. Indeed, it can be easy to forget the wealth of knowledge and skills that some teachers have at their disposal. Such knowledge is not limited to a familiarity with various activities, techniques and rules, but to a myriad of less obvious aspects: leading the children into the physical education area; changing between tasks; arranging groups; spotting potential problems *before* they arise, and so on. It is a mistake, though, to conclude that because some experienced colleagues do not produce detailed lesson plans they are not planning, nor that planning is secondary to actual teaching.

Research suggests that planning is one of the most significant factors affecting teacher effectiveness. Trainee teachers who plan their work in physical education (in comparison with those who do not) exhibit a number of important attributes associated with effective teaching, including:

- greater use of equipment and facilities;
- more directions;
- more careful and precise organization of lessons;
- clearer presentations;
- more specific feedback;
- greater variety and better progression of activities;
- better timing of lessons;
- greater ability to analyse pupils' needs;
- higher levels of activity and time 'on task' among pupils.

(Adapted from Mawer, 1995)

There are a number of important functions of planning that support effective teaching, some of which are discussed below.

Anne Williams (1996, p. 29) speaks of planning as 'articulation of thinking'. In other words, careful planning provides an opportunity for the teacher to think through the lesson, both in its entirety and its parts, before delivering it. Planning encourages the visualization of the lesson, its activities, its structure, and how it is to be delivered. Writing that plan down can give an even clearer idea of how the different elements relate to each other, and how well they address the set objective. This is of no small benefit if one considers the wealth of questions that lie implicitly within a plan, such as:

- How do I gain the children's attention and interest at the beginning?
- How do I best explain the theme?
- How are children to move from activity to activity safely and quickly?
- What teaching methods best suit the lesson objective?
- How do I organize pupils into groups for different tasks?
- How do I arrange the area, the equipment, the children?
- What vocabulary should I use?
- How do I calm down the children at the end of the lesson?

Physical education is a notoriously broad and wide-ranging subject. Not surprisingly, subject knowledge presents a major source of concern for novice teachers, even for specialists in the area (Mawer, 1995). Moreover, simply having a well-developed understanding of the divergent elements of the physical education curriculum is insufficient, as the effective teacher is one who can present the curriculum in a way that is meaningful to pupils. Lesson planning can serve as a valuable *aide-mémoire*, a summary of the key teaching points for a certain skill or the rules of a game. Once again, the act of preparing the plan will identify gaps in knowledge, and prompt reference to a textbook or guide. The information is then available to the teacher, should the need arise.

Planning can act as a warning. By offering an overview of the lesson ahead, it highlights necessary pre-lesson preparation of resources and possible sources of disturbance. By the nature of the job, teachers are constantly thinking on their feet. Planning allows them to think *before* the lesson, so that they can concentrate on other matters that arise *during* the lesson, such as responding to individual problems.

Finally, plans provide a useful record of the teaching and intended learning that has taken place. There are many times when it is important to have written evidence of work carried out, such as while a student teacher or during an inspection. As such, planning is a relatively simple, concrete means of showing that adequate care and attention have been taken in preparation of lessons. Less ominously, written plans provide valuable sources for future lesson ideas, as well as a basis from which later work can be developed.

THINKING ABOUT PLANNING

In planning, the teacher considers a number of related issues that determine the character of the lessons. One way of conceptualizing this is as a series of variables relating to the organization, presentation and content of the lesson (Figure 2.1). Each relates to a different aspect of the overall lesson, but they are inextricably linked together.

By making decisions about the different elements, both for the whole class and for individual children, the teacher begins to draw out a structure for his planning. Moreover, as will be seen below, a model of this sort provides a useful starting point for differentiating to meet the needs of individual pupils.

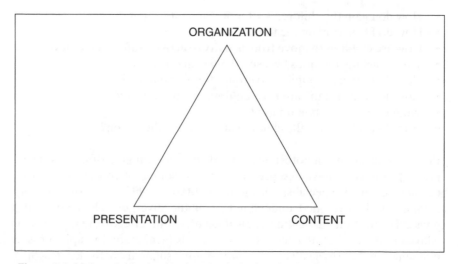

Figure 2.1: Main variables in planning physical education lessons

Organization refers to the social context of the teaching. Planning for organization ranges from relatively broad issues related to the character of pupil interaction – co-operative, competitive, individualistic – to more specific questions of the size of groups and the arrangement of pupils around the teaching area. As the teacher considers organizational variables, he might ask himself:

- Should the children be grouped or work individually?
- How shall I group the children?
- How shall we use the physical education area?
- How much pupil interaction is relevant?
- What are the different roles that pupils need to take?
- What is the appropriate behaviour and conduct for these activities?

Content refers to the identification of knowledge, understanding, attitudes and skills that the teacher aims to develop. In many cases, some of these questions will have been answered for the teacher some way in advance of planning, such as in the National Curriculum. None the less, this does not remove the teacher's role in determining the aspects of the curriculum to be focused upon and the way in which this is to take place. In planning for content, the teacher is answering a series of fundamental questions:

- What do I want to achieve by the end of the lesson/scheme of work?
- What activities will facilitate success of these objectives?
- What level of complexity will be required to meet the pupils' needs?
- How do I progress from one objective to the next?
- How quickly should pupils progress through the activities?

Presentation refers to the way in which the curriculum is taught to the pupils. Of course, the teacher needs to give careful thought to the best ways of presenting the relevant information to the pupils. He also has to consider the ways the pupils will be expected to show understanding or skills, and the most appropriate equipment for the activities. Typical examples of issues might include:

- What teaching strategies and styles are most appropriate for these objectives and activities?
- How will I expect the children to respond, or give evidence that they have understood the concepts or acquired the skills?
- What equipment is most appropriate to support this activity?
- How shall I organize my time during the lesson?
- Will I require other adults to help?
- Who will demonstrate the skills?

PLANNING THE LESSON

Kyriacou (1991) states that there are four major elements involved in lesson planning:

- deciding educational objectives;
- selecting and scripting the lesson;
- preparing the props to be used;
- deciding how to monitor and assess pupils' progress (discussed in Chapter 5).

Deciding educational objectives

The objectives of a lesson highlight the knowledge, understanding, skills or attitudes the teacher expects the pupils to acquire or develop during the lesson. Generally speaking, objectives should refer to the learning or behaviour of pupils, rather than that of the teacher. They should also be *reasonable*: in order to gain a clear idea of pupils' progress, objectives need to indicate something which the teacher expects the pupils to have achieved by the end of the lesson. Therefore, the teacher needs to break up the targets of a larger scheme of work into manageable elements. For example, a unit might have as its main objective the development of pupils' rugby skills. This is far too vague and ill-defined for a lesson objective. Depending upon the age and previous experience of the pupils, lesson objectives might refer to pupils' understanding of the backwards pass rule, the improvement of pupils' use of space in attack and defence, and the ability to perform simple touch tackles.

Selecting and scripting the lesson

Although physical education lessons necessarily involve physical activity, activity itself is not enough. Simply keeping pupils occupied with amusing games fails to fulfil the educative role of the subject, which demands that children *learn* something. The selection of the most appropriate activities to support such learning can be a complex task, and requires the teacher to focus upon the overall objectives and how a particular lesson can contribute to them. A central aspect of this process is breaking up a larger theme into distinct parts, and designing a progression through them so that they make coherent and intellectual sense to the pupils and support learning (Kyriacou, 1991). Physical educators can sometimes be quite poor at retaining coherence in activities, and too often children practise dry, meaningless drills which bear little or no resemblance to the theme of which they are supposed to be a part.

In planning the activities in a lesson, the teacher attempts to address the needs of the group being taught. Therefore, an awareness of the background knowledge and abilities in the class is of utmost importance. Previous experience of the group will give the teacher some notion of the quantity and pace of activities necessary. At the same time, it is always a good idea to 'over-plan', in the sense of having sufficient additional activities planned in case the work is too easy or too difficult, or is completed quicker than expected. The balance of challenge and comfort is a difficult one to strike: planning that is too ambitious can lead to pupils becoming anxious or frustrated; planning that is too easy can result in boredom.

Preparing the props to be used

By its nature, physical education usually involves the use of a range of equipment, from dance music to swimming floats, rounders bats and balls to maps and compasses. It is essential that these resources are prepared and made available by the teacher before the lesson commences. Adequate preparation of equipment can make a great difference to levels of pupil activity and consequently learning (Hellison and Templin, 1991), and bad preparation can result in wasted time, misbehaviour and accidents.

The first stage of preparing for a lesson might involve the identification and selection of equipment needed. The teacher should aim to match the equipment to the needs of the pupils. How old are the pupils? Do any have special needs that necessitate adapted resources? What are the previous experiences of the pupils? He also needs to ensure that there is enough equipment for the class being taught: in most cases, small groups or individual work is the norm.

Placement of equipment is an important and under-acknowledged skill. The teacher who leaves all the balls in the storage cupboard and then asks all the pupils to 'get a ball each' is the teacher planning for disaster. This potential problem can be easily overcome by making equipment accessible to pupils, perhaps by placing it at a number of spots around the area.

It is common to find certain types of equipment, such as large gymnastic apparatus, set up by a caretaker or older pupils at the beginning of the day, and for all classes to use this equipment before it is put away at the end of the day. The problem with this approach is that it implies that equipment needs are the same for all pupils, which is clearly not the case: resources for 10 year olds can be quite inappropriate for 5 year olds. It also denies pupils the opportunity to acquire important skills in selecting and setting up equipment. With guidance and time, almost all primary-aged pupils can set out almost all physical education resources, even gymnastics apparatus.

THE STRUCTURE OF THE LESSON

There exists a 'standard' approach to lesson planning (Bott, 1997; Gallahue, 1993; Mawer, 1995) which offers a useful model:

1 Introduction

At the start of the lesson, the teacher needs to:

- gain the pupils' attention;
- introduce the theme of the day's lesson;
- possibly review related work from previous lessons;
- physically prepare the pupils for movement.

The warm-up phase of the lesson is of enormous importance, and should never be omitted. It should involve gentle aerobic activity that steadily raises the heart and breathing rate and warms the muscles and tendons. The easiest way to ensure that the appropriate muscles are prepared for action, and that the children are psychologically prepared for the content to follow, is to make the warm-up resemble the main theme.

2 Skill development

In this section of the lesson, pupils practise specific skills associated with an activity. In dance, for example, pupils might practise certain dance actions; in gymnastics, they might perform a number of basic actions.

3 Climax

During this section of the lesson, pupils have the opportunity to apply the skills they have been learning or developing. This could be a dance, utilizing the various skills that have been practised, or a gymnastics sequence on apparatus, or a game.

4 Conclusion

The conclusion phase of a lesson is often forgotten in physical education, and this can lead to a number of problems. During the final phase of the lesson, pupils are both cooled down and calmed down by performing gentle, rhythmic exercise. The calming-down element is particularly important in primary schools, since children can become very excited during physical education lessons and need to be 'brought back to earth'.

OTHER IMPORTANT FEATURES OF LESSON PLANNING

Teaching points

As well as a description of the different activities that pupils will be carrying out, lesson plans need to include explicit teaching points, which highlight important details related to the way activities are presented and the way in which they are carried out.

- What are the key points of a new skill?
- What qualities of movement or technical details will the teacher be looking for?
- Are there any particular safety issues that need to be observed during an activity?
- Are there specific words or concepts that need to be introduced?

Questions of this sort help the teacher to ensure that the lesson promotes safe and worthwhile learning, rather than just activity.

Transitions

It is in the periods of transition between one activity and another that many problems of misbehaviour or safety occur. An instruction to 'get a ball' or 'get into groups of three' might be perfectly simple for adults, but can lead to chaos with 5 year olds. At least in the early stages of teaching, these organizational issues need to be carefully planned. Therefore, lesson plans ought to include some guidance on grouping pupils for a coming task and preparing resources.

Monitoring and assessment

In order to determine whether the lesson has been effective in facilitating pupils' learning, it is vital that the teacher monitors and assesses their performance and progress. Rather than being merely responsive to feedback, it is necessary for the teacher 'to be active, and to probe, question, check whether the progress and attainment intended are occurring' (Kyriacou, 1991, p. 25). There are many opportunities to assess pupils in physical education lessons. Of course, the teacher can observe and note pupils' reactions as they move through the lesson. However, if used alone, observation can be of limited value. Pupils can be highly skilled at concealing difficulties (Pye, 1988), and further strategies are necessary to probe their understanding or performance. Transition phases can be used for questioning. Moreover, physical education incorporates numerous opportunities for pupils to demonstrate their understanding, although this needs to be planned in a sensitive way to avoid placing the individual under undue pressure.

An example lesson plan is offered in Figure 2.2. Alternative models can be found in Gallahue (1993); Mawer (1995); PEA (1995); Read and Edwards (1992); and elsewhere in this book.

Creating context

Bott (1997, p. 30) describes the skill development phase as the most important part of the lesson, and Gallahue (1993, p. 198) states that 'only after the skill has been reasonably mastered should it be incorporated into game-like activities'. However, this is ignoring the great amount of skill development that occurs implicitly as a result of a well-chosen game or activity. This is especially

Lesson plan

Activity: Class:

Lesson objectives: Lesson preparation:

Previous experience/
outstanding issues:

Phase/timing	Activities (inc. differentiation)	Teaching/ safety points	Assessment
Preparation – organization and resource preparation			
Warm-up and introduction			
Transition – organization and resource preparation			
Skill development (Activity 1)			
Transition – organization and resource preparation			
Skill development (Activity 2)			
Transition – organization and resource preparation			
Climax			
Transition – organization and resource preparation			
Cool-down and conclusion			
Returning equipment			

Figure 2.2: An example template for a lesson plan

the case during the primary years, in which young children sometimes have difficulty identifying the context or meaning of a particular skill. For this reason, there may be times when the 'skill development' part of a lesson needs to be placed in context. For example, it would be ridiculous to work on the details of a competent swimmer's strokes before creating the context of that detail (by letting the child swim). In games also, specific skills only make sense in relation to the game of which they are a part. Children need to understand the game as a whole in order to appreciate how the different skill elements fit together. In this approach, the teacher's role is one of intervention, offering help with specific problems or extending a child's repertoire of skills. For this reason, an alternative model of planning some activities may be more appropriate:

- warm-up;
- game activity;
- skill development;
- game activity;
- conclusion.

Multi-activity approaches

Although it is less fashionable than it once was, multi-activity teaching has been common in primary school classrooms for years. Benn and Benn (1992) proposed a useful application of this approach to gymnastics. In essence, the structure of their lessons is very similar to the standard model, with the exception of the third phase, in which children rotate around five activity stations, each of which stimulates a basic gymnastics action (balancing, jumping, rolling, taking weight on hands and hanging/swinging/climbing). The advantages of this approach to planning and organization include greater variety during a single lesson, ongoing development of movement skills and well-balanced physical demands upon children's bodies. Although Benn and Benn focus their attention upon gymnastics, there is no reason why a similar model could not be applied to any other area of physical education, such as athletics, in which children could rotate around a circus of running, jumping and throwing activities in every lesson.

PLANNING UNITS OF WORK

In many ways, creating units of work is the most important phase of planning (Clark and Yinger, 1987). If the teacher is able to think through the overall objectives of the unit, the progression of activities and the necessary preparation, lesson planning becomes a relatively simple process of adding a level of greater detail and guidance on teaching approaches. Consider one approach to unit planning, which is adapted from early guidance for the English and Welsh National Curriculum (NCC, 1992) (see Figure 2.3).

Theme						
Age of pupils			Unit			
			Objectives			
Prior knowledge/experience			Time (no. of lessons)			
Lesson structure	Lesson 1	Lesson 2	Lesson 3	Lesson 4	Lesson 5	Lesson 6
Introduction						
Development						
Conclusion						
Resources needed						
Statutory requirements			Assessment criteria			

Figure 2.3: An example template for a unit of work

The virtue of viewing planning in terms of units rather than discrete lessons is that the emphasis is always upon an overall picture of the whole and the progression of skills and understanding within it, rather than one-off activities. Of vital importance in this process is an awareness of pupils' previous experience or knowledge of a particular area; and if the teacher is unable to ascertain information of this sort, he will need to consider simple assessment procedures.

In order to develop pupils' understanding, units usually focus upon a specific aspect of the physical education curriculum. Depending upon the age and experience of the pupils, units of work can take as their focus skills, activities or themes. Of course, this distinction is rather simplistic, as there is a great deal of overlap. None the less, it offers a convenient way of conceptualizing themes for units. Sample unit titles based upon each of these approaches are offered below:

Skills	Athletics	Running, jumping, throwing
	Games	Sending and receiving, controlling a ball using a stick
	Gymnastics	Supporting weight on hands, balancing on body parts
	Swimming	Stroke development, life-saving
Activities	Games	Mini-soccer, striking/fielding games
	Dance	Folk dance, jazz dance
	Outdoor activities	Climbing, hill walking, canoeing
Themes	Games	Attack and defence, tactics
	Gymnastics	Symmetry/asymmetry, partner work, shape
	Dance	The body, poems and stories

There are many ways of organizing units of work (see e.g. Bunker, 1994; Mawer, 1995; PEA, 1995). The most important features of a unit are that they give the teacher a clear overview of the lessons and objectives ahead (for the term or half-term), and that they offer a coherent pattern of progression, from relatively simple to relatively complex activities and concepts.

PLANNING FOR PROGRESSION

It is relatively easy for teachers to build up over time a collection of enjoyable and worthwhile activities for their physical education lessons. It is more difficult to use these tasks to develop children's skills and understanding through a progressive scheme. Indeed, the National Curriculum Council (NCC, 1992) describes this aspect of planning as 'one of the biggest problems that faces teachers'. Progression is facilitated by medium-term planning (such as in units of work), in which it is possible to locate individual activities within a larger scheme and to trace the progression of associated skills.

Williams (1996, p. 41) states that progression can be seen in the difficulty of the tasks achieved, in the quality of the response and in the context in which it is reproduced. By conceiving of planning in terms of progression, the teacher is encouraged to emphasize the development and extension of children's understanding and skills, and thus the acquisition of substantial educational goals.

Progress in difficulty occurs when pupils are required to perform increasingly complex or challenging tasks. There are many different ways of making tasks more difficult, including:

- extending pupils' skills repertoire (introducing the headstand; distinguishing between various soccer passes);
- moving from single to combined actions (passing – passing and moving to space; roll – roll to balance – jump to roll to balance);
- reducing the time or space to perform an activity (restricting the playing area; planning for quick decision-making);
- offering few options (limiting the range of 'allowed' actions in a gymnastics sequence);
- developing more abstract or strategic ideas (discussing moods and feelings in dance; considering defensive patterns during games play).

Progress in quality can be seen as pupils exhibit increasingly more sophisticated or successful performance of acquired skills. This can take a number of forms, including:

- better clarity or articulation or shape in gymnastics or dance;
- improved co-ordination in ball skills;
- better poise, grace or fluency in movement;
- more refined strokes in swimming or short tennis;
- better timing or positioning of strikes in softball or cricket.

Progress in context refers to pupils' ability to integrate actions into increasingly complex situations, such as:

- working with a partner and then in larger groups;
- working co-operatively and helping peers;
- taking more initiative and responsibility in planning, performing and evaluating tasks;
- applying skills learned in one context to a related one;
- understanding when and when not to use specific skills.

CONCLUSION

This chapter has suggested a number of ideas for developing planning and preparation skills for physical education. Like teaching, planning needs vary from individual to individual. Some teachers plan in great detail while others produce plans that are relatively brief. Whatever the style, however, planning and preparation are essential features of effective teaching.

KEY POINTS

- Be clear about what understanding or skill development you want to achieve during the lesson or unit of work.
- Be thorough in preparation for lessons. Identify the resources necessary, and make sure they are available and accessible to pupils.
- Identify appropriate lines of progression from relatively simple to complex skills or concepts.
- Monitor and assess your pupils' work in physical education, and use this information to inform your planning: the better you know the pupils, the better you can plan for them.

Chapter 3

Promoting a Positive Learning Environment

ANDREW LAMBIRTH AND RICHARD BAILEY

'Those who can, do. Those who can't, teach. Those who can't teach,
teach Physical Education.'
(Woody Allen, quoted in Graham, 1992, p. 1)

INTRODUCTION

There is a great deal of evidence, as well as common sense, suggesting that the
social environment in which learning takes place is of great importance to the
character of that learning (cf. Kyriacou, 1986; Wragg, 1994). Teachers' styles of
communication, their expectations and their responses to events during
lessons can have a great effect upon pupil behaviour, motivation and, ultimately, learning. This is no less important in physical education than in any
other area of the curriculum. In fact, it might be argued that the need for the
establishment of a positive learning environment is of even greater relevance,
due to the specific issues associated with pupils working and moving closely
together in large groups, with a variety of equipment and at different speeds.
Judith Rink (1993, p. 127) has argued that

> Physical Education classes should be characterised by an environment
> that is conducive to learning. [PE areas] should be places where all
> students can have positive experiences. Teachers and students should
> enjoy being there.

In the past, not all pupils looked back on their physical education lessons as
positive experiences. For many, the memories held of physical education
teachers' control strategies were as excessively strict, with a will to dominate
and engender fear in the children. One consequence of such approaches may
be a reluctance to participate in physical activities after leaving school
(Mason, 1995), and the associated risks to health and fitness of such with-
drawal.

This chapter begins by considering strategies for developing and maintaining positive and purposeful environments in physical education classes; environments that promote learning, motivation, respect and achievement. It goes on to discuss different approaches that encourage maximum participation by all pupils. Finally, effective methods of maintaining discipline and order, which are fundamentally important in all physical education teaching, are also examined.

POSITIVE CLIMATES FOR LEARNING

Chris Kyriacou (1991, p. 60) has identified a successful classroom climate as being 'purposeful, task orientated, relaxed, warm, supportive and [with] a sense of order'. The teacher's role in creating this climate is a key factor. He must give the impression, through a 'businesslike' style of presentation, that time must not be wasted and that nothing should be allowed to interrupt the important learning that is to take place. The teacher needs to appear confident and in control of the lesson, as well as enthusiastic and energetic. This impression is given by presenting well-planned lessons with activities that are challenging but attainable for all (see Chapter 2 on planning). In addition, just as the pupils should be appropriately dressed for physical activity, so should the teacher. This is partly due to the occasional need to demonstrate, but more importantly, it puts across a strong message to the pupils about the teacher's valuation of the activity.

In addition to this purposefulness, the teacher needs to create a supportive and caring environment. It can be argued that this caring atmosphere is particularly important in physical education, where some children are likely to feel self-conscious when involved in challenging physical activity, due to the unusually public nature of much of the subject. Pye (1988, p. 2) has called this approach 'solicitous tenderness'. The teacher needs to be warm, reassuring, kind and tactful – showing all the children that he cares about the development of their learning – and wanting to see them succeed can convey this warmth. In their own minds, children will implicitly ask questions of the teacher: 'Can this teacher organize and manage a stimulating learning environment?' and 'Can this teacher smile with us and care about our learning?' (Kyriacou, 1991). A number of studies (Mortimore *et al.*, 1988; Rutter *et al.*, 1979) support this view of a need for a positive learning environment. Indeed, without it learning is unlikely to occur, particularly in those children who are already anxious about this subject. The positive expectations of children's achievements shown by the teacher will help to promote the vital combination of self-respect and self-esteem so important for all learning.

MANAGEMENT OF LEARNING

The key task facing you as a teacher is to elicit and sustain pupils' involvement in a learning experience throughout a lesson which will lead to the learning outcomes you intend. (Kyriacou, 1991 p. 49)

Effective management of learning will require the teacher to maximize children's involvement in the activities that he has set. This will involve a combination of behaviour management techniques (discussed later in this chapter), secure planning, clear routines, and what could be described as 'stagecraft strategies' – skills designed to keep the attention of the class focused on the teacher and the learning.

At the beginning of the lesson, just as an audience would expect to see the actors on stage when the curtain goes up, it goes without saying that teachers should be ready to greet the children when they arrive or should accompany the children to the space themselves. For the teacher, this helps to ensure that the children arrive in an orderly fashion. Once again, as on the stage, the children also need to know when the lesson begins, so they are aware that from that marked point onwards their attention is on the 'action' of the lesson.

Teachers, like performers, need to fill the space with their own presence – it makes sense for the teacher to stand where all the children can see him and feel this presence. A clear voice is needed and eye contact maintained when talking to pupils. The teacher has to be the one generating the most interest in the room and in the near surroundings at all times. Like an actor, the teacher's intonation of speech and manner must invoke a sense of curiosity and excitement (Kyriacou, 1991). Children must want to feel the interest and purposefulness of the session. As with all audiences, the outside world's worries, excitements and fears tends to impinge on all types of present activity, and this needs to be extinguished as much as possible by providing stimulating distraction.

ESTABLISHING ROUTINES

Routines are procedures for performing certain tasks or behaviours which reoccur regularly (Siedentop, 1991). Establishing routines will enable teachers to manage time most effectively during sessions and so maximize learning. In order to effectively establish these routines there must be consent from the children involved. Establishing and communicating a clear rationale for these routines can form this consent. This will be achieved through negotiation with the children for each specific routine that needs to be in place. For example, children will understand the need for clear procedures for the distribution and collection of equipment, or the need to organize space for practice. The children, too, will want a smooth, well-managed session that allows maximum participation.

Younger children will need practice and regular reinforcement of routines before they are effectively in place. Teachers cannot presume, when inheriting a class, that the children will automatically know the essential routines for physical education sessions. In the cases where they are familiar with routines, the new teacher may well want or need to modify them (Rink, 1993). Teachers may find it worthwhile to spend some time establishing the essential routines through regular practising and reinforcement of desired behaviours. Praising desired behaviours during routines helps this reinforcement.

There are a number of essential routines important for successful physical education lessons, and these relate to the following aspects of planning and delivery:

- changing time;
- entering the PE area;
- distributing equipment;
- signals;
- the end of the session.

Changing time

In primary schools, changing clothes will often take place in the classroom. The teacher will need to monitor the changing process. The changing area should be arranged so as to maximize space to undertake the task. Ten minutes should be the maximum time for younger children to change. For older children, changing should last from five to seven minutes. Children should not be permitted to fool around while changing is taking place; this can be both hazardous (socks can slip far easier than shoes or feet on the floor), and time-wasting. Routines for the collection of jewellery or watches should be established. Often a class monitor can be appointed to collect items and then give them to the teacher.

Entering the PE area

A routine should be established for children to file into the teaching space together with the teacher. Children will need to understand the need to wait quietly for their peers to change before heading off. When the children enter the area they can either sit in a designated location, such as lines marked in the PE area or a bench at the side of the hall, or simply sit in a space. Older children can be taught to begin their own warm-ups as they enter the area.

Distributing equipment

Ideally, there should be several access points to the equipment to avoid congestion or rushing for access. Children will need to know how the teacher wishes the equipment to be moved and positioned around the space. The safe and effective handling of equipment will need rigorous training and reinforcement to ensure safe and efficient distribution.

Signals

Children are always eager to start an activity and will often be keen to climb equipment before the instructions are finished being given. To avoid this, teachers can preface their instructions with something like 'When I ask you to start, you will ...' It is essential that children know the start signal and the stop signal. In large outside spaces the teacher may wish to use a whistle. In enclosed environments the voice command should be sufficient. Instead of using a signal to stop immediately, it is often safer to train children to listen for the signal which means that they must 'bring to a close what they are doing' or 'immediately start to come down from equipment'. Signals are context-specific, so children will need to be instructed clearly about which signal they must listen for and what each means before the activity commences.

The end of the session

Routines for closing the session and lining up will need to be established. Children are often reluctant to finish physical activity, so these procedures will need constant reinforcement:

- calming-down activity;
- low, slow voice;
- concluding comments.

DISCIPLINE AND CONTROL

The overly strict and domineering approach to physical education teaching has been challenged in recent years (Graham, 1992). Today, teachers are aware of the intrinsic link between generally effective teaching and good control and management strategies. Teachers who can produce well-planned and well-presented lessons are also those who maintain the most order and engender a positive working environment (Rink, 1993).

There are numerous books on the subject of behaviour management (see e.g. Robertson, 1989; Smith and Laslett, 1993). Teachers often find this element of teaching one of the most challenging, and it is true that 'all teaching has an implicit tension underlying the activities that if pupils do not engage freely in the activities set up by the teacher, they will be coerced to do so' (Kyriacou, 1991, p. 84). However, creating a positive learning environment, as discussed earlier in this chapter, is the best way to maintain children's interest and engagement. Children respond well to a teacher who is competent and can exercise managerial control. Competency is shown by a teacher's knowledge of the subject and the enthusiasm he has for it. The nature of the learning offered will reflect this understanding and general competence. Children can feel insulted by incompetent, seemingly poorly thought-out sessions and this in turn can create poor behaviour (*ibid.*).

RULES

Physical education will require many of the regular rules of the classroom. Children have to learn the meaning of rules in different circumstances. They will need to be given examples of appropriate and inappropriate behaviour within these environments.

For rules to operate successfully they need to be negotiated with the children. A clear rationale needs to be mediated for each rule. The establishment of rules over which children feel they have 'ownership' helps to encourage a democratic climate, ordered by firm reference to reason. A society construed as being 'just' by its members, even the society of the primary school class, is a strong and stable one. The rules become an agreed social contract, with an understanding that those who knowingly break them also break from reason. Children will suggest rules they feel to be appropriate in certain circumstances. These suggestions need to be respected and discussed. The teacher will often need to rephrase some of these suggestions to make them more positive. A list of 'Don't do' and 'No' rules can have a negative effect on learning climates. It is also important to consolidate some of the rules so as to avoid long lists. An example of this would be 'Always do as the teacher asks' which is all-encompassing, or 'Respect everyone in the class'. Graham (1992) has suggested that rules can be posted in certain visible areas, thus encouraging consistency and reinforcement.

One list of rules might be:

- We listen when others are talking;
- We respect everyone in the class;
- We take care of equipment;
- We try our best;
- We always do as the teacher asks.

PROACTIVE STRATEGIES TO PREVENT MISBEHAVIOUR

Despite efforts to create caring, purposeful environments, some children may still misbehave. Effective class managers are able to monitor behaviour around the teaching area to pre-empt poor behaviour.

There are numerous monitoring techniques available to the teacher in physical education, including the following.

Scanning the PE area

This involves a conscious effort on behalf of the teacher to look periodically around the PE area to ensure 'on-task' behaviour. In general, the teacher's position needs to be one that offers a view of the whole class. Therefore, movement around the outside of the PE area can be a useful approach. In some cases, the teacher can walk over to children who appear to be having difficulty staying on-task. In other circumstances, calling across the area can be effective in letting children know they are being observed. In either case, the goal is to maintain a positive and purposeful learning environment.

Circulating

The teacher moves around the outside of the class observing and helping out children who appear to be having difficulty.

Eye contact

When talking to the class, it is important to ensure eye contact with all the children. It can also be effective behaviour control to establish eye contact with a child who is demonstrating disruptive or potentially disruptive off-task behaviour.

Using questions

Targeting children with a question often helps to maintain individual children's engagement with the session.

Teacher's strategic movements

It can be very effective to move into certain spaces in the PE area to ensure that children are aware of the monitoring of their progress. This also involves no vocal disturbance to the lesson.

Support

Skilful use of the teacher's time to help children who are struggling with an activity can ensure appropriate behaviour. A frustrated child unable to complete an activity is potentially a poorly behaved child.

Making changes

Effective monitoring of the progress that children are making will help the teacher to decide if changes to the plan for the lesson need to be made. Children working on tasks that are too easy or finishing their work early can become bored and disruptive. Equally, children working too slowly to finish within the given time may feel frustrated and, again, potentially disruptive.

When more serious cases of poor behaviour are present the teacher may decide that there is a need to implement strategies which aim to modify this inappropriate behaviour. These strategies have their roots in behavioural psychology. A teacher's response to different kinds of behaviour is central to the kind of reinforcement that children receive as a result of these behaviours. Teachers reward appropriate behaviour in various ways and do not reward behaviour that is inappropriate. Reward may be in the form of a simple remark or praise from the teacher, or there may be a merit system in operation. Children seen to be behaving well will win merit.

CHOICE

When rules have been negotiated and understood, reinforcement of these rules is all-important. The reinforcement can be made quite simply through the use of praise. Children who enter the hall before the start of the lesson know, as one of their routines, to sit cross-legged quietly. Praising all those who are complying can positively reinforce this routine. Those who are not initially doing as expected will, in most cases, change their behaviour in order to be praised, too. Many student teachers have been amazed at the effectiveness of such a strategy. Thus instead of spotlighting inappropriate behaviour, the teacher simply praises the appropriate conduct. As well as understanding the means to win praise and reward, the children also need to be aware of the consequences of poor behaviour. In order to instil this understanding in children, teachers need to be clear about how and when sanctions are delivered. For some children, the teacher may need to have a clear routine of warnings, 'time-outs' and further consequences. The most effective systems are worked on a whole-school basis, but sometimes teachers may need to have routines and systems that suit their class.

Clear steps to sanction can be the most effective. An example of a stage-by-stage system is as follows:

1. If a child misbehaves, breaking an agreed rule, this should be pointed out to them. This is best accomplished privately between the child and the teacher. The child has been warned.
2. If the child continues to break the rule the child can be given a 'time-out'. A time-out means time out from the immediate situation. This should be seen as a time to reflect and consider the wrongdoing. A time-out area is often allocated in a quiet part of the PE area. It is not generally advisable to send misbehaving children outside the teaching area.
3. If the child continues to behave inappropriately another warning is given. The child knows that if 'time-out' needs to be taken again there will be further consequences. This may mean that the child is sent to the head-teacher or, most effectively, a letter is sent home in addition to a phone call to the child's parents. In many schools these measures do not have to be taken. However, if the children know that this will happen if they behave inappropriately, in most cases they will choose not to. After all, why would one want to misbehave if the consequences of following the rules and working hard are praise and positive reports being given to parents? From stage one of this system, children are asked to make a choice, and in most cases they go for the one that brings pleasure. It is essential, therefore, that appropriate measures are set up to reward hard work and good behaviour.

CONCLUSION

The promotion of a positive learning environment is of fundamental importance in the effective teaching of physical education. However, the different pressures under which teachers find themselves mean that this is never a simple process:

> Teachers are expected to be good classroom managers. Administrators often consider teachers who exert strong control to be their best teachers, while parents and the community expect students to be taught self-control. Likewise students expect teachers to exert control and establish a positive learning environment. (Cruickshank *et al.*, 1995, p. 393)

This chapter has suggested that there are strategies for creating and maintaining learning environments that are well managed, appropriately controlled, and which facilitate pupil autonomy.

KEY POINTS

- The creation and maintenance of a positive learning environment is a prerequisite of successful physical education teaching.
- This environment should be characterized by a sense of purpose, support and order.
- Routines and rules help teachers manage behaviour and time, and help pupils focus upon other aspects of the lesson.
- Discipline and control strategies should be aimed at pre-empting misbehaviour and distraction, and at making it easy for pupils to chose compliance with the teacher's expectations.

Chapter 4

The Effective Use of Teaching Styles

TONY MACFADYEN

INTRODUCTION

The use of appropriate teaching styles makes an important contribution to children's learning in physical education. Different teaching styles affect many aspects of the teaching process, including the lesson's 'climate', and the teacher's ability to meet individual needs. Furthermore, an array of teaching styles is required to ensure that teachers have a broad enough armoury of techniques with which to meet the incredibly wide spectrum of objectives in physical education, including pupils' psychomotor, cognitive and affective development.

This chapter begins by considering various definitions traditionally associated with this topic, and pays special attention to the spectrum of teaching styles proposed by Mosston and Ashworth (1986). At the centre of the discussion is a debate about the advantages and disadvantages of the direct, teacher-centred styles compared to their indirect, pupil-centred counterparts. The chapter considers why a variety of teaching styles is important in primary physical education and what other factors may influence a teacher's choice of instructional method. Finally, it outlines some general guidance on teaching styles for primary physical education.

SORTING OUT THE TERMINOLOGY

Teaching style, strategy, method and instructional format are terms that have been used almost interchangeably in the educational literature and have led to a variety of interpretations. A number of writers have attempted to clarify the situation. Galton *et al.* (1980, p. 5) identified the nature of teacher behaviour during *interaction* with pupils as encompassing a 'teaching strategy' within the broader 'teaching style', suggesting that the former was the teacher's 'attempts to translate aims into practice'. Strategies, they claim, are implemented during the lesson through teacher–pupil 'transactions', which they term 'teaching tactics'. Once a teacher consistently utilizes a set of teaching tactics this is considered to be their 'teaching style'. For Siedentop (1991, p. 228), a teaching style is typified by the instructional and managerial climate that exists during the lesson, and is most clearly observed in the teacher's interactions with pupils. A teacher may thus be described as a 'live wire', 'cool' or 'businesslike'. Siedentop goes on to identify a teacher's instructional format as 'the different ways teachers organise the delivery of instruction, and particularly, how the student role changes as a result of the changing format' (*ibid.*).

The British Association of Advisers and Lecturers in Physical Education (BAALPE, 1989, p. 9) proposes that a teaching style is 'the general pattern created by using a particular set of strategies' and more recently Whitehead (1997) has suggested that it is the combination of strategies most commonly used, together with the personal characteristics of an individual. A teaching strategy is therefore a particular technique selected by the teacher for some specific occasion in order to achieve a certain objective. This chapter concentrates on teaching styles, and the terms are used in the same context to mean *the format of delivery* that a teacher utilizes.

THE SPECTRUM OF TEACHING STYLES

Mosston and Ashworth (1986) have proposed a spectrum of teaching styles which they see not as techniques or approaches but as 'a framework of options in the relationships between teacher and learner' (Mosston, 1992, p. 56). The spectrum incorporates eleven landmark styles along a continuum and is based around the central importance of decision-making in the teaching process, which governs all the behaviours that follow. These include such fundamentals as how students are organized and how the topic is presented. Decisions are grouped into pre-impact, impact and post-impact categories, and include all the conceivable options that need to be made during the teacher–pupil interactions. At the two extremes of the continuum are a direct, teacher-led approach, juxtaposed with an open-ended, pupil-centred style where the teacher acts as facilitator (see Figure 4.1). 'The spectrum defines the available options or styles, their decision structures, the specific roles of the teacher and the learner ... and the objectives best reached by each style' (*ibid.*, p. 29).

The comprehensive nature of the spectrum permits a clear view of two central human capacities utilized in physical education:

- the capacity for production (of new knowledge, movements);
- the capacity for reproduction (of existing knowledge, e.g. replication of ideas, movements,techniques).

This is one of the key aspects relating to the use of teaching styles: matching the appropriate style to the intended learning outcome(s) of the lesson. Each style has its own strengths and weaknesses that can render it more or less beneficial to pupil learning. As Mosston (1992, p. 28) has summarized: 'the

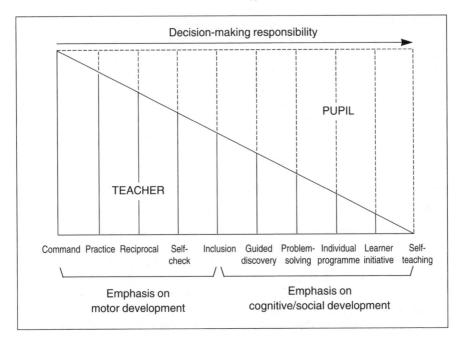

Figure 4.1: Styles of teaching physical education

fundamental issue in teaching is not which style is better or best, but rather which style is appropriate for reaching the objectives of a given episode. Every style has a place in the multiple realities of teaching and learning.'

It should be noted that in only exceptional circumstances would one style be adopted for the whole lesson. Furthermore, the two capacities mentioned above should be seen as complementary rather than mutually exclusive. After a pupil has discovered how to apply spin to a forehand tennis shot (*convergent discovery*) she will need to cement learning through repetition (*practice*).

THE LIMITED USE OF TEACHING STYLES

Observation of primary physical education lessons over recent years suggests an over-reliance on direct teaching styles (Severs, 1997). Harrison and Warburton (1998) report that government inspections for Wales indicate pupils' lack of opportunities to invent games and plan strategies, as well as receiving insufficient challenges for pupils to devise complex movement sequences in gymnastics. The same report suggests that teachers were paying insufficient attention to the appropriateness of teaching methods and that perhaps, in consequence, pupils lacked the opportunity to work independently.

Different reasons may explain this problem; one may be primary school teachers' concerns for safety. A second could be that most programmes begin with the teacher's preferences and undervalue or even neglect children's learning and development (Lawson, 1998). Third, as pupils' misbehaviour is of strong concern to teachers (Pieron, 1998), command-style tactics may be employed to keep a tight rein. Finally, the planning of indirect methods of teaching, combined with the production of supporting visual aids, can be seen as too time-consuming for over-pressed teachers who, quite understandably, decide a didactic approach will suffice where physical education is seen as less valuable. Research by Denton and Postlethwaite (1985) has highlighted the need for pupils to meet open methods much earlier in their school lives, and pupils' desire for greater choice in their work.

RESEARCH ON THE EFFECTIVENESS OF THE DIFFERENT TEACHING STYLES

Research on teaching styles is still somewhat patchy and equivocal, perhaps because of difficulty in measurement (Rink, 1993). However, Housner (1990) believes there is quite strong empirical support for the effectiveness of direct instruction. Moreover, Brady (1998) has found some evidence to suggest that when a task is practised repetitively, skill acquisition is enhanced. Research by Allison and Thorpe (1997) suggests that indirect teaching methods can also be effective in promoting skill learning, while Mawer (1995, p. 197) concludes that

> there appear to be considerable benefits in terms of both pupil learning gains and social development of teaching strategies that ... involve peer teaching or peer support ... provided the teaching programme is well structured and that pupils are trained for the role.

Anderson (1999) has suggested that strategic learners (those taught through a process-orientated style) are more likely to persist at a task despite failures, challenge themselves to use new skills and use their mistakes to alter subsequent attempts. Mosston (1992) believes there is enough evidence to attest to the value of each style in his teaching spectrum. The challenge, he believes, is how to use each style properly. However, Silverman (1991) suggests that when mastery of basic skills is the goal, direct instruction has the edge over indirect methods. However, if creativity or independence are goals, the situation is reversed.

THE STRENGTHS AND WEAKNESSES OF DIRECT STYLES

The use of direct teaching methods can be beneficial in a number of ways. A teacher who is new to a class may wish to establish his personality. Direct methods can be used to conduct a whole-class warm-up, to act as a motivational tool and set the tone for a lesson. The teacher's role in the teaching/learning process can be vital: in dance, for example, the teacher who leads off the lesson, even with a mediocre demonstration, can break down pupils' perceived barriers surrounding the activity. Furthermore, direct styles help keep the lesson 'tight' so the teacher can concentrate on his strengths, and not be exposed by a lack of experience.

The command style is useful in initiating pupils into purposeful activity, giving them an initial structured framework of 'security' from which the lesson can gain impetus. Many pupils look to the teacher for guidance, and in many cases the teacher's presence can provide the physical and mental support which pupils need when they are expected to attempt a skill perceived as dangerous (e.g. certain gymnastic activities). Moreover, it can be unwise for children to get into bad habits by practising the 'wrong way', particularly where safety is a concern. A command-style approach maximizes a teacher's ability to keep the lesson safe, since he has greater control over what goes on and where.

Many primary pupils may have insufficient understanding of their own ability to know at what level to attempt a task. The teacher's input will be necessary to cover any such misjudgements and ensure pupils work at an appropriate level. Even where a lesson is dominated by a different style, the teacher will always need to be 'at the ready' to intervene when required.

A teacher-centred approach is often the most efficient when a lot of information needs to be provided, and it can help teachers to effectively control large classes, whose unwieldy size can be discomforting. Equipment can be quickly placed in the right areas and pupils can be positioned in the appropriate spaces with a minimum of fuss, thus maximizing time on-task.

Many pupils are adept at copying what they see (Rink, 1993), so direct styles can often be effective ways of improving physical performance where pupils reproduce the desirable response to a skill, based on the teaching points set out by the teacher (e.g. a forward roll or a traditional dance). In these instances copying the most efficient style is highly profitable, since it saves time. As the teacher has overall responsibility for correcting faults, he can use his experience to ensure that pupils receive accurate feedback, a key component to skills learning (Pieron, 1998).

Some of the so-called direct teaching methods promote more than simply replication. In the *reciprocal style* the teacher specifies the task and the conditions under which it is to be performed, but pupils take over the implementation of instructions, which can help improve their communication, social and cognitive skills, as 'the act of playing the teacher role is an opportunity for the pupil to think through the task and how to approach it ... with greater understanding which facilitates practical learning' (Williams, 1993, p. 30).

Some critics argue that direct styles are restricting rather than liberating, and can impair the ability to retain and transfer information (Brady, 1998). Although pupils may be active for much of the time, it is not unreasonable to question how *purposeful* this physical 'education' is, since the explanation given and the task set are likely to be inappropriate for many pupils. 'The [teacher's] explanation ... is often too fast and scanty for some, too slow and laboured for the ablest and just right for the middle few' (Marjoram, 1988, p. 49).

Teacher-centred approaches can lead to the practising of skills in isolation (albeit technically correct) via drills which are often boring, appear remote and break down easily when children are required to use them in a game situation. Direct approaches can be very frustrating for pupils who have their own methods of working and in many ways inhibit cognitive development, since they 'fail to recognise the importance of involving students in the decision making process' (Hellison and Templin, 1991, p. 133). Weaknesses are clearly evident when learning outcomes are aimed at the creation of new ideas and movements, pupil analysis of performance, and personal and social development. In some instances, these approaches permit pupils little opportunity to plan and evaluate performance. If these aims are the teacher's focus, pupil-centred styles may have more to offer (Table 4.1 offers a summary of the features of direct and indirect teaching).

Table 4.1: Features of direct and indirect teaching

Direct teaching	*Indirect teaching*
Safety well controlled as teacher is central (militaristic)	Teacher on 'periphery'; appropriate for less dangerous activities
Pupils get to know information	Pupils get to know, and be able to use information
Limited differentiation	Excellent differentiation
Deliberate, calculated	Open, flexible
Pupil dependence	Pupil independence
Conditioned response	Self-regulation
Consumption	Construction
Product orientated	Process orientated
'Followership'	Leadership
Imitation	Imagination
Suits pupils who learn best by watching	Suits pupils who learn best by 'learning through doing'
Manipulation	Facilitation
Suitable for discrete, closed skills (e.g. volleyball serve)	Suitable for serial, open skills (e.g. finding space in invasion games)
Formal	Informal
Teacher is main resource	Greater use of material resources
Teacher as coach, leader	Teacher as mentor, 'enabler', co-investigator

THE STRENGTHS AND WEAKNESSES OF INDIRECT STYLES

Direct instruction does not suit all situations, and indirect styles therefore provide a valuable alternative to traditional methods of delivery. Teachers who are not very dynamic or lack confidence can compensate using other techniques provided by indirect teaching styles. Furthermore, open methods have strong principles underpinning them in their own right.

It has often been proposed that pupils only really understand if they are cognitively involved in learning a skill (Anderson, 1999). As Keighley (1993, p. 20) points out, 'physical activity does not guarantee mental activity and it is mental activity which produces learning'. (Some direct styles do make cognitive demands on pupils, but it is usually not the primary focus.) Thus Capel *et al.* (1997, p. 108) suggest that teachers 'should adopt teaching strategies that actively involve pupils in their own learning'. In this way learners may be able to transfer their understanding of principles that govern participation within one game to another setting (Schmidt, 1975). Anderson (1999, p. 45) has argued that pupils should be given 'the mental tools used to systematically manage the thought processes associated with . . . skill acquisition', which hints at a much wider brief than knowledge reproduction.

Indirect styles place emphasis on the cognitive domain, activate pupil involvement and draw on the strengths of children's imaginations in the learning process. This is particularly important in creative situations, such as developing a dance, or gymnastics sequences, because 'children will not innovate or travel unfamiliar paths when well trodden paths and established formulae are at hand' (Marjoram, 1988, p. 120). Indirect teaching methods tend to ask higher order questions (e.g. concerned with judgement, logic) that require open-ended, intellectually challenging responses. It is argued that execution of the skill is enhanced through exploration that provides a richness and wholeness to the learning experience.

By handing over responsibility, indirect teaching methods empower pupils and give them a sense of ownership of the lesson, so pupils feel that their ideas count. This can have considerable effects on their motivation. If pupils are to work independently, the teaching style adopted must give them this freedom: 'merely engaging in an experience that has the potential to make a positive contribution to affective or cognitive goals does not ensure that these goals are met. Learning experiences must be designed and developed for specific outcomes' (Rink, 1993, p. 7).

Generally, pupils will be motivated by tasks that are meaningful, interesting and enjoyable, but most of all they will be motivated by success. Pupil-centred methods provide excellent opportunities for differentiation (Hellison and Templin, 1991). They may take longer to set up than direct teaching methods, but, once established, they facilitate purposeful participation.

Critics of pupil-centred approaches might argue that it is too time-consuming; more time is spent thinking and discussing the activity than performing it. If open-ended styles are not carefully planned and controlled, lessons can easily 'drift', causing time to be wasted. If the work set is too broad, and virtually any pupil response will answer the question, standards of work can be low since pupils are insufficiently challenged (Williams, 1993). Teachers must also take care that pupils are mature enough to understand their own limitations when they are not successful.

VARIETY IS THE SPICE OF LIFE

Teaching physical education skilfully is a difficult and complex job. Practitioners need to be able to cope with pupils' different personalities, experiences, developmental stages and learning abilities as well as the very different nature of certain activities and the locations in which they must be taught. Thus, only the utilization of a variety of approaches would seem to suffice if pupils are to receive the breadth and depth of teaching they need and deserve.

A repertoire of teaching styles can be a potent weapon, helping to keep the class interested and enthusiastic. By mixing various styles the teacher can ring the changes, prevent an over-reliance on what he perceives as his most effective styles, and keep pupils from stagnating in a mental cul-de-sac. Research by Joyce and Weil (cited in Mawer, 1995, p. 144) suggests that pupils who are exposed to a 'dynamic disequilibrium' caused by exposure to new and different forms of teaching and learning will develop intellectually, and move towards a more advanced level of information processing.

It is to be noted that a teaching style is flexible only within the boundaries of what it is supposed to achieve (Mosston, 1992). As no one method covers all eventualities, 'the effective teacher will have the ability to switch, mix, and blend teaching strategies to suit his objectives and pupil responses' (Mawer, 1995, p. 228).

Teaching physical education can be unpredictable. A pupil will often raise an unanticipated issue that offers the lesson a new focus (e.g. introduction of new ideas in dance). The teacher who relies upon a single style may not be able to capitalize on such instances, whereas the teacher who can draw on different styles to suit the new situation is able to do so. It is sensible, therefore, for teachers to develop a range of strategies to increase their flexibility in teaching.

Primary physical education is the foundation for all that follows in this subject, and it seems logical to build a strong and broad base. This is surely more likely to be achieved using a variety of teaching styles that encourage different aspects of children's development rather than from a narrow platform that would be provided by the use of only one style. As there is no guarantee that pupils will initially understand a concept being taught, a repertoire of teaching styles allows the teacher to develop ideas from different perspectives, giving the pupil the chance to see problems in a fresh context.

Different children have their own ways of learning (some learn better from copying; others prefer to listen; others respond best to a combination of methods), so the teacher will need a variety of ways of 'connecting' with the pupils' preferred learning style to produce the best results. 'Appreciating that there are different types of learners can help us to understand that for some pupils, a framework on which to build is needed if they are to be creative . . . while for others, a very open approach will be successful' (Williams, 1993, p. 32).

OTHER CONSIDERATIONS

Teachers must consider a number of basic factors when deciding what style(s) to use and some of these are outlined below. The lesson must be safe, and the time, equipment and facilities available may influence what is possible. In a limited space the teacher may decide that closely directing pupils' movements is the only safe way he can teach, or in a short lesson, the practice style might best maximize the limited opportunity to learn.

There is little point in a teacher battling against antagonistic factors in pupils' learning for the sake of using a certain style, so it is important for the teacher to know his class. If a group of children seems to learn best using a certain approach, maximizing this potential is the sensible way to proceed. The teacher of physical education will need to consider wider issues too, such as the philosophy of the rest of the school and the way his colleagues teach.

Some activities by their very nature 'demand' to be taught in certain ways. In outdoor and adventurous activities the discovery of personal responses to different challenges necessitates a first-hand, problem-solving experience. The emphasis in dance upon emotion and aesthetic quality indicates the need for pupils to discover and express themselves. If the teaching style used does not permit the purpose of the activity to be expressed, it can blunt the activity.

The National Curriculum of Physical Education (DFE, 1995) states explicitly that pupils should be taught to plan, perform and evaluate. If teachers are to succeed in fulfilling these directives it is clear that the different learning outcomes promoted by various teaching styles will be required. The command/practice styles, for example, can enhance pupils' ability 'to . . . *practise* a variety of ways of sending . . . receiving and travelling with a ball', whereas the planning phase will be better served by guided discovery methods and evaluative skills, enhanced via self-check methods.

Pupils with special educational needs have been increasingly integrated into mainstream schools over recent years. This means that teachers now require an ever more flexible approach to cope with pupils' strengths and weaknesses, raising the importance of teaching styles that can modify the learning environment. 'In order to reach more students with diverse needs and different learning styles, and match the learner and the task goal, the teacher should use a variety of teaching styles' (Thompson, 1998, p. 6).

DEVELOPING TEACHING STYLES FOR PRIMARY SCHOOL PHYSICAL EDUCATION

It would be unwise to make any attempt to prescribe specific ways of using different teaching styles given the very different nature of primary school classes. It is for the thoughtful practitioner to decide when and where the use of a certain style will be effective. However, it is hoped that some general guidance will be of assistance to those considering development of their teaching styles repertoire.

Teachers quite clearly have the central role in creating significant learning opportunities for all pupils. This contribution can be made at the planning stage, so that during the lesson the teacher's role is more low key. It would seem sensible to give pupils independence gradually, through joint decision-making exercises, giving pupils greater control in small, manageable amounts. Pupils generally respond well to being trusted, and it would be unfortunate for pupils to react poorly to change that is too swiftly implemented, causing perceived 'failure' and a return to didactic methods. As Hellison and Templin (1991, p. 61) note: 'For inclusion to work, students have to understand how to do it and have to feel comfortable choosing easier challenges.'

By using only a couple of different teaching styles in the first instance, confusion for the teacher and pupils can be prevented. Using a *problem-solving* approach, to extend pupils' understanding of a topic previously taught didactically, is one such example, and pupils can be afforded the opportunity to choose equipment (from a limited range), lead part of the warm-up, and demonstrate to the rest of the class. The inclusion style is also an excellent method to start with, as both the teacher and pupil are fully involved in the decision-making; the former decides content and presentation but the latter chooses the degree of difficulty at which to work.

As pupils increase in competence and confidence in decision-making, they become ready to take more serious decisions. This can include drawing up sets of rules and regulations, planning the layout of the gymnasium, acting as coaches/referees, and even planning a negotiated scheme of work. It seems reasonable to argue that all primary teachers have some responsibility to develop the process of independent learning, so children are prepared to take on the responsibility expected of them at secondary level. As Anderson (1999, p. 46) points out, 'the longer students depend on others to think for themselves, the more likely they will continue to be dependent thinkers . . . throughout life'.

The characteristics of the pupils in a class are critical. Rink (1993) suggests that pupils of lower ability and non-conforming pupils perform better in structured environments characteristic of direct instruction. High-ability and motivated pupils seem to do better in an unstructured climate.

> The teacher, particularly the teacher in the junior school needs the flexibility to adapt and change game structures or to allow children to create their own games so that experiences provided for the children are appropriate to their age, ability and developmental level. (Williams, 1989, p. 17)

The year group being taught will tend to shape which styles can be most profitably utilized. Children have an underdeveloped information-processing capacity, which means they have problems selecting the right cues during motor skill learning. Teaching styles are required to present information so that pupils can concentrate on the most vital aspects. The work of Fitts and Posner (1967) is of help here. Pupils in the cognitive (beginners) phase are simply getting an understanding of what is required and therefore need basic guidance to the key factors of how a movement should be performed, so *command/practice* models may dominate. At the associative (intermediate) phase the basics are in place, so more attention is freed up to refine the skill; thus pupils may be suited to *reciprocal work*, the *self-check* or *guided discovery* styles. During the autonomic (advanced) phase, the pupil can undertake the action almost without thinking, so simply practising the skill is irrelevant. Further challenges are needed, such as having to work out how the skill is best used tactically, or developing the skill in some way (*divergent production*).

With regard to primary physical education, pupils could be seen to be at three main stages, and therefore may be ready to:

- comprehend what they are supposed to do (most basic);
- apply a skill proficiently on their own (increasing proficiency);
- consult, help others learn the skill (for 'skilled' pupils).

(Based on Anderson, 1999, p. 47)

Different teaching styles will be a prerequisite to dealing with these differences.

Many primary pupils will have little or no understanding of certain areas of the curriculum, suggesting that the teacher will initially have to play a central role. Young children often need very clear structures and boundaries, and constant 'reminders' to ensure safe, on-task activity in physical education. Therefore the more regimental methods of direct instruction are likely to dominate in the 5–7-year-old phase. Teachers of this age group may need the command style, for example, to keep a tight control on over-enthusiastic pupils who often lack self-discipline. Poorly behaved or immature children may not be trusted with implements and will require the close attention of the teacher.

Many young children will not be able to cope with the demands made on them by pupil-centred methods which, in order to work successfully, require children to have both developed verbal skills and a sound knowledge base to start from. Young children have short attention spans, so the teacher may need to intervene regularly to move children on to the next task. Older children will generally be more capable of benefiting from more child-centred approaches, as they can draw upon previously established motor responses. Severs (1997) believes that pupils can analyse others and give feedback from a fairly early stage, and many pupils are ready to take responsibility for learning by the junior years, which can mean involvement in decision-making. 'Some evidence exists that, even in Primary grades, children can be taught self management skills, that enable them to take increasing responsibility for planning and modifying the school environment' (Rink, 1993, p. 44).

The maturation of pupils' analytical skills can mean, in time, the development of pupils as assistant coaches who can operate successfully within the reciprocal style. This has major advantages regarding the immediacy and quantity of feedback which pupils may receive. Also by the junior years many children will want to work with more freedom than at a younger age, when they are more willing to uncritically accept rules and routines. The divergent style, for example, allows pupils to plan and follow their own devised pathways to reach a solution. Such approaches can help the teacher maximize the lesson's potential for an elite junior who may need separate instruction from the rest of the group.

CONCLUSION

How you teach is just as important as *what* you teach. It is paramount for teachers to be able to use a variety of styles interchangeably to meet pupils' differing needs. Only in this way can they ensure a safe, smooth and effective progression from one part of the lesson to the next. If we are to celebrate the diversity of talent that exists in the primary school we need an equally diverse set of teaching methods to enable children to reach their own level of excellence.

KEY POINTS

- Teaching styles are an integral part of children's learning. A teacher's main style of delivery will be influenced by many factors including their personality, preferences and skill. However, as *teaching* behaviour is independent of *teacher* behaviour, all teachers have access to the full range of teaching styles.
- Perhaps the key question in choosing a teaching style should be: 'Will it effectively get across the particular knowledge I want pupils to have?' Teaching for transfer of learning from one skill to another requires a different teaching process from that which is intended to be situation specific. Indirect styles will generally facilitate the former, whereas direct methods may be more profitable for the latter.
- The pupils in the class can be an excellent resource for managing the environment, generating ideas, instructing peers and motivating friends. The teacher must not feel he has to do it all himself; keeping too much central authority can hamper pupil development and make the teacher's life more difficult.

Chapter 5

Assessment, Recording and Reporting

SUSAN PIOTROWSKI

INTRODUCTION

Evidence from inspections of primary schools in England and Wales over a period of almost twenty years suggests assessment, recording and reporting (A, R&R) to be an aspect of the curriculum in need of some attention. The inspection of schools during 1990 to 1991 highlighted a general concern that 'Many pupils were not being given a sufficiently clear idea of their progress or an indication of how they might improve the quality of their work' (DES, 1992).

More recently, Clay (1997, p. 6) drawing on evidence from the Office for Standards in Education (OFSTED) Inspections of Primary Schools which took place during 1995 and 1996, concludes, 'assessment, recording and reporting are not well developed in Physical Education'.

The inspection evidence in England and Wales (Clay, 1997; DES, 1992; OHMCI, 1998) highlighted a number of weaknesses in relation to A, R&R in primary school physical education, including:

- school policies for A, R&R in primary school physical education are not always realized in practice;
- important links between planning, schemes of work, assessment and record-keeping are frequently not developed;
- systematic assessment and recording practices are not always related to the statutory orders in force;
- graded test and achievement certificates, such as those that might be used as part of sport governing body award schemes and which may not be sufficiently related to the expectations identified in statutory orders, are sometimes inappropriately used as a substitute for structured assessment;
- records of assessment are frequently not kept in primary school physical education and, even when information is kept, it is rarely used to build pupil profiles;

- report-writing tends to describe the activities covered and the attitudes adopted by the children rather than focusing on achievement and skill development. Clay (1997, p. 6) sees report writing in physical education as 'an area in need of further development in many primary schools'.

A variety of reasons for these observed weaknesses in addressing A, R&R in primary school physical education could be hypothesized. One possible explanation is that even with the introduction of statutory orders for physical education in England and Wales, teachers remain unclear about what they should expect children to achieve in physical education, and hence what they should be assessing. The importance of clarifying expectations with regard to pupil achievement in primary physical education, if significant improvements in A, R&R are to be made, will be a central focus of this chapter.

The chapter will focus on:

- the nature and types of assessment;
- the role and purposes of assessment in effective teaching and learning in physical education;
- identifying appropriate expectations as the basis for assessment;
- linking expectations with planning and assessment;
- methods of assessment;
- recording;
- reporting.

WHAT IS ASSESSMENT?

In an educational context, 'assessment' can be defined as a process which involves making 'relevant, appropriate and accurate judgements about pupils' achievements' (DES, 1991, p. 42). These judgements involve making comparisons of what the pupils know, understand and can do in relation to specific, predetermined criteria or learning objectives (criterion-referenced assessment), or comparisons of what the pupils know, understand and can do in relation to others (norm-referenced assessment) or comparisons of what the pupils know, understand and can do in relation to their previous achievements in the same activity (ipsative assessment).

Regardless of which method of comparison is used to make an assessment of pupil attainment and progress, the difficulty of reaching accurate judgements in the context of physical education should not be underestimated. Teachers are largely judging practical performances which, by their very nature, are transitory. The actions are often fleeting and there is usually no permanent record in the form of written, painted or crafted objects for the teacher to view and return to in formulating a judgement. Video recordings can be used, but even they have their limitations and require considerable skill if they are to be used effectively.

For assessments to be accurate they must faithfully reflect what the pupils know, understand and can do. This means that the judgements must be valid and reliable. In order to be valid, the assessment must get as close as possible to the reality of what the child knows, understands and can do (Sutton, 1990). For example, to make a valid assessment of a child's swimming skills, the judgement must be based on the pupil's swimming performance and not on a written test.

For the judgement to be reliable, it is necessary that the same judgement is reached under the same conditions, on different occasions. The written test could be a reliable means of assessing a pupil's knowledge of stroke technique if the same teacher would reach the same assessment of the child's knowledge if the script were marked on different occasions or if the same marks would be given by another teacher marking the test. Reaching a reliable judgement requires understanding the variables that can affect performance, such as the influence of the context of the assessment; the standards applied in assessing, for example how many times; the period of time required to say that the child has genuinely attained, rather than perhaps demonstrating an apparent ability through luck; and the influence of teacher expectations (Sutton, 1990). The question nevertheless remains of why assessment should be central to the provision of physical education in primary schools.

THE ROLE AND PURPOSES OF ASSESSMENT

Assessment is integral to effective teaching and learning

Assessment is not necessarily integral to all teaching but it is integral to good or effective teaching and learning. Leah *et al.* (1997, p. 158), claim that 'as a PE teacher assessment is an essential part of your teaching'. This is true within the context of the National Curriculum for Physical Education (NCPE) but it is possible, in principle, to teach physical education without assessment. For example, a physical education teacher could communicate the essential teaching points for a pupil to learn a skill such as a forward roll. The pupil may grasp these points and perform the roll perfectly. It is possible that the child has been taught and this could be confirmed by a third person, even though the teacher may never observe the outcome of that teaching, nor provide any feedback. In truth, however, teaching is likely to be far more effective if the outcome is observed and feedback given to correct mistakes and reinforce what is sound. Teaching is also likely to be more effective in developing pupils' learning if the content of what is taught is related to previous assessment. This provides an informed basis as to the pupil's current stage of development and what is now needed if that pupil is to progress. More accurately, therefore, assessment is essential to good or effective teaching and therefore should be an essential part of teaching physical education. Assessment, as noted by Robinson (1995, p. 9), 'should be an inseparable part of curriculum planning and delivery'. Spackman (1998b) is among those who affirm that assessment is integral to good teaching in physical education. She writes, 'ongoing ... assessment of children's work in PE is at the heart of good teaching' (*ibid.*, p. 4).

The purposes of assessment

It follows from the earlier definition of 'assessment' that a primary function of assessment is to provide information relating to a pupil's level of attainment in relation to set criteria, the achievements of others or in relation to a previous level of attainment. The process of assessment may serve a number of functions. It can:

- identify the strengths and weaknesses of individual pupils; it can confirm correct responses and highlight where improvement is needed;
- confirm the progress being made by pupils;
- provide an informed basis for feedback on progress and attainment for
  - the pupils themselves
  - other stake-holders such as parents, other teachers, or school inspectors
  - the teachers, with regard to the effectiveness of their role in promoting pupil learning;
- provide a basis for planning future lessons and the emphasis needed within these;
- motivate some pupils, especially those driven by a need for achievement and social approval;
- identify the best performers and provide a basis for selecting pupils for school representation;
- provide information for grading or prediction.

Assessment can be formative or summative. Formative assessment involves using the information collected by the assessment process to indicate the most appropriate next step in the learning process (Latham, 1990). Summative assessment takes place at the end of a specific learning period, such as at the end of a unit of work, and its purpose is to summarize pupil achievement. Summative assessment identifies achievement, to date, at given intervals.

WHAT TO ASSESS? THE KEY TO EFFECTIVE ASSESSMENT IN PRIMARY PHYSICAL EDUCATION

As the introduction to this chapter makes clear, there is an accumulation of evidence suggesting that assessment procedures are not sufficiently well developed for the purposes of effective teaching and learning in primary physical education. This is likely to be for a number of reasons, one of which may be that teachers remain unclear as to what it is children should be learning and hence what it is they should be assessing, recording and reporting in and from these contexts. Wetton (1988, p. 17) like many teacher educators, found herself constantly being asked by nursery and infant teachers 'What should children be able to achieve in PE when they are five, six or seven?' She recommended the development of 'a framework that will allow them [teachers] to observe perceptively . . . [and] some easy method of recording the information they gather.'

Although Wetton was writing prior to the introduction of a statutory framework for physical education in England and Wales, there is still a need for the kind of framework proposed by Wetton, not just for infant teachers but for the entire primary age range. The NCPE provides an example of a useful general framework but is insufficiently detailed for assessment purposes for most primary physical education teachers. Teachers require a thorough understanding of the fundamental movement abilities and skills needed for achievement in the range of activities that make up the physical education curriculum, and detailed understanding of the stages of their progression.

The key to improving assessment in primary school physical education is to clarify expectations regarding pupil attainment, and the expected stages of progression. For the primary school physical education teacher, these expectations can be derived from a clear understanding of:

- the aims of the subject;
- any curricular framework in place which defines broad expectations – especially where these are subject to statutory order;
- detailed understanding of the fundamental movement abilities and skills (and their stages of progression) required for achievement of the aims of the subject.

Clarifying expectations: the aims of physical education as the starting point

Physical education is uniquely placed within the school curriculum to cater for those dimensions of physical development which develop the kind of whole-body control and co-ordination required for participation in sport, dance and exercise contexts. It is also uniquely placed to help pupils to appreciate, through physical activity, the effects of exercise on the body. It is well documented (see Whitehead *et al.*, 1997) that many concomitant benefits may follow from this development, such as benefits to physical growth, intellectual development, health, social and personal development, self-esteem and self-image.

The range of activities that could be included under the umbrella of sport, dance and exercise contexts is vast. Nevertheless, it is a common feature of these contexts that they require pupils to develop fundamental movement abilities and motor skills which in their development are combined and applied in different ways, either in individual, partner or group contexts. The skills are applied with increasing levels of autonomy as individuals become more adept at learning how to improve their performances in the light of their previous attempts.

The significance of (statutory) curricular frameworks for clarifying expectations

The aims provide a very broad framework of expectations which, if met, characteristically define the physically educated person. However, physical education teachers are still left wondering what level of attainment is appropriate to expect from most pupils of particular age ranges. Statutory, national subject frameworks which are now in place in many countries throughout the world, more locally defined curricula, or frameworks that may have been put in place in individual schools, attempt in their various ways to translate the broad aims of the subject into a framework of progressive expectations for pupils of particular age ranges. Where a statutory subject framework is in place, this must provide the starting point for defining learning objectives and, by implication, the focus for assessment. The introduction to this chapter has already shown that inspectors, focusing on A, R&R in primary physical education in England and Wales, have identified serious weaknesses where A, R&R has not been sufficiently related to the expectations identified in the Statutory Orders. Many commentators (such as Gilbert, 1992, and Robinson, 1995) agree that the expectations identified in the NCPE in England and Wales should be the starting point for learning objectives/assessment in physical education in these countries.

The proposed NCPE in England and Wales for Curriculum 2000 (DfEE/QCA, 1999) provides an example of a curricular framework from which learning objectives (and hence a focus for assessment) can be drawn. This particular curricular framework will be used as an example throughout this chapter of how A, R&R can be mapped against broad learning objectives. Readers assessing physical education in contexts which are not subject to the Statutory Orders in force in England and Wales can perform the same exercise in relation to the curricular contexts within which they are working.

Proposals for the revised NCPE identify a broad framework of expectations which are detailed in an eight-level Attainment Target (AT) for physical education. In assessing a pupil's level of attainment, teachers are required to judge which of the eight descriptions 'best fits the pupil's performance' (DfEE/QCA, 1999, p. 181). The eight-level descriptions chart clear stages of progression for pupils aged between 5 and 14 years in relation to the following four strands of development: (1) acquiring and developing skills; (2) selecting and applying skills; (3) evaluating and improving performance; and (4) developing knowledge and understanding of fitness and health. Implicit within the eight-level descriptions are stages of progression which it is important to identify in clarifying more precisely the learning objectives/assessment focus. In relation to acquiring and developing skills, for example, progressions are evident which chart development from:

Level 1: copying and exploring simple skills, repeating them with basic control and coordination and beginning to link them appropriately; to

Level 2: remembering and repeating simple skills with control and co-ordination, varying skills, actions and ideas and linking them appropriately; to

Level 3: selecting and using skills, actions and ideas appropriately; to

Level 4: performing skills with precision, control and fluency; to

Level 5: consistently performing skills with precision, control and fluency; to

Level 6: selecting and combining skills, techniques and ideas and adapting them accurately and appropriately, consistently showing precision, control and fluency; to

Level 7: as above, but with consistent demonstration of precision, control, fluency and originality; to

Level 8: consistently distinguishing and applying advanced skills, with consistently high standards of precision, control, fluency and originality.

Similar lines of progression can also be traced in relation to development with respect to (2) selecting and applying skills, (3) evaluating and improving performance, and (4) knowledge of fitness and health. In relation to the eight-level AT, most primary-aged pupils are expected to attain levels 1–3 between the ages of 5 and 7 and levels 2–5 between the ages of 7 and 11.

An Attainment Target of this kind may go some way towards addressing the uncertainty that some teachers feel in wondering what it is pupils should be learning and hence what it is they should be assessing in physical education. However, it is unlikely that even with this level of detail, the descriptions are precise enough to bring about significant improvements in assessment practices in primary schools. For example, in assessing pupils' attainment in relation to Level 1 which encourages pupils to copy, explore and repeat simple skills, primary teachers may still be left wondering which simple skills it is appropriate for pupils to acquire and develop if the overall goals of physical education are to be achieved. The expectations identified in the AT are inevitably broad, partly in response to the need, explicitly stated in the original proposal document for the NCPE in England and Wales (DES, 1991, p. 43), to 'allow for flexible interpretation to accommodate pupils with disabilities and difficulties'. Hence in relation to Level 1 of the process of acquiring and developing skills, the broad and general nature of the expectation allows all pupils to achieve – even those with severe special needs, who may be able to copy, explore and repeat a simple skill such as picking up a ball. However, while the broad and general nature of the expectations has the advantage of being accessible to all, it can still leave many teachers, particularly non-specialist teachers of physical education, unclear as to what most pupils aged 5 to 11 should be able to achieve in relation to the aims of the subject.

In order for significant improvements to occur in relation to A, R&R in primary school physical education, general curricular expectations need to be supplemented by a more detailed understanding of appropriate expectations for particular age ranges. In the context of physical education, if teachers are to be more effective in assisting pupils to develop, apply and reflect upon the skills needed to perform successfully in sport, dance and exercise, they will require a sound understanding of motor skill development (cf. Gallahue and Ozmun, 1995). The inclusion of clear expectations in relation to children's motor skill development adds an element of greater prescription and helps to guide teachers' observations in the assessment of pupils. Reference to more precise criteria of this nature is likely to be particularly welcome to those teaching in primary schools without specialist knowledge of physical education. For primary generalists, it is more and not less prescription of pupil expectations that is required to engage in the process of meaningful assessment in physical education.

Clarifying expectations through an understanding of fundamental movement abilities and skills and their stages of progression

Achievement of the aims of physical education is dependent on the acquisition of certain fundamental movement abilities and skills, such as running, dodging, balancing, stopping, twisting, bending, stretching, reaching, lifting, pushing, pulling, jumping, climbing, catching, throwing, kicking, dribbling, rolling a ball and striking an object with an implement. A considerable body of research exists (see References in Chapter 7) which details the ages and stages of fundamental movement ability and motor skill development. Meaningful assessment in physical education during the primary years needs to be related to this body of knowledge to ensure that the fundamental movement abilities and skills are developed.

This knowledge of motor skill development should include a thorough understanding of the stages of progression for the acquisition of some of these motor skills. Gallahue and Ozmun (1995) detail the developmental sequence for several fundamental movement abilities and skills. If teachers of physical education develop a clear understanding of the developmental sequences for skills such as throwing and catching and so on, they can use assessment purposefully to identify faults in technique which, if not corrected, may limit pupils' ability to achieve in physical education later on in their schooling.

The development of movement abilities and skills provides a clear focus for assessment in primary physical education. When a more detailed understanding of motor skill development is accommodated within a curricular framework which acknowledges that further stages of progression occur through selecting and applying these skills to particular activity contexts, as well as evaluating and seeking to improve performance, we have an example of a framework which provides a useful model for identifying appropriate expectations for primary physical education.

LINKING EXPECTATIONS WITH PLANNING AND ASSESSMENT

Units of work are developed from the general expectations and should specify clear learning objectives which are designed to achieve broad curricular expectations, underpinned by sound and detailed knowledge of motor skill development. The learning objectives identified in the unit of work are generally developed with continuity and progression during a series of lessons. Each of the objectives can be broken down into more specific learning outcomes which identify what the pupil should be able to do and know as a result of learning which takes place in each lesson. These outcomes are directly observable and assessable (see Spackman (1998a) for further details of this process of linking assessment criteria to planning which is designed to

achieve the expectations detailed in national or local curricular requirements). This chapter goes beyond the work of Spackman in arguing for
greater recognition to be given to the importance of a detailed understanding
of motor skill development when translating the general statements included
in broad, curricular frameworks into more precise learning objectives.

The identified objectives/learning outcomes provide the assessment
criteria in relation to which the teacher must then collect specific evidence of
the child's attainment. It is good practice for pupils to be aware of the assessment criteria. They should know what it is they are to learn. The methods by
which evidence can be collected are varied.

METHODS OF ASSESSMENT

Informal methods of assessment largely rely on ongoing observation and
verbal interaction. More formal methods, such as those employed during
times specifically set aside for the purpose of assessing, might take place at the
end of a unit of work.

There are no nationally produced test materials for assessing physical
education in England and Wales. Most assessment in physical education is
based on a continuous process of observation which is guided by having clear
learning objectives/assessment criteria. Judgements about *how* actions are
performed rather than *which* actions are performed are more difficult to
make, and need to be guided by the identification of clear teaching points in
lesson plans (e.g. the feet should be turned out in the correct performance of
breaststroke leg kick) and a clear understanding of how motor skills develop
from their basic to mature patterns.

In reaching accurate judgements of pupils' progress and attainment in
relation to appropriate expectations, teachers will need to collect evidence
across differing activity contexts. In common with the SCAA (1996, p. 21)
guidelines for 11 to 14 year olds, reaching reliable judgements for primary-
aged pupils will need 'to take account of strengths and limitations in
attainment across a number of areas of activity and over a period of time,
rather than by focusing on one activity'.

Some pupils may need to use a range of forms of communication (perfor-
mance-based, written or verbal) to demonstrate what they know, understand
and can do. Williams (1996) identifies a range of methods which may be
appropriate to use in collecting evidence of attainment in physical education:

- observation (direct observation, photographs or video recording) of
  pupils' performance;
- pupil self-assessment or peer assessment (using given or negotiated
  criteria);
- written materials;
- group discussions;
- answers to questions;
- pupils' explanations or descriptions.

RECORDING

Elaborate recording arrangements are not required in England and Wales by the National Curriculum. However, manageable recording systems do serve a useful purpose. Spackman (1998a) suggests that recording provides a useful reference to:

- supplement the ability to recall;
- develop individual education plans;
- report or give feedback to children, parents and others;
- inform planning and to differentiate lesson material.

Recording systems should:

- be kept simple and manageable – recording routine observations and comments in a quick and easy way (e.g. checklist plus space for comments);
- relate to the intended learning outcomes for each unit of work;
- be easily understandable by anyone else who may consult the record.

Part of the recording of evidence of pupils' progress and attainment in relation to expectations during the primary phase should involve charting pupils' progression in relation to fundamental motor skill development which will be included in the learning outcomes of planned lessons. This evidence will be collected from across the range of the activity areas taught. To ensure that the record kept is readily accessible for use by others, it might simply record comments detailing the achievement of specific learning outcomes in relation to the expectations. A form for maintaining each pupil's record of achievement may resemble that given in Figure 5.1.

The example of recording shown in Figure 5.1 is for completion by the teacher. It should be remembered that pupils can also be involved in self-assessment and in keeping their own records of attainment. An advantage of self-assessment is that pupils are explicitly aware, through the assessment criteria, of what they are to learn. They may be encouraged to maintain records through, for example, the completion of checklists, worksheets, or through keeping an ongoing diary or record of achievement.

REPORTING

Reporting includes both formal reporting to other stakeholders such as parents, as well as informal reporting to pupils on their progress. There is a statutory requirement in England and Wales to report to parents annually, in relation to the statutory expectations.

The expectations derived from the (statutory) curricular framework together with an understanding of motor skill development can be used as guidelines for the purposes of reporting to parents. These descriptions will

A Comments	B Comments	C Comments	D Comments
L1 Gym Date (unit 2) 1/6 LO1: explores actions on hands and feet Gym (unit 2) 8/6 LO2: able to repeat bunny jump Gym (unit 2) 15/6 LO3: able to link landing from straight jump with bunny jump	L1 Gym Date (unit 2) 15/6 LO3: able to link jump with bunny jump	L1 Games Date (unit 1) 5/2 LO5: describes own and partner's throwing action	L1 Games Date (unit 1) 29/1 LO4: describes faster heartbeat after warm-up

Name of pupil: Ben Jones   Key: A = Acquiring and developing skills
                                              B = Selecting and applying skills
KS1: Year 1   C = Evaluation and improvement
                                              D = Knowledge and understanding of fitness and
                                                    health
L1 = Level 1   LO = Learning outcome

Figure 5.1: Example of recording pupil attainment

require translation into 'parent-friendly' language. The substance of the report, as Spackman (1998a) suggests, can be based on evidence of progress and attainment in relation to selected learning outcomes as reflected in the evidence recorded in the pupil's record of attainment. Methods of recording and reporting pupils' attainment should be accurate, informative, useful and yet economical in terms of the teacher's time. This can be accomplished by using the narrative from the pupils' record to contribute to a pupil's report. For example, the report might include the following statement, based on the record above:

> Ben has achieved Level 1 standard of attainment. In gymnastics, he has developed confidence in performing skills such as jumping and taking weight onto hands. He has demonstrated an ability to link a controlled landing with a bunny jump. In games, Ben is able to describe the increase in heartbeat which occurs during the warm-up phase of the lesson. He is also able to describe what he and others are doing when

they perform a good throwing action. Ben is now working towards attainment at Level 2 through developing more control in his performance.

During the upper primary years one would expect the report to reflect more advanced forms of progression. An extract might read:

Jane has reached Level 3 standard of attainment. She has developed a strong throwing action with a good sideways stance and appropriate follow-through. She is using this to good effect in basketball where she consistently and appropriately uses a one-handed shoulder pass with precision and control. Jane is working towards Level 4 standard of attainment through beginning to develop tactical knowledge which enables her to interact well with the rest of the team and to adapt her actions in response to the opposition.

In summary, the report should:

- relate to the recorded evidence of attainment;
- be positively constructed in focusing on what the pupil knows, understands and can do (while the report can give indicators for future progress, care should be taken to avoid reporting in a manner which influences pupils from a young age to conclude that they are 'no good at PE and never will be');
- relate pupils' attainment to any statutory targets;
- be informative and comprehensible by the intended audience by avoiding language that is too technical at one extreme or too bland at another.

CONCLUSION

The purpose of this chapter has been to give an insight into the principles and processes of assessment in primary school physical education. The **key points** that have been emphasized and which are central to good practice in A, R&R in primary school physical education are:

- Assessment is an essential part of effective teaching and learning.
- Effective assessment in primary physical education requires identifying clear expectations for this age range.
- Policy and procedures for assessment in primary school physical education must be related to the expectations defined in national or local curricular frameworks.
- Motor skill development should not be ignored in identifying clear expectations for primary physical education. It highlights important milestones which can help teachers to focus with greater clarity on the expectations embedded in more general curricular frameworks.

- Objectives and specific learning outcomes for units of work and lesson plans should be drawn from the expectations. Learning outcomes and assessment criteria are synonymous.
- Records of assessment which are simple and manageable and which record attainment in relation to learning outcomes should be maintained.
- Reporting should be based on progress and attainment in relation to selected learning outcomes.

Chapter 6

Including *All* Pupils in Primary School Physical Education

RICHARD BAILEY AND
CHRISTOPHER ROBERTSON

INTRODUCTION

> There are strong educational, as well as social and moral, grounds for educating children with SEN, or with disabilities, with their peers. This is an important part of building an inclusive society. (DfEE, 1998, p. 1)

> Physically disabled children in mainstream schools can find integration ends at the gym door. (Fisher, 1988, p. 6)

Primary school physical education lessons have always involved teaching pupils with a range of abilities and needs. Streaming is almost unheard of in this area, and while mixed ability teaching can present a challenge, most teachers accept it as part and parcel of their role. Accepting a challenge, however, does not mean that teachers find it an easy one, and many have expressed concern regarding their ability to meet the increasingly wide range of needs presented to them. Changes to policy and philosophy in a number of countries have resulted in the inclusion of children with increasingly severe difficulties: children who earlier might have been considered the concern of specialist, separate schools. As Jowsey (1992, p. xv) put it: 'All teachers ... are now teachers of children with special educational needs.'

A cliché, perhaps, but it remains true that *all* children in school have particular needs and may require special attention from time to time. Their needs are individual to them, and this is no more or less true for children with physical or learning disabilities. It is neither wise nor possible to provide simple solutions to 'problems' of this sort. The aim of this chapter is to introduce teachers to important information that will enable them to be in a better position to respond to the individual needs of their pupils. Of course, it needs to be acknowledged immediately that the subject is a broad and complex one, far beyond the scope of a chapter such as this. The information offered here should never be seen to replace specialist support from informed, appropriately qualified colleagues and literature, and simply taking the time to talk to the child.

This chapter will consider how teaching more inclusively in physical education can and should be seen as a positive and exciting opportunity. It will outline some key principles of good practice, highlighting, too, the particular roles and responsibilities that physical education specialists can fulfil. An assumption that the chapter as a whole makes is that a good teacher of physical education has a uniquely valuable combination of skills, knowledge and understanding that can be used to significantly enhance the provision made for pupils with special educational needs. In working with this assumption in mind, it is implicitly suggested that physical education specialists could, in future, see their roles in relation to special needs and inclusive educational practice both changed and enhanced.

The following themes will be used to address this initial commentary in more detail:

- the need for all pupils to receive a positive physical education experience alongside their peers;
- progress in policy from special to inclusive education;
- physical education for all: curriculum and pedagogy;
- understanding pupil needs;
- meeting needs effectively: classroom practice.

PHYSICAL EDUCATION FOR ALL?

When considering children with different needs and conditions, teachers need to be very careful that they do not lose sight of that which is most important. It can be easy in our discussions of various conditions, disabilities and impairments to forget that we are dealing with young children with the same need as their peers: to be children (Robertson, 1999). Children have an intrinsic need to experience what Bruner calls the 'culture of childhood' (1983, p.121): to play, act and be included with their peers. There is a huge body of evidence showing that physical activity is a vital component in the healthy development of all children (see, e.g. Bailey, 1999a; Malina and Bouchard, 1991). Regular and positive physical activity is a necessary condition of normal physical, emotional and social development. As the only formal exposure to physical activity that some children may have, a varied, positive physical education experience is essential. However, some authorities have raised doubts that children, especially those with more severe physical and learning disabilities, receive such an experience (Jowsey, 1992). Whether this is due to negative attitudes, poor training or lack of support, many teachers feel unprepared to deal with some children in their class.

All children require regular, quality physical education, and it may be that children with disabilities or learning difficulties require an even greater amount than their peers. Competence in physical skills and activities is a significant factor in children's experiences of school and their overall quality of life. Success in physical skills is seen by primary-aged children as more valuable than success in classroom-based activities, and participation in such activities is seen as a key factor in the development of social relationships and self-esteem (Bailey, 1999b). Unfortunately, many children with special educational needs experience less physical activity than their peers (Brown and Gordon, 1987), and this seems to include those children without a disability related specifically to movement.

There is a danger that the child denied the opportunity of physical activity will suffer a number of disabling consequences. Aside from the well-established risks of low levels of activity (such as obesity, high blood pressure and weak bones), there are risks to the child's potential social relationships and self-esteem:

> To the degree that a child's activity pattern is distorted by impairment, socialization occurs outside a normal context, and a child cannot fully gain the competencies required to dwell easily within the home, community, and society. (Brown and Gordon, 1987, p. 828)

There is a further risk that the difficulties experienced by a child with special educational needs will develop into a 'spiral of failure', whereby early difficulties with activities lead to attempts to avoid those activities, which result in less practice and so even greater difficulties (Ripley *et al.*, 1997).

FROM SPECIAL TO INCLUSIVE EDUCATION

Gulliford and Upton (1992) trace the origin of the phrase 'special educational need' to the late 1960s, as a response to an increasing dissatisfaction with the language of handicapping conditions, and a greater awareness of the number of children experiencing difficulties in progressing and adjusting to ordinary schooling. The Warnock Report (DES, 1978) was an important attempt to address this issue in the United Kingdom. It rejected the notion that there are two types of children: those with and those without a handicap. The nature of individual needs is far more complex than such a crude division implies: whether an individual's condition constitutes an educational handicap depends upon many factors, such as the school's expertise and resources, the child's personality, the quality of support, and the encouragement within the family and community. It is entirely conceivable that a child with a disability can, in many contexts, perform as well or better than her peers, given appropriate support. By focusing upon a child's 'need' rather than her 'handicap', the emphasis has shifted from a mere description to a statement of the educational help and provision required (DES, 1978).

The notion of special educational needs has continued to receive endorsement through successive central policy documentation (in the United Kingdom, for example, through the Education Reform Act, 1988, and the Code of Practice, 1994). However, some people have raised concerns. Jean

Gross (1996), for example, points out that a special educational need was originally something a child *has* in certain circumstances, and perhaps for a certain
period of time, while it has often come to mean something that a child *is*.
Inflexible conceptions of special educational needs prevent the teacher from
understanding fully the particular needs of pupils, and can lead to a pes-
simistic approach towards children who are failing, neglecting the real
obstacles to achievement.

It is for these reasons, among others, that many educators and policy-
makers have started to refer to *inclusive* rather than *special* education. This
change is considered more than rhetoric, reflecting a conviction that nothing
short of a radical reappraisal of the structure and character of schooling is
needed if it is to adequately meet the needs of all its pupils (cf. Jenkinson,
1997). These views certainly have an important international reference point:
The Salamanca Statement (UNESCO, 1994, p. 11):

> The fundamental principle of the inclusive school is that all children
> should learn together, wherever possible, regardless of any difficulties
> or differences they may have. Inclusive schools must recognize and
> respond to the diverse needs of their students, accommodating both
> different styles and rates of learning and ensuring quality education
> to all through appropriate curricula, organizational arrangements,
> teaching strategies, resource use and partnerships with their communi-
> ties. There should be a continuum of special needs encountered by
> every school.

Here we see the expectation that education for all children, regardless of their
differing abilities, will begin and continue in their local neigbourhood schools.
In the United Kingdom, recent policy documents (DfEE, 1997, 1998) have sig-
nalled that inclusive educational policy development is here to stay for the
foreseeable future. The full implications of this have barely been anticipated,
but they must be at least twofold. First, pedagogic practice will need reshap-
ing, and this chapter offers some insights into how this might be done. Second,
school organization will have to become infinitely more flexible than it is at
present.

CURRICULUM AND PEDAGOGY

Recent reports and guidance documents in both physical education and
special educational needs years have led to restatements of the importance of
including all pupils in lessons (QCA/DfEE, 1999a, 1999b). One highly influential report from the United Kingdom physical education community (cf.
Sugden, 1991) considered developing concepts of disability (WHO, 1980) in a
purposeful way and placed important emphasis on four principles which
should inform the planning and content of a physical education programme
for children with special educational needs:

1. *Entitlement* – that all pupils have a right to fully participate in worthwhile activities.
2. *Access* – to be achieved first and foremost by the provision of appropriate and challenging learning experiences and assessment mechanisms, allowing for modification when required.
3. *Integration* – that pupils, even when following an adapted curriculum, should be doing so alongside their peers.
4. *Integrity* – that physical education lessons should be demanding, motivating and exciting educationally.

These principles provide useful guidance for teaching physical education to all children. Planning in physical education, if it is to allow for the inclusion of all pupils, should have sufficient flexibility to ensure that they can learn together. It should also offer sufficient progression of meaningful activities to allow every pupil the opportunity to experience a sense of real achievement. Centralized policy-making, if it is to follow the inclusive model, must take care not to exclude through unnecessary prescription. Recent changes to the National Curriculum for England and Wales (QCA/DfEE, 1999b) serves to illustrate this point. While there is a clear commitment to greater flexibility in provision, there remain instructions, for example, that children should be taught to swim 'using recognized arm and leg actions, and strokes on front and back' (*ibid.*). This seems laudable enough, but it excludes many pupils with physical and/or learning difficulties who may learn to swim well, but not by using orthodox strokes (Association of Swimming Therapy, 1981). In addition, the early-level descriptions for physical education introduced in the same document outline language and cognitive skills that would exclude some children with learning difficulties from evidencing motor abilities.

Debate of this kind should certainly reflect on positive developments made to date in both curriculum design and provision. Account will also need to be taken of deep-seated kinds of stereotyping that pervade societal views of physical activity, that associate it inextricably with contrived notions of beauty and perfection (Barton, 1993; Oliver, 1996). One way of re-conceptualizing difficulties of this kind is to view physical education much more in terms of play and physical development than restrictive notions of skills or techniques (Bailey, 1999a). According to this conception, all pupils can achieve and progress.

UNDERSTANDING PUPIL NEEDS

The term 'special educational needs', though it can be regarded as less disparaging and more educationally useful than those of the past (retardation, subnormality, and so on) has significant limitations. In one sense it is very vague, telling us little about the nature of difficulties experienced by a child. In another sense it is unhelpfully stigmatizing, lumping many different children together as 'SEN', but failing to recognize individual differences or needs.

Perhaps a more useful way of understanding needs is to view them in three ways, each of which interconnects with the others (adapted from Norwich, 1996):

1. *Individual needs* – arising from characteristics different from all others.
2. *Exceptional needs* – arising from characteristics shared by some, such as developmental co-ordination disorder, visual impairment, high movement ability.
3. *Common needs* – arising from characteristics common to all.

This typology of needs allows for a more complex and humane view of needs. It helps teachers to consider a range of needs and their educational implications, and it also ensures that a singular view of needs does not predominate. In physical education this would mean that an individual's particular difficulties, strengths and interests are given careful consideration. It would also mean that shared characteristics are taken account of when they are relevant. For example, when teaching specific motor skills to a young child with Down's Syndrome, it might be useful to understand aspects of motor learning that such youngsters could find difficult or easy, and to utilize appropriate professional advice and research evidence. This would ensure that teaching is optimally informed and likely to be most effective. This is not the same as working with crude assumptions such as 'all Down's Syndrome children are . . .' Moreover, the use of this typology would enable a teacher to always keep in focus the important inclusive imperative, that children should have the right to learn together. In practice, this typology should be used flexibly, enabling particular needs to be addressed as priorities. Clearly too, the three kinds of needs outlined here are not incompatible, and could be addressed simultaneously.

This approach to understanding special educational needs also allows for the possibility that biological, psychological and social factors can interact to both cause and ameliorate a child's learning difficulties (Cooper, 1996). Knowing about these factors can be very useful in considering how best to meet a child's needs in physical education. In this regard, Sugden and Wright (1996) have devised a simple framework for identifying pupils with special educational needs in physical education. They distinguish between children who have a special educational need which is *primarily described in terms of their movement skills* (such as physical disabilities and movement difficulties), and those who have a special educational need in physical education, but which is *secondary to other needs* (including learning difficulties, hearing and visual impairment, behavioural problems). As will soon become clear, this is not a strict and precise division, and not every child in these groups will have difficulties in physical education. Nevertheless, it serves to emphasize the needs that may arise in the specific context of a physical education lesson.

The understanding that such frameworks can provide us with in physical education is best exemplified by looking at two examples: a child with cerebral palsy (primary movement difficulty), and a child with emotional and behavioural difficulties (secondary movement difficulty).

Example 1: cerebral palsy (CP)

This is a non-progressive disorder caused by early damage to the part of the brain responsible for movement. The degree of movement difficulty associated with CP varies considerably, from a slight problem with walking to very severe disability, and also from difficulty with only one limb to difficulty with all limbs.

Some possible implications for physical education are:

- There is a tendency for a pupil with CP to deteriorate in physical efficiency, unless she takes part in some form of regular systematic physical activity.
- Functional ability is more important than style, and sometimes quite prolonged sessions of experimentation, with educators and child working together, may be necessary to finally decide upon the most appropriate positioning and approach to a task.
- Pupils with spasticity need careful positioning to enable them to perform to best advantage. Spasm can be increased by fear, excitement or tiredness.
- Periods of relaxation at the start of or during lessons will probably produce better results in children with spastic CP.
- Spatial, perceptual and organizational problems are common and could severely affect a pupil's performance in physical education, but could also be improved by specific teaching.
- Holding and supporting is often difficult, and care is needed in climbing activities. Some children, especially those with ataxia, may have balance problems, and may be more prone to falling than other pupils.
- Dressing and undressing can often cause difficulties, which can be partly alleviated by allowing plenty of time, providing a calm, quiet environment and helping with sorting and organization.
- Grasping and releasing objects may be slower and more of a challenge than normal, and moving objects can therefore be very difficult to deal with.

Clearly, the implications described here would not necessarily be relevant to every child with CP, but a good understanding of them could be very important. More significantly, perhaps, some of the teaching approaches that might follow from a consideration of these implications would be of value in teaching all children. (Further information on physical disabilities, medical conditions, sensory impairments and their educational implications, including those relevant to physical education, can be found in Haskell and Barrett, 1993; Jowsey, 1992; Kenward, 1997; Wright and Sugden, 1999.)

The second example, that of emotional and behavioural difficulties, is inevitably briefer, for it refers to motor difficulties as a secondary characteristic. Nevertheless, the implications are still significant.

Example 2: emotional and behavioural difficulties

Possible implications for physical education include:

- Although there may not be identifiable movement difficulties, behavioural difficulties may interfere with learning.
- Educators will, in most aspects of physical education, need to establish clear rules regarding behaviour, taking account of safety factors.
- Some pupils with emotional and behavioural difficulties may excel at physical education and this needs recognition, praise and recording.
- Some children with emotional and behavioural difficulties, especially those with poor self-esteem, may find the public nature of physical education difficult.
- Some activities may trigger difficult behaviour, so educators will need to consider carefully when intervention needs to assert that such behaviour is unacceptable, and when confidence-giving support strategies are required.
- It should be recognized that standards of behaviour should not be regarded as absolute, especially for children who are emotionally vulnerable, and that it may take time for them to learn 'rule expectations'.
- Some pupils with emotional and behavioural difficulties may have specific problems associated with a known condition, such as Attention Deficit and Hyperactivity Disorder or Autistic Spectrum Disorders. Educators need to know the possible implications of these with regard to teaching/learning approaches, particular behaviour patterns and possible motor difficulties.

IDENTIFYING AND ASSESSING NEEDS

> Without a detailed assessment, an intervention programme cannot be geared to the needs of the individual child. (Sugden and Henderson, 1994, p. 20)

It is important that teachers know about their pupils if they are to be in the best position to help them. The benefits of early identification and assessment of children's needs are well established (Robertson, 1999), and teachers play a pivotal role in this process. The sort of information that needs to be considered in physical education includes:

- pupils' existing knowledge and skills;
- pupils' hearing and sight;
- their understanding of language;
- their emotional needs;
- conditions that may be associated with movement difficulties, whether directly or indirectly.

The specific methods that teachers use to identify and assess individual needs depend upon a number of variables, including time, resources and the child's need. What follows is a simple, developmental model of assessing needs.

Initial identification of children with special educational needs in physical education may arise through *informal observation*. This may be made by a teacher during physical education lessons or by parents watching their child play. Teachers, of course, observe throughout the school day, and build up a great source of information regarding the different strengths and weaknesses of the pupils in their classes. They become aware of those children who have problems paying attention, co-operating during activities, or comprehending explanations. They may also notice children who appear to have sight or hearing problems, or those children who appear 'clumsy'.

Following an expression of initial concern, the teacher carries out more *focused observation* in order to gain further, more detailed information about the difficulty. This might involve keeping a diary of a particular child's activities and difficulties over a period of time. On the other hand, physical education offers numerous opportunities to observe performance and problems across the whole class. For example, as part of a games scheme of work, the teacher could plan for partners to pass a ball between two markers, and note those children who experience difficulty. Many schools have produced simple activities that assess children's handwriting or reading skills, and it would be relatively easy for the physical education curriculum leader to devise an observation framework (or adopt or adapt an existing checklist, such as Sugden and Henderson, 1994), which could assist all teachers in developing a clear picture of their pupils' movement strengths and weaknesses.

If informal and focused observations suggest that a child might have difficulty in movement that is likely to interfere with their experience of physical education, a more formal assessment may be necessary. A number of *diagnostic tests* or *assessment frameworks* exist that offer the professional (whether it be a class teacher, special needs co-ordinator or other specialist) an individual, formative assessment of the child's needs (such as Henderson and Sugden, 1992). The virtue of these schemes is that they offer detailed information on the nature of a child's individual need so that they can inform broader assessment frameworks (such as the Code of Practice in England and Wales: DFE, 1994).

CONCLUSION: THE ROLE OF THE CLASS TEACHER

Primary school teachers are facing increasing demands on their time and expertise. Some have expressed doubts that they are capable of meeting the needs of an increasingly diverse school population (Jenkinson, 1997). This feeling of powerlessness may be even greater during physical education lessons, in an environment that is quite distinct from the more familiar classroom, and in which different special needs, related to movement, arise.

There remains a danger of 'medicalizing' (Oliver, 1990) special needs, through which teachers come to conceive of conditions purely in terms of clinical intervention. Of course, it is important to be aware of the character and implications of different needs in order to adapt the teaching and the curriculum appropriately, but this does not reduce or alter the vital educational role of the class teacher. 'A child with myopia is the responsibility of an eye doctor who prescribes lenses which are necessary for learning, but this does not diminish the responsibility of the teacher' (Norwich, 1999, p. 92). Norwich's quote highlights two related issues. First, that whatever the special need, the teacher always has a central role to play in educational decisions. Second, that an integrated approach to addressing the needs of children is of utmost importance. Different professionals have different expertise, and an adequate approach must recognize the roles that each can make. Teachers may need to access advice and guidance regarding certain aspects of a medical condition or physical impairment, but it should be remembered that clinicians and psychologists are not experts in classroom practice, nor in the delivery of physical education lessons (Ripley *et al.*, 1997).

There is another danger in this regard, and that is in the belief that teaching children with special needs is of a different character to teaching other children. While there are important aspects of a child's need that should be considered, the fundamental principles of teaching and curricular design remain the same. A brief scan of the implications for teaching of various conditions, such as those given above, reveals that almost all apply to all children; some may simply require greater emphasis in particular situations. There are circumstances in which it is important to develop knowledge and expertise that goes beyond general good practice, and this may involve the teacher seeking specialist help. However, this is not 'high specialism' (Robertson, 1999, p. 78), associated with working in clinical settings. It is knowledge supporting good practice. The central point, however, is that

> special needs teaching (is) not ... something different and distinct from other forms of teaching, but as an extension of good professional practice. (Sugden and Wright, 1996, p. 121)

In fact, it may be that mainstream class teachers are in the best position to work with children, especially with regard to initial learning, in which enthusiasm and making learning fun are more important factors of teaching than those which emphasize particular skills and techniques (Bloom, 1985). Moreover, as was discussed at the beginning of this chapter, children's primary need is to *be* children and to be *with* other children. Physical education offers a distinctive and unequalled opportunity to address this need.

KEY POINTS

- Physical activity and playing alongside peers are both fundamental needs of all children; physical education may be the only structured and safe activity that some children experience; therefore, it is of paramount importance in children's education and development.

- Considerations of special needs in physical education should be made primarily in terms of children's movement abilities.
- Identification of movement difficulties usually begins with the class teacher; therefore, observation, assessment and recording are of particular importance.
- Special-needs teaching is an extension of good, general class practice; it rarely involves skills that are alien to a good class teacher.

Chapter 7

Movement Development and the Primary School Child

RICHARD BAILEY

INTRODUCTION

> Children are not simply small adults. Indeed, they differ from adults qualitatively as well as quantitatively. (Sharp, 1991, p. 70)

In order to create an environment that encourages learning and achievement and reduces the risks of injury and frustration, the teacher of physical education needs to be sensitive to a number of physical and psychological aspects of child development. These include:

- the role of movement and physical activity in development;
- the phases of movement development during the primary years;
- children's physical growth during this period;
- the way children handle information as they move and develop;
- their motivations in relation to physical activity.

These features of child development will be considered in this chapter, and practical implications for planning and teaching will be identified.

THE IMPORTANCE OF PLAY AND PHYSICAL ACTIVITY FOR THE CHILD

> Play is what young children do when they are not eating, sleeping, or complying with the wishes of adults. Play occupies most of their waking hours, and it may literally be viewed as the child's equivalent of work. Children's play is the primary mode by which they learn about bodies and movement capabilities. It also serves as an important facilitator of cognitive and affective growth in the young child, as well as an important means of developing both fine and gross motor skills. (Gallahue and Ozmun, 1998, p. 193)

Jerome Bruner (1983, p. 121) has described the 'culture of childhood' as characterized by action, play and movement. Likewise, Jan-Roar Bjorkvold (1989) has emphasized the role that physical activity (and music) play in the lives of children, and goes on to suggest that any schooling that disregards such experiences creates a harmful and dispiriting tension. He expresses this view as a clash between 'child culture' and 'school culture': the former centres upon the importance of play, physical proximity and movement; the latter upon study, physical distance and inactivity. Physical education stands alone as the one area of the curriculum in which children have the opportunity to fully experience and benefit from their natural culture.

Some writers have suggested capitalizing upon the power of movement to develop children's achievements in other areas (Bailey, 1999b). Movement-based activities can create an environment that is enabling and 'fun'. It may be that such activities are capable of generating empowering situations, in which children relax and enjoy learning. By 'camouflaging' learning as games and play, teachers can encourage children who have built up defences to lower their 'affective filters' (Gildenhuys and Orsmond, 1996, p. 105), their frustrations and anxieties, and to develop their skills and understanding incidentally as physical activity is explored and solved. Moreover, as movement is universal, children become involved in experiences that bridge differences in social or cultural background, ability or intelligence.

Research suggests that competence in physical activities is a significant factor in children's experiences at school and the quality of their lives. Children would rather take part in physical activities than any other endeavour in their experience. They would also prefer to succeed in these activities than in classroom-based work (Roberts and Treasure, 1993). A number of studies have highlighted the central place that physical competence has in the developing social relations of childhood. In his classic study of social status in teenagers, Coleman (1961) found that sporting prowess was the major factor affecting popularity in boys during adolescence. More recent research (e.g. Weiss and Duncan, 1992) has supported Coleman's findings, while extending their application to all ages of children and both sexes. Children, it seems, gain acceptance by being perceived as 'good' at activities that are highly valued by their peers. At the same time, children who have not developed a base level of physical competence suffer from poor social relations, which has a consequent impact upon their developing self-esteem (Evans and Roberts, 1987).

The promotion of regular physical activity is an important aim of a physical education programme. An enormous amount of research evidence is being collected that strongly endorses the commonsense view that regular exercise is a vital factor in the maintenance and improvement of children's levels of health, both physical and psychological. In terms of physical development, a strong positive correlation has been found between physical activity and numerous indicators of healthy functioning, including bone density and mineralization, regulation of body weight and fat, and regulation of blood pressure (Bailey, 1999a). In relation to psychological development, studies have found a positive relationship between regular physical activity and a reduction in anxiety, stress and depression (Dishman, 1986), with increased levels of self-esteem and self-concept (Gruber, 1986), with improved academic performance (Shephard *et al.*, 1984), and with a greater ability to deal comfortably with everyday challenges and pressures (HEA, 1997). All this research seems to support a recent consensus statement, in which it was concluded that:

> There is substantial evidence that regular physical activity produces multiple beneficial physiological and psychological outcomes during adolescence. The strength and consistency of these findings lead to recommendations for all adolescents to be physically active on a regular basis. (Sallis and Patrick, 1994, p. 311)

UNDERSTANDING DEVELOPMENT

Sometimes it is the most obvious things of which we most need reminding. As the quotation at the beginning of this chapter reminds us, children are not small adults. In order to maximize learning and achievement, it is vital that the teacher acknowledges the different ways in which children behave and respond, and adapts teaching accordingly. This is the basis of developmentally appropriate physical education: teaching and learning should be planned, delivered and assessed in terms of the varied needs of children. One of the problems that has bedevilled physical education since its beginning has been the well-meaning but ultimately damaging effects of enforcing adult values and expectations upon young children's physical activities. Small children playing within large teams, with inappropriate equipment, in huge playing areas to adult-designed rules is a recipe for frustration and failure. Developmentally inappropriate activities may contribute to many children's increasing dissatisfaction with physical education lessons as they move through their compulsory schooling (Macfadyen, 1999), and the alarming drop-out from regular physical activity once those lessons end (Mason, 1995).

In order to understand the concept of developmentally appropriate physical education, it will be useful to clarify a few terms. *Development* refers to the lifelong process of change by which individuals acquire competences in different areas. It is usually characterized by increased sophistication in organized and specialized functioning as a result of both biological and environmental factors. One important factor is *maturation*, which refers to the biologically determined progression towards a mature state; another is *learning*, which encompasses an individual's experiences, whether planned (as in teaching) or not. The relative influence of these two factors to overall development (nature or nurture?) has been the source of debate for many years, and will no doubt continue. Most authorities agree, however, that development is a consequence of interaction between both factors (Gallahue and Ozmun, 1998; Sugden and Talbot, 1998). It may be that learning is particularly emphasized in some aspects of development (perhaps in the acquisition of physical skills and abilities) and maturation is emphasized in others (skeletal growth). Nevertheless, it is seldom an either/or situation: skill development may be constrained by cognitive ability, physical growth or strength, which seems to be somewhat genetically influenced; skeletal growth can be impaired by damaging experiences, such as malnutrition or over-training.

Development is a complex, dynamic process. While it is possible and sometimes useful to focus upon certain aspects of overall development, those aspects ought never to be considered as isolated from the total human being. A change to one aspect of a child's development will have many implications for others. In terms of children's movement development, it is important to recognize that there is an interaction between physical make-up and movement experiences. Some theorists have taken this view a stage further, by emphasizing that the specific demands of a task are further factors in the interaction between children and their experiences, and that these different elements (the resources which children bring with them, the learning they experience and the tasks they carry out) are not only influenced by one another, but also modify one another (Gallahue and Ozmun, 1998; cf. Wright and Sugden, 1999). A simple summary of this model is offered in Figure 7.1.

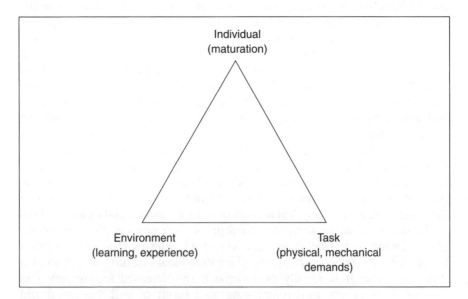

Figure 7.1: A transactional model of children's development

This 'transactional' model stresses the optimistic role that adults can play in child development, and underlines the importance of teachers adapting the experiences children receive in schools to meet their individual needs. Rather than assuming fixed or linear relationships between the child and her environment, the teacher can choose activities and contexts which they consider most appropriate (Wright and Sugden, 1999).

THE DEVELOPMENT OF CHILDREN'S MOVEMENT SKILLS

> The entire period of childhood may be viewed as a sensitive period for mastering fundamental movement skills and being introduced to a wide variety of sport skills. (Gallahue, 1993, p. 86)

Children are in the early stages of a lifelong process of learning how to move, control and co-ordinate their bodies in response to the different challenges that face them. There is a well-established series of stages of movement development, and although the sequence is the same for most children, there is some variation in the ages at which individuals reach phases. Delays in movement development could be an early indication of an underlying problem or condition, or may be the result of impoverished experiences.

The development of movement skills is from basic, generic movement patterns to increasingly specific and specialized actions. In part, it is a process of acquiring new skills whereby a child learns how to sit up, then stand, walk, run and skip. It is also a process of refinement of those skills, so children come to perform movements with increasing control and fluency (Haywood, 1993). This distinction between acquisition and refinement of physical skills is an important one, especially to the teacher of physical education, who constantly has to move between aims related to the extension of pupils' movement abilities (their movement vocabulary) and to the quality of its application.

From birth, children begin to explore and develop their movement potential. Through play, imitation and instruction, they acquire increasingly sophisticated and specialized skills that help them face the challenges presented during life. One way of conceptualizing movement skills development during the primary years is given in Figure 7.2. Each phase is

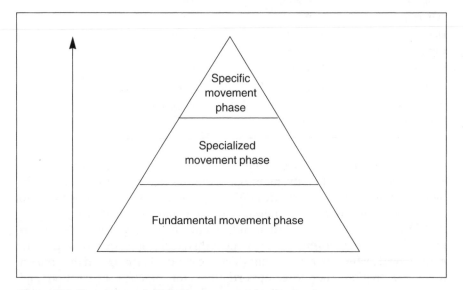

Figure 7.2: The phases of children's movement development

characterized by qualitative and quantitative changes to children's movements. A recognition of the phase of movement development which a child has reached is of basic importance in designing appropriate physical education experiences.

FUNDAMENTAL MOVEMENT DEVELOPMENT

From about 2 to 7 years of age, children lay the foundations for a lifetime of movement. This period is one of exploring and extending their capabilities, and the quality of a child's movement experiences is of central importance. At this stage, children need the time and space to acquire and refine the basic skills of stability, locomotion and manipulation, upon which later abilities, such as sporting skills, are built. While many children may not have developed fluency in the performance of these skills, most will be able to perform actions with reasonable control. The generic movements associated with this phase are summarized in Table 7.1. It is vital that children experience the full range of these skills and, as Sugden and Talbot (1998, p. 18), have pointed out: 'Any programme should incorporate width of experience rather than depth in order to provide the basis for the more specific skills that appear later.'

Table 7.1: Generic movements. *Source:* Based on Gallahue (1993)

Locomotion	Manipulation	Stability
Walking	Handling	Bending
Running	Ball rolling	Stretching
Leaping	Throwing	Twisting
Jumping	Kicking	Turning
Hopping	Punting	Swinging
Climbing	Striking	Balancing
Galloping	Volleying	Rolling
Sliding	Bouncing	Starting
Skipping	Catching	Stopping
Bouncing	Trapping	Dodging

Unfortunately, there is growing evidence that many children do not experience appropriate movement opportunities necessary for the development of basic movement abilities (Walkley *et al.*, 1993), and this is likely to have a damaging effect upon later development and participation.

Children actively explore their movement capabilities. Although there is probably a strong maturational element at this stage, there are also important roles played by the environment in which the child is learning and the context for the activities. Therefore, opportunities for practice, instruction and encouragement are all vital. Children usually find the performance of their skills satisfying in themselves, and play is generally the medium for learning and practising these skills. Since play is associated with feelings of joy and pleasure, practice can become positive and rewarding (Bailey and Farrow, 1998). Wherever possible, the teacher should aim to build upon these feelings in physical education lessons.

SPECIALIZED MOVEMENT DEVELOPMENT

The period from 7 years of age until puberty is often described as the 'skill hungry years' (Maude, 1996; Williams, 1996). It occurs between the periods of rapid development in infancy and puberty, and represents a time of relative stability for children, during which they can extend their physical competence in different contexts. Children have established the fundamental movement skills of locomotion, stability and manipulation, and are now keen to develop their expertise in new and challenging situations. It is therefore a particularly exciting time to teach physical education. Having acquired a reasonable level of competence in the 'basics', children of this age range seek out opportunities to increase the range and quality of their movement. Children of this age are enthusiastic, and often highly motivated to develop their physical skills (Bailey, 1999b).

One way in which the child's understanding of movement is developed is in the area of more formalized activities. While younger children will have experienced simple games, these children are now ready for greater structure, more explicit rules and more clearly defined roles. More structured activities should only be introduced slowly and incrementally, but children's greater understanding of form means that they are better able to cope with the responsibilities of simple rule-bound games. This active desire on the part of most children during this phase to develop their skills means that motivation is rarely a problem for teachers. At the same time, the fact that this is an optimum time for learning physical skills means that the teacher must not waste the opportunity. Failure to capitalize upon children's desire and readiness to improve can lead to long-term under-performance and even dis-enchantment with physical activity.

By developing the basic skills learned and practised during the early years, children are able to perform more specialized, stereotypical actions. They do this by refining, combining and elaborating upon their fundamental movement skills, as illustrated in Figure 7.3.

PHYSICAL GROWTH

Children's physical growth, that is, the development of the skeletal structure and muscularity, is of great relevance to the present discussion.

All children follow a similar pattern of physical growth in terms of stature and body weight. However, there are significant differences between individuals in the timing and degree of change (Malina and Bouchard, 1991). Changes in size and proportions of the body can have major effects upon the

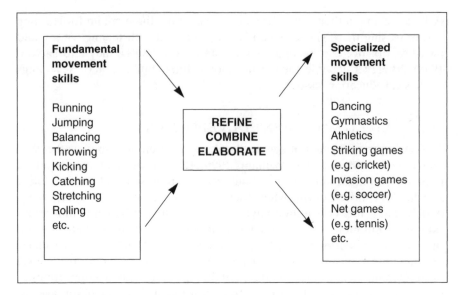

Figure 7.3: The relationship between fundamental movement skills and specialized movement skills

ways in which children perform physical skills, and consequently, some under-standing of these factors is useful to the teacher.

The general pattern of growth follows a four-phase pattern: rapid growth during infancy; more steady development during the junior years; a further period of rapid growth during adolescence; and slow gain until adult stature is reached at about 20 years of age. There is a well-defined *growth spurt* during adolescence, during which children undergo a sharp increase in both stature and weight. Some children also undergo a relatively small *mid-growth spurt* at about 6 or 7 years of age.

This pattern is followed by both sexes, although there are differences in timing and degree of change that result in obvious variations as children mature. Before adolescence, sex differences are insignificant. Girls generally enter adolescence earlier than boys, and their period of accelerated growth finishes earlier, too. There is great variation in timing of the adolescent growth spurt, with girls generally entering this stage between 7 and 10 years, and boys between 8 and 13 years. However, there can be up to four years' difference in developmental age between children of the same chronological age (NCF, 1994). During this time, there are gradual changes to children's physiques, including a relative broadening of boys' shoulders and a broadening of girls' hips.

During the growth period of childhood, the head doubles in length, the trunk trebles, the arms quadruple and the legs increase fivefold (NCF, 1994). Thus, children become progressively 'bottom heavy' as their physiques mature. Clearly, these changes to children's proportions can have a significant effect on performance of skills. Balance, dexterity, co-ordination and timing of actions can all suffer as some children appear temporarily clumsy and suddenly unable to move with the control they exhibited when younger. This can be a frustrating time for children, and patience and support are essential qualities of the teacher in such situations.

In any class of 10-year-old girls and boys, there is likely to be a mix of pre-pubescent and pubescent children, and consequently there will be wide variations in physique and physical abilities. Not all activities will be suitable for all children within a class, and so differentiated tasks may be needed to maximize learning and reduce risk (Smith, 1991). One other aspect of physical growth of particular importance to primary school physical education relates to bone development. It is well established that physical activity is a pre-requisite of bone health (Armstrong and Welsman, 1997; Malina and Bouchard, 1991). The intermittent muscular contractions and weight-bearing of typical physical play seem to be associated with wider, denser bones in both children and adults. However, inappropriate activities can be damaging, and a brief outline of the process of bone development will explain why. As children develop, their skeletons change from relatively soft cartilage to more rigid bone. In the arms and legs, bone development occurs from the centre outward and at the ends. Between these areas are plates of cartilage, which are sites of growth. These plates are the 'weak link in the transmission of force, and are most susceptible to injury in children' (NCF, 1994, p. 5). Very strong muscular contractions, such as landing from height, explosive starts, bouncing and squatting actions, can be harmful to soft, still forming bones; they should therefore be avoided.

PSYCHO-SOCIAL DEVELOPMENT AND MOVEMENT EXPERIENCES

One significant manner in which children differ from adults relates to the way they handle information. Whereas teenagers and adults are selective in how they scan the environment and identify relevant features, children are far more exploratory and disorganized, and are less able to identify relevant stimuli (Connell, 1993). Ross (1976) identified a developmental change in the character of children's attention. Infants aged up to 6 years are often *under-exclusive*, as they tend to focus upon one object (for example, a ball) with relative disregard for other features of the environment. Older children tend to become somewhat *over-inclusive* in their attention, considering a huge range of factors as they play. They are easily distracted, they heed noise too much and often find it difficult to focus upon important visual cues. It is only as they approach the teenage years that children habitually attend in a more *selective* way.

Children have a limited 'pool of attention which can be allocated at will' (Connell, 1993, p. 80), and they learn better ways of handling information as they mature. However, teachers can help younger children learn to deal with information more effectively by restricting the amount of information and gradually introducing cues. In almost all cases, it is better for children to work in small groups than large. The precise number of children in a group is variable, depending upon the purpose of the activity, the space and the available resources. Small-group work makes them much better placed to recognize relevant cues for action. It also ensures a far greater level of activity and participation, and therefore greater opportunity for challenge and improvement.

Small-sided activities are also a solution to the inherent complexity of much of the physical education curriculum. Although 7 year olds are ready to take part in activities with a prescribed rule structure, such as a game, many present quite complex social problems: What is my role? What are their roles? What are they likely to do? How will they respond to my actions? (Lee, 1993). These can cause difficulties. Small-sided activities reduce the variables, so that children are better able to develop an understanding of an activity's requirements. By gradually developing work in pairs, then in threes and fours, and by offering the chance to play in different positions, teachers can initiate children into the rules and roles of an activity in a way that is manageable yet challenging.

Improvement in information processing seems to be attributable partly to the development of generalized programmes for executing an action. These programmes may be refined through a process of trial and error elimination (Bailey and Farrow, 1998), during which the child learns the relationship between certain movements and outcomes. The wider the range of experiences the child has, the better able she will probably be to generalize the use of skills to new events. It is therefore important for children to practise skills in a variety of conditions rather than in restricted ones (Haywood, 1993). For example, children should use a range of equipment in different types of situations.

Almost every aspect of physical education requires children to deal with a number of tasks at the same time. In dance, pupils might be moving their bodies in time with others; in gymnastics, they might be performing a travelling pattern while crossing a bench. Some children will be unable to perform the different tasks properly, especially if such tasks require their entire attention. It is important, therefore, that as well as introducing new skills and activities, the teacher does not forget the development of basic movement competence. The child needs time to practise and 'play' with the basic movement skills. Repetition is rarely considered in terms of general teaching, but in physical education (and, it is suspected, many other areas of the curriculum) it is vital if children are to develop their full potential. By practising and repeating these actions they become relatively automatic, and the child's mind is freed up to give attention to more complicated aspects of the game that require greater thought or decision-making (Bailey and Farrow, 1998). For example, children can repeat sending skills to such an extent that they perform them without significant attention, allowing them to focus upon other variables in a game situation, such as the position of team-mates or the goal.

Another factor of child development that is of relevance to the present discussion is motivation. A large number of studies have suggested that two perspectives on achievement can influence children's behaviour and work in the school environment (Nicholls, 1984; Roberts and Treasure, 1993). A mastery perspective, or a task orientation, occurs when children focus upon demonstrating their ability or competence at a task, and where the emphasis is upon self-improvement or self-comparison. An example of this approach is when children try to develop the accuracy of a throwing action towards a target. A competitive perspective, or an ego orientation, on the other hand, is characterized by children seeking to compare their ability or performance with others, for example, during a running race.

A common assumption seems to be that the competitive orientation is the norm for children, especially in the physical education environment. However, research suggests that this is not the case. While teenagers often exhibit a competitive goal orientation, younger children seem to be far more influenced by mastery goals as well as social approval than by competition (Roberts and Treasure, 1993). Although boys are more competitive than girls, in the junior age range both tend to be more concerned with the improvement of skills and the overall development of physical competence than being favourably compared with their peers.

Some writers have stressed that the 'motivational climate' created by adults can have a powerful effect upon the way children perceive a task (Ames and Archer, 1988; Roberts, 1992). Teachers' responses to the child's activity can conflict with and sway the child's assessment of the situation:

> By giving certain cues and rewards, and making explicit expectations, significant adults structure the sport context so that task or ego involved conceptions of ability are the criteria by which performance is evaluated. (Ames and Archer, 1988, p. 10)

This motivational climate deserves serious attention by teachers, as it relates closely to the behaviour of children. Children who have adopted a mastery orientation are able to select challenging tasks, persist despite set-backs and remain interested in the activity. They also seem able to develop positive relationships with peers. Some of this may also be true for children with a competitive perspective. However, evidence suggests that with these children there are greater risks of problematic behaviours emerging. When children have a high perception of their competence, they tend to exhibit the same qualities as children with a focus upon mastery. However, for children with low perceptions of ability, their behaviours tend to be characterized by poor motivation, avoidance of challenge and lack of persistence (Haywood, 1993). The negative reaction to competitive situations may be more apparent in girls than boys (Sports Council, 1993). In addition, the competitive frame can be very fragile and a child's confidence in her own ability can be damaged by failure or difficulty (Dweck, 1986). Whatever the perceived ability, children with a competitive orientation to their participation are the ones who are most likely to give up sport once they leave primary school (Roberts and Treasure, 1993).

None of the above should be understood as a criticism of the competitive aspect of physical education. On the contrary, competition forms a distinctive feature of the subject, and one that many children enjoy. The key point, however, is one of emphasis. Competition might form the environment of participation but it should not be the goal; it is the medium, not the message. An unwarranted emphasis upon winning can, in the long term, lead to a rejection of the whole enterprise. Ironically, by emphasizing the importance of doing one's best, trying to beat previous performances or improving skills, the teacher is likely to encourage enjoyment of the competitive element (when it is present and appropriate) in physical education lessons as well.

CONCLUSION: START WITH THE CHILD

There is a great deal of evidence to suggest that children benefit enormously from positive, challenging physical activities. This is one reason why physical education in schools is so important for children. The physical education lesson is an opportunity for children to develop their physical skills in a structured, supportive environment. For some, it may be the only chance they will have. Physical education is regularly cited among the most popular subjects (Birtwistle and Brodie, 1991), and the teacher can build upon these positive feelings associated with physical activity to make a clear and necessary contribution to children's movement and overall development. It was in recognition of this fact that the 1964 UNESCO Council, in setting guidelines for curricula in developing countries, recommended the following:

> An individual, whatever his ultimate role in society, needs in his growing years a due balance of intellectual, physical, moral and aesthetic development which must be reflected in the educational curriculum and timetable. . . . Between 1/3 and 1/6 of the total timetable should be devoted to physical activity. (Cited in Shephard, 1984, p. 8)

Sadly, children in the United Kingdom currently receive fewer hours of physical education than any comparable country in Europe (Armstrong and Welsman, 1997), and recent government initiatives (QCA, 1998) seem set to reduce this time still further. Time will tell the consequences. Nevertheless, every teacher of children in the primary years has a great role to play in supporting regular, varied and enjoyable physical activity.

KEY POINTS

- Movement and physical play are fundamental factors in healthy overall development in children.
- Development is best thought about in terms of a transaction between children, their environment and the tasks they carry out.
- It is important that the teacher of physical education is aware of the different stages of movement development, and adapts his aims and methods accordingly.

- Children's bodies need regular and varied physical activity, but this must be appropriate and safe.
- Children process information, pay attention and are motivated to perform in ways that are often unlike those of adults. Planning and teaching should always reflect these facts.

Chapter 8

Co-ordinating Primary Physical Education – Leadership Matters

TONY MACFADYEN AND JEAN O'KEEFFE

> The effectiveness of a teaching programme can be consistently enhanced if individual teachers are given responsibility within the school for both planning and oversight of the course in relation to particular aspects of the curriculum. (HMI, cited in Cox, 1987, p. 31)

INTRODUCTION

Adequate and competent provision of physical education in primary schools is dependent on a multitude of factors. These include such variables as first-class teaching, high expectations of pupils, effective curriculum organization and planning, sound systems of assessment, recording and reporting, and the continuing professional development of staff (OFSTED, 1995). These, and other factors which underpin the effective delivery of the subject, are within the realm of the subject leader. Thus achieving the conditions which facilitate effective provision is a critical and demanding task.

This chapter is divided into three main parts. In the first section the concept of leadership is examined, including an investigation of the functions, theories and styles of leadership, as well as consideration of the attributes and competences of a leader. In the second section, consideration is given to the interpersonal skills and modes of communication of which the leader needs to be aware in order to help his effectiveness. Finally the chapter looks at the importance of holding a vision and considers how the leader may need to negotiate change, as well as providing a practical example of important issues that need to be considered for a physical education policy. Therefore, it aims to raise awareness that will inform and, where possible, improve practice.

The role of the subject leader has been strongly supported in the field of primary physical education, since an effective subject leader can be of immense value to the profile and provision of physical education (BAALPE, 1999; Chedzoy, 1996; TTA, 1998). Blake (1998, p. 110) has referred to an 'acknowledgement that those teachers who effectively coordinate Physical

Education in Primary Schools have a major impact on the way their colleagues teach and, in turn, the overall quality of the Physical Education provided.'

The Teacher Training Agency's (TTA) exemplification of the core purpose of the subject leader highlights the substantial responsibilities of the post:

- the provision of professional leadership and direction for the subject;
- the exemplification of high standards of teaching and learning and the development of appropriate documentation;
- to support, guide and motivate teaching and auxiliary staff;
- to evaluate, monitor and review the effectiveness of current teaching and learning, the curriculum offered and progress towards agreed targets for the pupils and staff.

(TTA, 1998, p. 4)

Raymond (1998) identifies two pivotal responsibilities for the post: co-ordination and subject leadership. The realm of co-ordination emphasizes the need to harmonize, work together and establish routines and appropriate practices. The function of subject leadership encapsulates the provision of information, the exhibition of expertise, the offering of direction, a dedication to raising standards, and guidance in the development of the subject. Thus, Davies and Ellison (1994, p. 52) believe the subject leader should act as

an exemplar to colleagues; encourage others, listen to concerns and provide action plans; assume responsibility for managing the subject within the school, e.g. documentation, planning, implementation, assessment, record-keeping and evaluation.

LEADERSHIP

The functions of leadership

One of the most powerful factors contributing to the effective co-ordination of physical education is strong and positive leadership. This is significant because 'the management of schools has changed from an emphasis upon control, to leadership to bring out the best in people' (Mortimore, cited in Kitson and Merry, 1997, p. 159). Curriculum leaders need a multitude of relevant skills if they are to foster the optimum environment in which improvement, achievement and success can flourish. Leadership, therefore, is about a concern for people, motivating and managing teams as well as creating appropriate structures that all contribute to the fulfilment of an overall plan (vision). Eastwood and Buswell (1987, p. 36) describe the function of leadership as 'defining objectives, planning, communicating, delegating, supporting and controlling; doing, observing, discussing, evaluating and doing again; fulfilling the task, building and maintaining the group and developing the individual'. Leadership thus concerns a process of influencing both individuals and groups towards identified targets.

Theories of leadership

Theories of leadership are well documented and include the trait and situational theories, the behavioural model, and the transactional and transformational theories. Chelladurai (1990) has proposed a 'Multidimensional Model of Leadership', originally developed for athletic situations, which conceptualizes leadership as an interactional process. Chelladurai hypothesizes that the effectiveness of the group's performance and the members' satisfaction are dependent on the congruence of three forms of leader behaviour: 'required', 'preferred' and 'actual'. If each of the behaviours agree and complement each other, optimal performance and member satisfaction will result. *Required* leader behaviour refers to the notion that a situation will demand specific behaviours from a leader. *Preferred* leader behaviour concerns the preferences of the members of the situation. For example, 'some members want to stress achievement, others affiliation. Age, gender, skill, and experience influence what guidance . . . and feedback they prefer' (Weinberg and Gould, 1995, p. 212). *Actual* leader behaviours relate to the true behaviours exhibited by the leader. Similarly, Martens (1987) has proposed that effective leadership is directly related to:

- situational factors (specific situation and environment in which leaders are operating);
- member characteristics (the actual attributes of the staff and pupils of a school);
- leadership qualities and leadership styles.

Clearly, physical education leaders must be aware of the school's overall aims, and their colleagues' attitudes, if they are to offer the appropriate support, guidance, reassurance and vision. It may be important, for example, that subject leaders propose specific physical education changes in step with the school's overall plans. BAALPE (1999, p. 15) focus specifically on four strands of leadership for physical education, 'each of which when fully employed contribute in a balanced way to overall effective subject leadership':

1. Visionary (holding a vision for the future of the subject).
2. Impact (promoting and generating enthusiasm for physical education).
3. Strategic (application of their experience, knowledge and understanding of the physical education curriculum to the planning and delivery of the subject).
4. Interpersonal leadership (which 'relies on the Subject Leader having the skills and attributes to ensure effective communication . . . of the ethos, standards, importance and significance of Physical Education in the school' (*ibid.*, p. 15).

Styles of leadership

Effective leaders can alter their styles and behaviours in order to tailor them to the demands of each situation. As Raymond (1998) notes, the secret is to be able to manoeuvre in and out of styles according to different circumstances. Thus effective leaders utilize a variety of styles and strategies of leadership depending upon the organizational context and their interpretation of themselves and others in the group. Management and leadership behaviour can be viewed most clearly as a continuum (Figure 8.1).

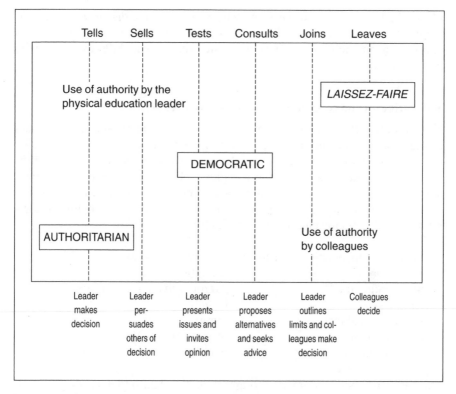

Figure 8.1: The leadership continuum in physical education

An *authoritarian* leader is usually described as task-oriented, someone who places utmost emphasis on getting things done at the expense of positive interpersonal relationships. A *democratic* leader is often more concerned with interpersonal relationships and can be characterized as a relationship-oriented leader. This style of leadership aims to keep the lines of communication open, maintain positive social interaction and ensure a feeling of well-being throughout the organization (Weinberg and Gould, 1995). Juxtaposed to the authoritarian leader is *laissez-faire* leadership typified by a lack of interference, and a very relaxed approach, where individuals are left (trusted) to manage quite independently.

Day and colleagues (cited in Chedzoy, 1996, p. 26) highlight the concept of an 'enabling leader', someone who encourages and demands of fellow teaching staff the greatest contribution to the fulfilment of a vision:

> Enabling leaders self-consciously bring to the act of management the highest standards of integrity, responsibility, justice, equality, discipline and love ... they also have an unfailing belief that this is a requirement of all the members of the school community, not just those with desig-nated leader functions.

Physical education co-ordinators may be well advised to discover and experi-ment with the various leadership principles in order to learn how and when to apply them in their own situations, rather than learn skills that might be inappropriate.

The attributes and competences of an effective leader

Unfortunately, there is no definitive set of characteristics that can ensure suc-cessful leadership. This is why, according to Weinberg and Gould (1995, p. 203), 'it is easy to think of people who are great leaders, but it is more diffi-cult to determine what makes them leaders'. However, it is quite clear that a leader's personal qualities can have a significant effect. Research into the characteristics associated with professional and effective leadership reveals a multitude of expected characteristics which are listed below:

Personal impact and presence.	Energy and vigour.
Assertion.	Empathy.
Self-confidence.	Adaptability and versatility.
Enthusiasm.	Reliability.
Intellectual ability.	Integrity.
Commitment.	Intrinsic motivation.
Innovation.	Ambition.

Furthermore, good leaders are thought to hold a clear understanding of their own values, beliefs and goals, as well as those of their followers (Southworth, 1998).

The competences of an effective leader would seem to include:

- A knowledge and understanding of the subject area, for example, the process of teaching and learning, current research or specific subject content.
- The ability to solve problems and make decisions.
- The ability to communicate clearly and understand the viewpoints of others.
- The ability to organize and manage self, others and change.

(Based on Raymond, 1998; TTA, 1998; Weinberg and Gould, 1995)

Nevertheless, it is imperative to remember that this favourable compilation of attributes and competences is not solely sufficient in a leader's quest for achievement, improvement and successful leadership.

INTERPERSONAL SKILLS AND EFFECTIVE COMMUNICATION

Effective leadership is heavily reliant on expert interpersonal skills and the ability to communicate successfully with colleagues. Interpersonal skills of a leader encompass the ability to work alongside others effectively, to lead discussions, and advise and support other staff. These skills form the basis of good communication, enabling the leader to get to know fellow staff, their strengths and weaknesses, and their feelings towards physical education. A leader who understands his staff is more likely to get the best out of them compared to a leader who is too distant. The physical education leader must endeavour to listen to colleagues' worries and offer guidance and feedback in order to develop confidence and positive levels of self-esteem among team members. Whitaker (1997, p. 123) has written on important interpersonal skills for teamwork that include: 'thinking; listening; handling ideas; supporting other team members; providing encouragement; sharing feelings; self-discipline'.

Effective leadership requires the co-ordinator to establish relationships with colleagues that are honest, open and trusting and facilitate meaningful two-way communication that enables opinions, beliefs and concerns to be shared freely, without fear of intimidation or embarrassment.

Communication

Research by Jack (1995) concluded that an apparent lack of communication between the headteacher, physical education curriculum leader and general teaching staff resulted in confusion as to what each person expected of each other. A host of factors appears to contribute to effective communication which Weinberg and Gould (1995) believe occurs in three fundamental ways:

1. *Intrapersonally* – the communication we have with ourselves.
2. *Interpersonally* – this communication involves at least two people in a meaningful exchange.
3. *Non-verbally* – involving non-verbal cues, which are critical in receiving and imparting information.

Raymond (1998) has suggested that communication can assume formal, informal, upwards/downwards/sideways, oral and written modes. Productive methods of communicating in the primary school can thus include discussions, consultations with individuals or groups, memos, notices, letters, newsletters, official meetings, agendas, minutes of meetings and written reports (cf. Robinson, 1993). When disseminating or seeking information, consulting or negotiating with others, it is vital to select the most appropriate format for communication. For example, in these days of e-mail, leaders must be careful to fully utilize face-to-face communication, particularly on sensitive issues. In no situation should e-mail be used to save confronting a difficult issue; this usually only serves to make the situation worse.

MEETINGS

Meetings can be ideal vehicles for communicating effectively, but in the current teaching climate teachers are heavily burdened with a significant range of obligations and responsibilities. Thus in contemplating any meeting, the leader should evaluate and establish if any alternative method of communication would be more appropriate. Meetings are typically employed as means of sharing knowledge, expertise and opinions, consulting colleagues, engaging in decision-making, disseminating information, planning work collaboratively and hearing guest speakers (Harrison and Theaker, 1989).

> In order to maximise the talents, ideas and contributions of those attending a meeting, the leader needs to exercise control. Poorly conducted meetings cost the department dearly in terms of time, results and goodwill. (Robinson, 1993, p. 97)

Since the chance to meet formally with colleagues in order to discuss physical education matters may be irregular, the physical education co-ordinator should ensure he is well prepared by:

- defining the purpose of the meeting;
- establishing the optimal format;
- meticulously planning the content;
- organizing and preparing the venue;
- issuing relevant documentation prior to the meeting;
- ensuring participants are aware of what will be required of them.

Partnerships

The establishment of sound partnerships is an important tool to improve the quality of delivery in physical education. A curriculum leader is more likely to increase the probability of attaining his set goals if he can enlist the support and guidance of the potential human resources at his disposal. By skilfully combining the individual strengths, abilities and resources of each agency, the provision of physical education can be enhanced. It would seem that the key is to forge each of the individuals and groups into a universal team, who can collaborate efficiently to reach common, agreed, high quality objectives. Physical education leaders therefore need to identify potential partners within and outside of the primary school. A list of figures to consider might include:

Senior management

Teaching colleagues/curriculum leaders

The board of governors

Ancillary school staff

Parents

Local community

Sports development officers Local universities and colleges

INSET providers

Neighbouring schools and their teaching staff

Advisers and consultants

Local sports clubs

Educational and health authorities

Governing bodies of sports

The headteacher

The support provided by the headteacher for subject leaders is an important feature in the achievement of high standards in primary schools (OFSTED, 1995). The headteacher can provide immense support in many ways, including financial investment and training, ensuring adequate physical education on the timetable, and advising on documentation. Having the headteacher 'on side' cannot be overvalued, and co-ordinators are well advised to play a proactive 'political' role in the school to win the support of senior management; for example, by sending them developments on all new initiatives, ensuring regular bulletins for assembly, and inviting senior managers to meetings, to observe lessons and support extra-curricular activities.

External advisory support

External agencies such as local education advisers and sports development officers can provide substantial support by running after-school clubs and providing practical information and ideas through demonstration taster lessons, providing resource materials, delivering INSET, and by acting as reference points for advice on difficult matters (Casey and Plumb, 1988).

Neighbouring schools

In any context, but particularly where the physical education leader is a generalist teacher, it may be particularly useful to explore the sharing of specialist subject support within clusters of schools (CCW, 1994). The benefits of sharing staff with expertise in physical education can include collaborative planning of schemes of work and joint in-service ventures. Pain and colleagues (1997, p. 41) believe 'collaboration with another school or schools in a cluster can result in the pooling of considerable expertise either for more specialised teaching or to raise the confidence of others'.

Parents

Regular, informative communication with parents can result in noticeable support which, if used wisely, can be invaluable for improving curricular and extra-curricular provision. Newsletters, pupil diaries and school notice-boards can all be effective methods of winning support.

Fellow teaching colleagues

In many primary schools the class teacher is responsible for teaching his own class physical education. It is therefore vital that a curriculum co-ordinator positively influences the teaching practices of each and every class teacher so that the school consistently delivers a high standard of physical education. The skilled utilization of support materials will be an essential factor in this process. Consultation with fellow subject leaders is also important to share good practice, reflect on progress and secure cross-curricular links for physical education.

The mentorship role

The physical education leader can act as a 'mentor' for all colleagues. However, it may be particularly necessary to support the induction of a newly qualified teacher. Clark (1989, p. 14) explains the mentorship role as that of an 'experienced guide. A sponsor who believes in what one does, promoting and showing the way.' This would seem sensible, given that 'there is a concern that newly qualified teachers at Key Stages 1 and 2 are not equipped to teach the minimum requirements of the National Curriculum for Physical Education' (SCAA, 1996, p. 13). Thus the physical education leader has an essential duty to welcome and embrace new staff into a supportive and encouraging environment if he expects continued high standards.

ENVISIONING THE FUTURE AND NEGOTIATING CHANGE

The purpose of a vision is to create a coherent strategy that facilitates the 'department' to increase its effectiveness. Before any progress can be made towards the realization of a vision, however, there needs to be an assessment of the current position. A physical education leader can improve his team's capacity by working towards a vision that has been devised by the staff team, thus reflecting their aims and aspirations. Davies and Ellison (1994, p. 35) suggest that 'every school depends for its future on having a "vision", a blueprint of a desired future state, [which] should be shared by all concerned'. It is a primary responsibility of a physical education leader to share in the formulation of such a vision.

Innovations are rarely neutral, sometimes threatening and often notoriously difficult to achieve (Sparkes, 1991). As teachers are central to the process of change, negotiations often need to be approached sensitively. The leader may need to weigh up situations so that those teachers who lose in one innovation, benefit through change the next time (*ibid.*). Change can involve high personal cost and little reward for teachers, so its implementation requires a strong rationale, and the physical education leader must be able to articulate how and why any change will be beneficial. Cross and Harrison (cited in Davies, 1995, p. 6) suggest that 'change only occurs when teachers believe in the need for it, know where it is going, are committed to it and have some ownership of it'.

One of the primary ways to create a structure for change is the preparation of appropriate documentation, since educators have been made increasingly accountable in recent years. Curriculum policy documents are the written expression of the school's beliefs and practices and imply a clear commitment that is open to inspection.

PREPARING A PHYSICAL EDUCATION POLICY

Outlined below is a possible format for the construction of a physical education policy document.

- *An introduction.* The document should review the aims and ethos of the whole school (its mission statement) and outline the philosophy of the school with specific regard to physical education. The introduction should also relate to national requirements where appropriate.
- *A physical education policy statement.* This should contain the collective vision for physical education and a rationale, justifying the place and purpose of the subject within the school. The aims and objectives for physical education within the school should be detailed and clarified. The statement may identify what the majority of the children will know and understand, and the types and range of performance they will demonstrate at certain points in their development. In essence, the policy statement should give any visitor to the school a sense of the school's ideology regarding physical education (Dunn, 1998).
- *A physical education school development plan.* This identifies immediate and long-term objectives and targets for the future of physical education within the school. It might include a plan for the physical education leader's personal development, and the programmes of INSET for the professional development of the staff.
- *Curriculum documentation.* Clearly stated plans concerning the actual delivery and teaching of physical education should be included, and related to national guidelines where appropriate. It can also be useful to include sample units of work and lesson plans in this section.
- *A statement of the skills, knowledge, concepts and attitudes to be explored by pupils in physical education.* Statements exploring pupils' expected progression, and consistency and continuity of experience, can also be included here.
- *Guidance regarding teaching and learning in physical education,* including the employment of a variety of teaching styles.
- *Guidance regarding the use and of storage resources, the deployment of apparatus and equipment, and the care and utilization of facilities.*
- *Guidance on the deployment of teacher assistants in physical education.*

- *Information on a special educational needs policy.*
- *Guidance on assessment, recording and reporting systems.*
- *Policy statements* on:
  - entitlement;
  - equal opportunity and access;
  - cross-curricular liaison;
  - differentiation;
  - behavioural management (detailing common agreed procedures and routines);
  - contingency arrangements (such as wet-weather programmes);
  - the budget for physical education;
  - inter-school liaison;
  - extra-curricular provision (including a rationale, the aims and objectives, the extent of activities);
  - links with the wider community (including outside agency involvement);
  - the integration of information and communication technology.
- *Mentorship*. A statement considering the responsibility of the physical education leader in the induction of newly qualified teachers and staff needs.
- *A health and safety policy.* This section specifies the appropriate clothing for physical education and the procedures for accidents and emergencies.
- *The physical education leader's role specification.*
- *A subject evaluation statement.* This explains quality assurance procedures undertaken by senior staff with regard to physical education.

It is advisable to regularly review the documentation so that it accurately reflects the match between policy and practice and is used to reduce any differences between them.

Monitoring and reviewing progress

The leader should undertake to monitor the provision of physical education, collecting and recording observations and breakthroughs in physical education in order to provide an insight into progress – or not! 'Evaluation is (or should be) primarily concerned with doing things better, both now and in the future' (Davies and Ellison, 1994, p. 117). A review of physical education permits the leader to take recent changes into account, and improvements over time will serve to boost the morale, confidence and self-esteem of the team.

Administration and resource management

The subject co-ordinator's role involves managing people, procedures and resources. Consequently this necessitates carrying out a range of administrative duties that require sound organization of some or all of the following:

- the Physical Education Curriculum Policy Document;
- newsletters;
- agendas and support documentation for meetings;
- a reference library of relevant resource materials and articles;
- timetables for physical education, the use of the school hall and playing fields, and extra-curricular activities;
- physical education displays and notice-boards;
- physical education events and residential experiences;
- guest speakers and INSET providers;
- information on pupil 'statements' and needs, and how it may affect their participation in physical education.

It is clear that the physical education leader must make maximum use of the limited time available if he is to complete the requisite duties. 'The effective management of time will play a key part in determining the quality of your success as a curriculum leader and it is necessary to keep this under constant review' (Harrison and Theaker, 1989, p. 8). Thus thinking ahead, anticipating and evaluating expected workloads, setting realistic and achievable targets and prioritizing issues will be essential.

Resource management

Teachers, other adults, pupils, the facilities available, displays, literature and equipment can all be considered resources at the leader's disposal. It is important for the leader to establish routines for the care and safe use of equipment; however, this is an ideal opportunity to structure the collective responsibility of all staff towards a common goal.

Professional development

This is perhaps one of the most critical aspects of the subject leader's role. He is a resource for other teaching and non-teaching staff, offering advice, guidance, support and motivation. However, this is made more difficult as 'the unique nature of the practical work in Physical Education can often mean that it is a more difficult task for [the leader] to share his/her practical experience and expertise with colleagues' (Blake, 1998, p. 109). Areas in which colleagues seek advice and support from the physical education leader might include issues such as subject knowledge, lesson planning, class management strategies and teaching styles, assessment, record-keeping and reporting, and safety.

Teacher development is an integral part of school improvement. As physical education 'presents the teacher with a number of challenges which demand additional . . . working routines to those encountered in the classroom' (Rowe, 1995, p. 15), it seems that the physical education co-ordinator has a special responsibility to work closely with colleagues to help them develop new skills. Organizing and managing staff development courses is an integral facet of the role of the subject leader whose initial priority will be to assess the needs of the staff. Possible methods of data collection include observations, discussions, official meetings and questionnaires. Running in-service training based on staff requests ensures that, as far as possible, their needs will be met and demonstrates the leader's ability to listen.

It is important to acknowledge that different staff will be at varying stages in their professional development, so the physical education leader's intervention should relate to each teacher's personal context. The physical education leader can act as a critical friend who should carefully consider 'how their comments and critiques will feel to the recipients. This doesn't mean never to criticise but to be sincere and sensitive to how others are feeling' (Weinberg and Gould, 1995, p. 234). Asking a teacher to run a specific staff development session can be an excellent way of utilizing their strength, encouraging collective responsibility and gaining worthwhile information at the same time. Almond (1997, p. 31) has recommended that physical education leaders should provide teachers with chances to 'acquire a caring pedagogy, an informed and intelligent "practical knowledge base" and adequate opportunities for them to feel confident and competent in making available the very best of Physical Education to all young people'. Therefore, a realistic and manageable programme of in-service training may include:

- focused discussions regarding relevant and topical issues, and the review of current literature and resource materials;
- practical workshops;
- visits from guest speakers and advisory teachers;
- demonstration teaching and team teaching;
- summarizing key points from courses attended.

The physical education leader can act as a positive role model for colleagues. It is imperative that the leader demonstrates personal good practice: 'as a coordinator your own reputation and the reputation of the subject will be closely linked to the "image" you create' (Raymond, 1998, p. 31).

CONCLUSION

It is hoped that this chapter has provided prospective and developing physical education leaders with ideas and guidance for further consideration within their primary schools. Providing consistently high-quality learning opportunities for pupils in physical education is not an easy task, but should remain a priority for all subject mentors. Strong, dynamic leadership can go a long way to achieving this aim.

KEY POINTS

- There are different styles and strategies of leadership. The effective leader will be able to move in and out of various styles to suit different occasions accordingly.
- Many elements make up the successful delivery of physical education, so partnerships within and outside of the school will be important to cover the different aspects.
- Many non-specialist teachers find teaching physical education intimidating. The subject leader must try to alleviate any such anxiety by fostering an environment where improvement and achievement can flourish.

Chapter 9

Creating a Safe Learning Environment in Physical Education

TONY MACFADYEN

INTRODUCTION

> Safety ... does not consist merely of the absence of accidents but a positive mental and physical security which comes from the knowledge that all the teacher's responsibilities have been recognised and met. (O'Connor, 1987, p. 25)

The concept of safety should be a priority throughout the planning and delivery of physical education lessons. This is because, of all the curricula subjects, physical education probably has the greatest potential for creating situations where accidents resulting in bodily injury can occur.

During the course of physical education lessons children are expected to move their bodies vigorously, run and change direction at high speed, jump over apparatus, strike with implements, make use of limited space, work in areas that may not have been constantly monitored and are open to the elements, operate in and by deep water, and much more. It is thus incumbent on all those involved in promoting and conducting physical education to contribute to the provision of a strong safety culture that allows pupils to undertake a range of exciting and challenging activities, many of which have inherent risks, without coming to harm.

By being aware of potential hazards and taking appropriate action to prevent them and by following good practice, teachers can ensure that the level of risk of an accident is minimal. Roberts *et al.* (1995) have advised that safety precautions should become habitual in situations such as teaching, since an awareness of risk is an important prerequisite of effective prevention.

The purpose of this chapter is to explain how primary teachers can reduce the chance of pupils being physically damaged in the course of a physical education lesson by considering the application of some of the key safety principles. The first section examines the duty of care teachers have with respect to physical education. This is followed by a consideration of the contribution which teachers need to make to risk assessment and their role in reducing the level of danger. The third section discusses a selection of other factors that can have a significant bearing on the level of risk of accident in the physical education lesson. The final section looks at the importance of pupils' awareness of safety issues.

DUTY OF CARE

While most primary schoolteachers would probably consider the provision of a safe environment to be part of their normal professional functions (cf. Clay, 1997), it has to be remembered that teachers and schools have a significant responsibility for safety which is underpinned by law. Teachers in the UK are considered to be *in loco parentis* and this responsibility includes a duty of care for the safety of the pupils in their charge. The level of care to be taken by those in physical education was at one time based on what might be expected of a reasonably prudent parent. However, the British Association of Advisers and Lecturers in Physical Education (BAALPE, 1995, p. 23) has noted that

> Over the years it has been established through the courts that a school teacher should be expected to know a good deal more about the propensities of children than might a prudent parent. Add to this that some aspects of Physical Education have a high level of risk and required awareness and a higher duty of care is now expected of Physical Education teachers.

In order to provide this higher duty of care it would seem to be essential for those teaching physical education to have training, qualifications and experience appropriate for the activities with which they are involved. They should also be able to apply their knowledge of the changing structure and nature of the growing child to assist in safeguarding the well-being of pupils in their charge.

Qualifications

In order to deliver a higher duty of care over the full range of curriculum physical education, teachers at primary level need to be knowledgeable about the full range of activities likely to be taught, and to be able to plan, present and evaluate lessons effectively, taking into account such fundamentals as progression and differentiation. Given the time restrictions with respect to physical education within some Initial Teacher Training (ITE) courses (in Britain, the average time available for physical education on Primary PGCE courses is 23 hours, and on undergraduate courses 32 hours: Warburton, 1999), it could be supposed that not all newly qualified primary teachers will feel confident about conducting lessons safely over the whole range of activities. Even when deemed qualified, a teacher should not attempt to teach an activity or skill above his present level of competence.

Teachers without the necessary expertise can upgrade their qualifications in a variety of ways. In-service courses may be made available through local, national and academic providers and many governing bodies of sport have designed courses for teachers. In addition to physical education qualifications, it is advisable for those teaching physical education to have basic first aid training, while a thorough knowledge of the school's accident and emergency procedure is essential.

Knowledge about young people

It has been emphasized elsewhere in this book that knowledge of children's development is an important factor in the appropriate application of physical education in the primary school. Teachers need to be aware of safe exercises for young children and the safety implications of pupils' individual differences in partner work; for example, where children of the same age, but at very different stages of growth, may choose to work together (see Chapter 6).

Safety for pupils with special needs

Familiarity with a school's policy on pupils with special needs is essential in maintaining a safe environment in physical education. Pupils' medical conditions (e.g. asthma, diabetes and arthritis) can affect practice, and teachers will need to know how to avoid putting a pupil in danger. Unless specifically forbidden, children with an impairment (medical/sensory/physical) should actively participate in lessons, albeit with some precautions when required. For example, a pupil with epilepsy who is subject to 'absences' can readily participate in low-level gymnastics but will be ill-advised to climb high apparatus due to their potential loss of consciousness.

Safely integrating pupils' individual needs into physical education can present a real challenge to teachers. The teacher will usually need to consider a number of issues in this regard:

- How can the chosen physical activity be safely adapted/modified to best meet the individual's needs?
- What are the implications of the identified impairment for the pupil, teacher and other class members?
- Will extra support be required, and if so, how can it be most effectively employed?
- For pupils with a sensory impairment, what communication issues need to be addressed to ensure the pupil remains safe?

(Based on Perkins, 1997)

Teacher as leader

The quality of teachers' leadership is a vital principle of safety, as teachers can set good examples to pupils at a time when role models are very important. Personal presentation and clothing can set the right example and teachers can emphasize through their words and actions the importance of safety in physical education: 'The prevention of accidents largely depends on the skill, knowledge and example of the teacher' (DES, 1980, p. 1).

Welch (1978, p. ix) has suggested that 'accidents are part of the constant trial and error process of living', and to some extent this is paralleled in physical education. Teachers will therefore need the ability to anticipate, think quickly, and intervene appropriately to prevent minor accidents, resulting from pupil explorations, becoming serious. This means monitoring the whole class all the time. Teachers can prevent accidents by knowing their pupils, by ensuring pupils are physically and mentally ready for the challenge ahead, controlling the lesson adequately, teaching skills in a progressive way, and not expecting pupils to do something far beyond their current ability. Lessons that are built on previous experience, have clear aims, are well structured and effectively paced are likely to be safer than those where preparation is sparse.

RISK ASSESSMENT

The identification and management of risk is an essential part of every teacher's duty, so that even some of the most exciting and challenging activities can be attempted by pupils without risk of injury. The trick is to reduce the level of danger by a series of strategies and procedures, yet still retain those elements which an activity can provide, such as a sense of adventure, mastery of a task, expenditure of effort, challenge and individual expression, which pupils enjoy so much and which contribute to their development.

Risk assessment consists of a set of procedures through which hazards and those who may be harmed by them can be identified, and then control measures devised to prevent the possibility of accidents from occurring from the foreseen dangers. 'Risk assessment emphasises the estimation and quantification of risk in order to determine acceptable levels of risk and safety; in other words to balance the risks of an . . . activity against its . . . benefits' (Cutter, 1993, p. 2). Effective risk assessment should mean that the only risks which pupils face are those that are an inherent part of the activity. The National Coaching Foundation (1986) defines inherent risks as *the risks left over* when everything possible has been done to make an activity as safe as possible.

The ways in which identified risks are managed need to be recorded. BAALPE (1995, p. 44) advises that the process of risk assessment 'should form an integral part of Schemes of Work and lesson planning'. The same authority also states that risk assessment should be applied when foreseeable risks or hazards may occur. Due to the nature of the subject, it would seem sensible to appraise most activities in the physical education curriculum, at the same time noting that some require more attention than others. Thus activities can be placed on a continuum according to the perceived level of risk they exhibit (Kelly, 1997). Most dance activities may be placed at the lower end of the continuum, with some gymnastics or outdoor pursuits at a higher point.

As a result of a risk assessment exercise it may be concluded that a particular activity is potentially too hazardous for inclusion in the school's physical education programme, at least in certain forms. Trampolining, weight-lifting, some athletic throwing events and some games, for example, are generally considered unsuitable for primary schools. Some activities and equipment are actually prohibited by some education authorities. At a local level it may be necessary, following a risk assessment, to preclude an activity from the physical education programme, because it is not possible, given prevailing conditions, to reduce identified risks to a reasonable level. Banning netball because the surface of the only playing area becomes too uneven or slippery to move about without fear of accident illustrates the point.

Such is the breadth of the physical education curriculum that even specialists may not have an in-depth knowledge of all the activities being undertaken in their school. In such cases it would be wise to call for advice from an expert when required.

Negligence

In recent years, a number of authorities have noted the mounting legislation and growing litigation in physical education (Eve, 1997; Harrison and Watkins, 1996) which has meant more serious accidents are often subject to an enquiry. Kelly (1997) notes that current law considers *the environment, supervision* and *instruction* to be the three key areas of an investigation. Being found to be negligent in an incident is probably a teacher's greatest anxiety. However, by showing that they have taken reasonable precautions and have followed standard practice (for example, they can be seen to have carried out the relevant safety rules and followed the accident procedure after an accident) teachers can help to protect themselves from the likelihood of litigation.

OTHER FACTORS AFFECTING SAFETY IN PHYSICAL EDUCATION

Research suggests a safe and orderly environment is usually paramount for learning to take place (Hill and Hill, 1994). Noticing and dealing appropriately with hazards is an ongoing responsibility for those teaching physical education and they may be assisted in their endeavours by considering the following factors. It should be noted, however, that the following points do not make up an exhaustive list. Teachers should refer for detailed guidelines to definitive texts on safety at the end of the chapter.

Premises

While each physical education activity will have its own distinctive risks, there are generic potential hazards arising from the nature of facilities in which lessons take place. Thus, for activities that take place indoors, special attention must be paid to the design and construction of the accommodation, the floor surface and obstructions, while outdoors the playing surface and general environment need to be examined and any necessary precautionary procedures implemented.

Indoor facilities
Design and construction of the accommodation
Since 90 per cent of primary schools do not have their own purpose-built sports facilities (NAHT, 1999), it seems inevitable that the majority of physical education lessons will not be carried out in purpose-built rooms. While some account of the needs of physical education might have been taken in the provision of the school hall, teachers conducting lessons in such areas should be on the look-out for dangerous features. These might include doors that open inwards, protruding handles, radiators and low-level unprotected glazed areas. The space adjacent to these hazards must be cordoned off in an obvious way and called a 'no go' zone. Activities that include running and other fast movement must be organized in such a way that children could not possibly come into contact with the dangers, or should not be included in the programme.

Floor surface
Although non-slip, even floor surfaces required for physical education may well be found in the school hall, teachers should always be alert to situations that can change conditions. Dirt brought in on outdoor shoes, spilt drinks and leaks can all turn a normally safe floor into a dangerous one. Inspection of the floor area should take place before the start of the lesson and arrangements should be in place for dirty floors to be swept and spillages mopped up as soon as they are discovered.

Obstructions
Teachers must be aware of furniture, a piano or other equipment that may intrude into a multi-purpose working area. Co-operation and negotiation with other teachers and supervisory staff is the key to ensuring as much space for safe movement as possible. Temporarily redundant items should always be stored in the same designated space and in such a way that sharp corners do not protrude. The selection of appropriate activities, good organization of the space available and sufficient margin between activity and storage areas should help prevent collisions between pupils and furniture.

Outdoor facilities
The playing surface
It is expected that in the majority of primary schools the outdoor playing surfaces on which physical education lessons take place will be grassed or hard surfaced. Poorly maintained surfaces which are pitted, bumpy, or covered with loose material are likely to be unsafe for many physical activities, especially those involving moving balls, running, and quick changes of

direction. Teachers should remember that certain weather conditions can turn normally safe playing surfaces into unacceptable ones. Frost, rain and dew can all make some surfaces unsuitable for use, as can occasional car-parking on the hard playing area that can result in the deposit of oil patches. It is important, therefore, that the playing surface should be inspected before all lessons. Some areas that are not easily scanned and are vulnerable to outside abuse should be thoroughly checked for dangers. Pupils may be involved in a sweep search of the area so long as they can be relied upon not to touch or pick up any dangerous objects they might come across. Children should be instructed to draw the teacher's attention to any offending items found and these can be removed with the right amount of care.

General environment

Appraisal, similar to that of indoor premises, is required before each physical education lesson held outdoors. For example, the state of boundary fences and the position of activity spaces in relation to them will need consideration. In addition, the teacher must remain vigilant throughout the lesson as conditions may change; an orienteering course can become unsafe because of the entry of a delivery vehicle to the school grounds.

Swimming pools

Public swimming pools have well-established safety regulations that are normally strictly enforced by trained staff. Teachers should be aware of the regulations, and support the on-site professionals. When a school's own pool or a private pool is utilized, similarly strict safety regulations should be adhered to, including staff qualifications and staff:pupil ratios.

Equipment

Two main kinds of physical education equipment can usually be found in primary schools: gymnastic equipment (fixed and portable), and portable equipment.

Gymnastic equipment

Gymnastic equipment can be both fixed and portable. Although anchored to a wall or ceiling, fixed apparatus (ropes, ladders, rings) often moves in and out on trackways, or is hinged and has to be manually set up to form a climbing frame. Portable gymnastic equipment includes pieces such as bar boxes, nesting tables, balance bars and benches, some of which have to be assembled before use. Both kinds of gymnastic equipment may be treated in a similar way by teachers, except that in the case of portable apparatus special consideration has to be given to approved methods of lifting and carrying by children and to the neat and safe storage of this kind of apparatus, since dangerous situations may arise from poor handling of equipment or untidiness.

Many teachers of physical education do not feel confident in using gymnastic equipment, and are uneasy about the possibility of injury to their pupils arising from falls and mishaps when it is incorporated into their lessons (BAALPE, 1995). Teachers' misgivings in using apparatus probably arise largely from their limited experience and their lack of subject knowledge.

When, as is often the case, children are involved in setting out gymnastic equipment, a three-part checking protocol should be completed by the teacher before anyone moves on to any piece. Part one involves the teacher checking that the equipment has been correctly positioned and that each piece occupies sufficient space to allow movements on to, from, through and over it without fear of pupils bumping into walls or other obstructions, or interfering with other activities. In the second part of the checking process the teacher should ensure that the apparatus is stable, has been properly assembled and should note particularly that any locking pins/fixing bolts implicated in the assembly process are securely engaged. The third part of the inspection routine should concentrate on the condition of the equipment. Occurrences such as accidental collisions or vandalism could cause splinters to be present in wooden beams, or vibration may cause screws or bolts to work loose. Should any problems be discovered, the apparatus should be taken out of use immediately. All those teaching physical education should feel secure in the knowledge that the apparatus they are using is inspected on a regular basis by professional engineers according to the manufacturer's recommendations.

Portable equipment

Bats, hockey sticks, rackets, goal/net posts are examples of the type of equipment that might be found in a primary school. They may seem innocuous enough when stacked in the store cupboard, but they can constitute a hazard and may bring harm to the user, or those around her, if they are not of a suitable size and weight (see Chapter 7 on child development), or kept in good condition. Worn or soiled handles that can cause a performer's grip to slip can turn a striking implement into a missile.

Clothing and jewellery

Children heat up and cool down relatively quickly compared to adults and can therefore suffer from heat stress in too warm an environment or from hypothermia when it is too cold. For these reasons children must be properly protected when they may experience extremes of temperature (for example, on warm days, visits to an under-heated swimming pool or to playing fields subjected to a bitingly cold wind). In hot conditions children should wear loose, lightweight clothing and where necessary be protected from the sun's rays with long-sleeved vests and hats, with parts of the skin still exposed treated with a high-factor sun cream. Conversely when it is cold, children should wear sufficient layers to keep out the chill: a shivering child is less likely to be alert to potentially dangerous situations developing around her. Shoes worn in physical education lessons should be flexible and have flat soles resistant to slippage on the surface being used. For gym and dance, bare feet are often most appropriate. Children should not sacrifice suitability to fashion, for example; laces should always be tied up rather than simply tucked in.

There are very few jewellery-related accidents in schools because there are usually procedures already in place to prevent them. It is important that all teachers of physical education ensure that compliance with these procedures, which normally require removal of ornamental jewellery and other personal effects before the start of the physical education lesson, remain standard practice. The exceptions are where jewellery is worn for cultural reasons. In this situation, cases should be dealt with sensitively on an individual basis. Children and their parents are often more receptive to the argument of removing jewellery once the consequences of an accident have been explained. Where jewellery is kept on, careful thought needs to be given to how the adornments can be adequately covered (e.g. surgical tape/wristbands).

EDUCATING PUPILS

It is clear that the teacher plays an essential role in producing a safe and secure physical education environment in which pupils can learn. Teachers should work to a general set of rules in all their lessons to provide pupils with a framework to adhere to. Young children in particular will need tight control, as they often have difficulty realizing the implications of their actions. At certain times, teachers will need to instruct pupils when and where to move to, so everyone remains safe.

Children must not begin their tasks on the apparatus until the safety checks have been completed by the teacher. Pupils will need to be taught this restraint assiduously, and constantly reminded of the protocol as the equipment is likely to prove a great attraction. In the further interests of their safety the children will also have to be taught that only an appropriate number of people can be allowed on each piece of equipment at any one time.

It is suggested that teachers will need to find a balance between instructing pupils on exactly what to do, and helping them to increase their own understanding and awareness of safety. Teachers who over-regulate and simply continue to tell pupils what to do, can produce pupils who are unable to act on their own initiative, which can lead to a genuine failure to know what the rules are, and even reaction against them (Welch, 1978). Older children may be resentful of too much teacher intervention as they learn to come to terms with their own ability and the amount of risk they can safely take. Accidents are less likely to occur if children understand what causes them, and if they are allowed to take responsibility for their actions. The Council of Europe (cited in Boucher, 1977, p. 139) suggests that 'training of the child at all ages in active participation in safety behaviour is essential'. This is recognized in England and Wales' National Curriculum of Physical Education (1995) which incorporates a specific section on safe practice that pupils should be taught. This will clearly have to be a gradual process during the primary years as children mature and become increasingly able to take on more complex safety principles.

Schools may be advised to make explicit in policy documentation how pupils' responsibility for their own and others' safety will be developed year on year. For example, Benn and Benn (1992, p. 97) suggest 'a good school policy will phase in the demands of handling apparatus alongside the development of other areas of learning in gymnastics'.

CONCLUSION

Safety in physical education is the teacher's first priority and should never be compromised. This chapter has suggested that safe practice underpins good practice and that safety considerations should be a natural starting point for each lesson. Accident prevention is multi-faceted but can be effectively managed through commonsense, responsible risk assessment.

Anxiety about teaching physical education can become a real drain on the teacher's energy, and detract from pupil learning. The best way forward would seem to be to plan a framework that can cope with foreseen eventualities and to use appropriate regulations to guide the implementation of sound curricular physical education.

KEY POINTS

- Safety precautions cannot remove all risks, but can eliminate unnecessary dangers.
- Teachers should admit their limitations and not compromise safety in an activity about which they are unsure. However, teachers should gradually increase their expertise through continuing professional development.
- Teachers can, and should, teach children about the potential dangers that exist in physical education so that pupils come to know and understand how to use safety procedures. At the same time, teachers must realize their role as a risk manager and recognize and cater for the inexperience of children.

Part II

Content of Primary Physical Education

Chapter 10

Teaching Athletics

TONY MACFADYEN, RICHARD BAILEY AND MIKE OSBORNE

INTRODUCTION

> Athletics is essentially the experience of walking, running, jumping and throwing activities in various competitive situations. If taught well it lends itself to the development of each student's potential in physical activity and enables them all to play a full part in observing and communicating with peers in seeking to improve their performances. It is an exciting activity provided the material and its delivery are student-centered and not merely repetition of Olympic events. (O'Neill, 1998, p. 17)

Athletics can quite rightly claim to be the 'vocabulary' of sport, as virtually every other sporting activity to some extent involves running, jumping and throwing. Children also run, jump and throw as part of their natural play, and these abilities need to be developed in order to act as a foundation for progress in other movement spheres. The important aspect is the development of *personal competence* in all three areas and not the application of artificial adult competitive categories to them. Writers such as O'Neill (1992) and Beaumont (1990) have suggested that for too long the traditional ways of teaching athletics, that place 'events', and by implication techniques, at the heart of the lesson are inappropriate in the primary school. In support, the fundamental intent of this chapter is to suggest that any athletic activity should be made to fit the child and not the other way round.

In order to teach athletics to pupils in the primary school in a safe, enjoyable and effective way a number of issues need to be addressed, including the place of athletics within the wider physical education curriculum, the appropriate content for primary school children, and effective approaches to teaching these activities. These elements form the framework for this chapter.

THE PLACE OF ATHLETICS IN THE CURRICULUM

Athletic activities concern the pursuit of the fulfillment of individual potential. Pupils strive to improve performance against measurements and/or others in maximizing their performance in terms of time, height, length or distance. Athletic activities build on children's natural capacities to run, jump and throw. They promote all-round physical development – speed, strength, stamina and flexibility. (DES, 1991, p. 14)

Athletics occupies a peculiar place within the physical education curriculum. On the one hand, it involves the development of certain familiar and specialized skills. For example, it could be argued that any member of the public could list characteristic athletics activities, such as long jump, high jump, discus, javelin, sprinting, long-distance running and so on. On the other hand, the essential elements of athletics, namely running, jumping and throwing, which make up the basic ingredients of almost all other physical education skills, may not be similarly acknowledged. A footballer, for example, needs to run to reach a ball, jump to head it or to be able to throw it back into play. The relationship between these two dimensions of the subject – the specialized and the generic skills – is not always made clear, especially during the primary years.

In recent years, there has appeared to be a move to marginalize the place of athletics within physical education in the UK (QCA, 1998), and this is unfortunate. The chapter on movement development (Chapter 7) makes clear the need to offer children a range of activities that establish fundamental and specialized movement skills, without which proper functioning becomes impossible. Thus children up to the age of 6 or 7 must practise the core skills of locomotion, stability and manipulation. Thereafter, they need to refine, combine and elaborate these skills into increasingly specialized contexts. Athletics stands out as the ideal medium for facilitating such development, particularly when a personal developmental model is employed.

One problem may be that many people hold rather stereotypical conceptions of the subject. Comments by authoritative figures in the world of athletics like Dick (1987) have perhaps only served to accentuate the problem:

I feel most strongly that the beginner athlete must be well taught, with teachers and coaches committed to ensuring that the various 'technical models' are established before moving on to competition or advanced training.

Given the wide variety of movement activities which children need and deserve, and to discourage the replication of stereotyped adult athletic events, it is important for teachers to understand that it is the teaching of *athletic activities* that is appropriate for young children, not adult *athletics events*.

O'Neill (1992, p. 12) has suggested that 'no other key activity area within Physical Education has modeled itself so uncompromisingly on the adult format in the way Athletics has'. One reason for this may be the laudable yet often counter-productive promotion of criterion-referenced National Governing Body awards that risk putting the event before the child. Used appropriately, National Governing Body awards can be a useful teaching aid, but they should not replace appropriate educational objectives.

The skills listed above – long jump, javelin and so on – certainly make up the content of adult athletics. Aspects of these events may have a role as children grow older, but the teacher of younger children needs to understand that these skills are built upon a foundation of earlier learning. As has been emphasized throughout this book, it is inappropriate to unreflectively adopt adult activities when working with children. For example, before a child can throw an adult javelin, she can develop the technique of throwing other equipment, such as quoits, bean bags, balls of different sizes and weights, and foam javelins. (Shuttlecocks taped together provide a cheaper home-made projectile!)

The fundamental movement patterns of the different throwing, running and jumping techniques are essentially the same, but the simpler actions reflect the particular stages of development of a still maturing child. Moreover, the standards of adult performance can place the child's body under potentially damaging stress. Well-meaning attempts to mimic full versions of athletic events can inhibit learning and motivation, and disincline the child to later participation. Why should a 6 or even a 12 year old be expected to run maximally for 100 metres when the required physique to do so is that of a Linford Christie or Merlene Ottey?

The point is well made by David Gallahue (1976, p. 48):

> Without a clear understanding of children we become teachers of content rather than of children. If we are to maximize our effectiveness as teachers of children we must know, understand, and accept children for what they are and not 'adultise' them and force them into being what we expect them to be.

Thus the teacher needs to be clear that athletics in the primary school aims to lay the necessary foundations for later performance. It does not attempt to replicate that performance. This does not mean that there is no place for skill learning. On the contrary, there are many skills that need to be developed. Some of these are best developed in an atmosphere of play and exploration. Others require specific teaching, and this will be discussed later.

There is another dimension of athletics that deserves acknowledgement, and that relates to health and fitness. Fry (1995) uses the term 'athleticism' to refer to those attributes that are transferable to all aspects of physical activity, such as stamina, strength, power, speed and agility. The contribution that physical education can make to developing children's health (Harris, 1989; Sleap and Warburton, 1992; and see Chapters 7 and 14 of this book) is part of the important debate about lifestyle and activity patterns of children. Athletics is particularly well placed to play a role in this respect. Stamina can be developed through taking part in longer distance running; strength through appropriate use of jumping activities; speed through sprinting; agility through obstacle and dodging events. There is some evidence that physical fitness gains made in childhood track into adult life (Simons-Morton *et al.*, 1988). However, as the research is equivocal it would seem more appropriate to use athletics as a vehicle to 'hook' children on to physical activity. If this is to work, children need to be motivated and to feel good about their participation. Therefore, the content and delivery of the subject by primary teachers is crucial. If pupils are to come to love athletics, it needs to be a positive, enjoyable and fun experience. Wetton (1997) has rightly stressed that children's social relationships, as well as learning, are best encouraged in an environment in which children are happy.

CONTENT AND ACTIVITIES

The sections that follow draw a distinction between activities and content suitable for 5 to 7 year olds, and 7 to 11 year olds. In practice, of course, there is no strict distinction. It is highly likely that some infants could benefit from the more structured activities suggested for older children. Likewise, the games suggested for younger children can easily be used with 7 to 11 year olds, whether as warm-ups or as enjoyable variations within the lesson. What is important is that activities should suit the children's physical and cognitive stage of development.

APPROPRIATE CONTENT FOR 5–7 YEAR OLDS

The years from 5 to 7 are a period during which children continue to develop the building blocks of movement. The main message is, keep it simple. Some children will begin to be ready for more specialized skills (which will be discussed below), while many continue to require practice in the fundamental movement skills.

Young children need to learn to work together in simple co-operative and competitive situations. There is a risk in athletics of placing too much emphasis upon the competitive aspect. This an important feature of athletics, but it needs to be introduced gradually and in a way in which all children feel their efforts are valued. It should be noted that children can compete in various ways, not only against their peers. In some games (for example, 'What's the time, Mr Wolf?') children can 'compete' against the teacher. In others, they compete against themselves ('How far can you throw the bean bag? Can you beat that?') or against a standard (when competing for certain athletics awards). The personal commitment and effort that leads to progression is the important feature of primary school athletics; even at elite adult level, 'personal bests' are celebrated and reported, and it is this aspect that must be emphasized throughout the teaching and learning of all athletic (and perhaps all other) activities.

For example, children can keep diaries of personal improvement rather than the teacher simply recording achievements in a book.

Breadth rather than depth of experience is important at this stage (Sugden and Talbot, 1998), and the teacher needs to plan for a wide range of activities that provide varied and exciting challenges, and expose children to different ways of learning that encourage exploration of a wide range of responses. Littlewood (1998, p. 28) sees this period as the 'Foundation Development Stage' and suggests that 5 to 7 year olds' athletic experiences should centre around spontaneous play, informal activities, co-ordination and movement skills. Children should generally work on whole-body movements. A simple approach to planning is to adopt the classification of fundamental movement skills presented in Chapter 7:

- locomotion skills;
- manipulation skills;
- stability skills.

Locomotion refers to the ways children move their bodies from one place to another. The simple enquiry, 'How many different ways can you move around the area?' can result in innumerable actions. The most fundamental actions include walking, running, side-stepping, jumping and skipping.

Manipulation is about sending and receiving objects, including balls, bean bags and quoits. Athletics tends to focus upon projecting these objects, either as far as possible or towards a target. The basic skills include throwing, rolling and pushing objects.

Stability, in this context, refers to balance and awareness of the position of one's body in relation to an area and other people. The ability to maintain and adjust one's balance is fundamental to both manipulation and locomotion skills, and thus stability skills are central to all movement development. In relation to athletics, important skills include starting, stopping, avoiding and changing direction.

This classification makes clear the close links between athletics and other areas of physical education, such as games, gym and dance. When is running part of athletics or part of games? When does stability cease to be part of gymnastics and become part of athletics? A case in point is the National Curriculum for Physical Education (1995) for England and Wales. Athletic activities are not featured as a discrete unit at Key Stage 1, but closer inspection of the other activity areas reveals that pupils should be taught 'to develop and practise a variety of ways of sending . . . a ball and other similar games equipment' and 'elements of game play that include running, chasing, dodging' (DFE, 1995, p. 115).

It is vital that children explore the limits and possibilities of their movement through athletics. As stated earlier, the children require a *breadth* of experience. Consequently, the teacher needs to plan for them to experience a range of challenges, using a variety of equipment. This chapter does not aim to offer a comprehensive list of tasks for the teacher; there are numerous such texts that can be consulted (cf. Gallahue, 1976; McGeorge and Almond, 1998; Wetton, 1992). There follow some examples of activities that are appropriate for the 5 to 7 age range. Using locomotion as an example, children can explore their movement by taking numerous different emphases (Tables 10.1 to 10.6).

Table 10.1: Locomotion skills

Skills	Example activity
Travel to collect	'Fill the basket' – the teacher throws bean bags around an area, and the children attempt to return them to their basket before the teacher can throw them out again.
Travel to jump	Run and jump over a barrier (such as a rope or mark on the ground).
Running for distance	'How far can you run in five seconds?' 'How far can you run in two minutes?'
Running for time	'How fast can you run the distance?'
Jumping for height	Jumping high in the air, or small bounces on the spot.
Jumping for distance	Use markers to measure distance jumped. Legs straight or bent? Arms still or swinging? How few jumps to cross the area?

Table 10.2: Activities to develop locomotion skills

Animals	Children pretend to be different animals as they move around the area. Different animals move in different ways: cheetahs move quickly; elephants move slowly and heavily; mice scurry in different directions, dodging others.
Jumping	A series of hoops are placed in lines.
Relay	Teams jump from hoop to hoop towards the finishing line. Children can be encouraged to explore different jumps: which takes you furthest? Which is further?
Bean game	In this extremely popular game, children travel around the area reflecting different 'beans': runner beans run; Mexican jumping beans jump with small bounces; jelly beans wobble; and so on. Children can think of many more beans and associated actions.

Table 10.3: Manipulation skills

Skill	Example activity
Send to self	Throw object into the air and catch; throw, bounce and catch. How high? How many?
Send to partner	Roll, throw or push to partner. How accurately? How far? How many?
Send to target	Aim to hit hoops, skittles or baskets.
Different actions	Roll, push, one-handed throw, two-handed throw, overarm, underarm, sling, front-facing, sideways-facing. Which actions help send the object furthest? Which are most accurate?

Table 10.4: Activities to develop manipulation skills

Pursuit	Children form a circle. Younger or less able children can sit close together, while older or more able children can stand a set distance apart. Either by handing or throwing, children pass a ball around a circle. Then a second ball is added. Can one ball catch up with the second? Three balls? Four?
Skittles	In a circle around a number of lightweight skittles, children throw or roll a soft ball, trying to knock them down. As the ball rebounds or misses, the receiver carries on until all are hit.
Golf	All ages enjoy this simple game, which is included in the Youth Sport Trust's 'Top Play' scheme. Groups devise their own course of hoops, baskets and other targets. The player throws a bean bag to each target in as few throws as possible, then moves on to the next. How many throws to complete the course? Can you beat your record?

Table 10.5: Stability skills

Skill	Example activity
Starting and stopping	Starting from standing, crouching, lying. Controlled and 'soft' stops.
Changing directions	Avoiding others, dodging and weaving.
Static balance	Freeze and balance on the spot; holding different body shapes. Two feet. One foot.
Dynamic balance	Walking along lines on the floor or low gymnastic beams or benches.

Table 10.6: Activities to develop stability skills

Frozen bean bag	All children in a group place a bean bag on their heads and slowly move around an area. If the bean bag slips off, that child 'freezes' on the spot until a friend replaces it. For extra challenge the teacher can add other tasks: balance on one foot; touch your toes; and so on.
Stop and go	One child stands behind a line at a distance from the others. She calls 'Go' and the others begin to move towards the line. On 'Stop', they must freeze. Any wobbles start again. The first to cross the line becomes the caller.
Tom and Jerry	In pairs, one child is Tom; the other Jerry. The teacher calls 'Tom', who tries to tag Jerry, and vice versa.

APPROPRIATE CONTENT FOR 7–11 YEAR OLDS

As children progress through the primary years they need to learn skills that are more specialized and occur in specific contexts. Drawing on the broad base of movement skills developed earlier, children's increasing maturity and efficiency in running, jumping and throwing activities means it is useful to begin to frame these activities in terms that are more recognizably 'athletic'. These activities are really refinements, combinations and elaborations of earlier skills, but the contexts in which they occur are more structured (cf. Littlewood, 1998). Taking the National Curriculum for Physical Education (1995) in England and Wales as a case in point, athletic activities, not featured as a discrete unit at Key Stage 1 (5–7 years), is featured at Key Stage 2 (7–11 years) where children should be taught 'to develop and refine basic techniques in running ... throwing ... and jumping' and 'to measure, compare and improve their own performance' (DFE, 1995, p. 117).

It is the core elements of the activity that should still be considered, so events can still be stripped of their overly technical complications. In the high jump a three-stride approach will still suit many pupils; in the long jump it is the speed of the run-up that should be emphasized, so a nine-pace approach is adequate. As children generally become more capable of working with their peers, they can increasingly learn to operate as a team, for example, in relay competitions.

Older children can also begin to learn other skills necessary for athletics participation. They can practise timing their friend's run; they can measure the length of others' throws or jumps and record these results. These skills are just as essential as the physical movements, and add a further dimension to their understanding of the activities. As class teachers will often teach their own class, there will be excellent opportunities for cross-curricular links, and these may include:

- Mathematics (comparison, estimation, recording findings and decimal notation);
- English (relating events, collecting data, description and text vocabulary);
- Science (using instruments, types and uses of materials, forces and energy).

The three key elements of athletics – running, jumping and throwing – should remain the focus for children at this age.

Running

Running is natural, but it is also a skill that children can develop and many children enjoy competitive running races. However, they do form unusually public displays of maturation (as well as ability), and this can be harmful to some children's confidence, especially if the teacher places unwarranted emphasis upon the outcome. As they grow older, children begin to compare themselves with others (cf. NCF, n.d., p. 12), and they are often very aware of any difference. However, reinforcing and rewarding these differences is of dubious educational worth, and can be harmful to children's self-esteem and continued enthusiasm (Fry, 1995). Children who try their best but never win are quite naturally going to lose motivation and develop low self-esteem. The goal for teachers is for each child to have a sense of achievement, so the teacher needs to plan for inclusive opportunities in order for all class members to improve. Instead of racing pupils against each other, lesson content can include activities that investigate the contrast between sprinting speed and the pacing required for running 250 metres, and how running style may be affected by each type of running. Offering children the chance to set and improve upon their own standards and to work as part of a group can be invaluable learning experiences.

In most of the examples given below, children run for a certain time and attempt to improve upon the distance they cover. This reduces crude comparisons, since maturation can make a nonsense of direct comparisons between children. It also removes a potential class management problem: what do the early finishers do while the rest are running?

Sprinting
- Timed sprints: lines of cones five metres apart are placed down a 'track'. Children observe and record how many cones their partner 'covered' in five seconds (teacher may time and blow whistle, older pupils can 'time' each other).
- Estimated sprints: How many do you think you can reach in three or six seconds?

Longer distances
- Track runs: markers for 25-metre intervals. How far did you run in one minute?
- Varying pace: follow my leader/changing strides.

Relays

- Partner or very small teams (three or four) to carry out short distance tasks (picking up or replacing bean bags, or passing batons). Care should be taken not to force children to run too great distances. Four 'legs' of 20 metres is fun, challenging and allows for more time to practise the baton change-overs.

Hurdles

- Low barriers.
- Lines on the ground.

Jumping

Children love to jump, and jumping can take many forms:

- For distance from standing:
  - from one-footed take-off;
  - from two-footed take-off.
- For height:
  - from straight on;
  - from an angled approach.

Throwing

There is very little justification for primary children to take on the javelin, shot, discus or hammer, although the use of modified and mini-equipment can make 'replication' of the adult form worthwhile. Children can use a variety of throws:

- overarm;
- underarm;
- round arm.

Across all the athletic tasks pupils should also be fully involved in the timing, measuring and recording of performances, as well as taking turns to teach each other.

DEVELOPING QUALITY IN ATHLETICS

The three main elements of athletics – running, jumping and throwing – are core skills that all children should understand in order to develop and progress. Thus effective teaching and learning in athletics would focus upon these fundamentals, and the basic principles that underpin them.

In running, these are:

- to look straight ahead;
- to keep a strong, straight back;
- to use the arms (in a balanced pumping action);
- to lift the knees straight and (fairly) high;
- to use the front part of the feet (not the heels).

In the jumps, these are:

- to keep a strong, straight back (Fosbury Flop is not appropriate for this age group);
- to take off with one foot (unless specifically doing a standing broad jump);
- to 'drive' the non-take-off leg upwards quickly and powerfully;
- to 'drive' the arms upwards to help provide lift;
- to approach high jumps from an angle (about 45 degrees);
- to 'grit' their teeth (to avoid injury);
- to combine speed plus height when jumping for distance.

In the throws, these are:

- to start with weight on the back foot (the same side as the throwing arm);
- to 'drive' with the back leg;
- to rotate the hips;
- to resist and lift with the front leg (the opposite side to the throwing hand);
- to transfer weight up and over the front foot;
- to throw at about 45 degrees for maximum distance;
- to follow through and end up on the 'new front' foot (i.e. right foot for right-handers).

TEACHING ATHLETICS

Many athletic activities have clear competitive aspects, and many older primary children love to compete. However, competition and success are not always compatible. Used appropriately, competition can be a powerful motivator; however, where it is used unthinkingly, it can destroy the confidence and ambition of many children. Furthermore, as athletic activities take place on a public stage and are generally individual in nature, there is a need for sensitivity in teaching and comparing children. Children do not need to solely compete against each other. Challenges can be:

- against others;
- against self;
- against set standards;
- against self-selected standards;
- co-operative.

Athletics lends itself to a variety of teaching styles. As McGeorge and Almond (1998, p. 8) point out, even

> a teacher with little experience of Athletics can provide essential guidance and understanding by concentrating on empathy rather than a very didactic approach. This can be done by adapting the competition events … to ones which allow the pupils to really feel the event.

Direct teacher instruction may be required for teaching events safely. Even if pupils are not throwing dangerous implements, teachers can instruct pupils in good safety habits. A list of some of the main safety considerations is given below:

- establish a safe and controlled routine;
- count all the equipment out and check that it is all returned;
- equipment should not be played about with or mishandled;
- be aware of the dangers of operating on wet surfaces;
- equipment should be transported in a safe manner and stored securely;
- children should always stand behind the throwing line when it is not their turn;
- pupils can be made aware of safe distances between throwers;
- throwers should check the landing area before throwing and must not collect their implement before being instructed to by the teacher;
- hard surfaces should be protected to ensure a soft landing.

Almond (1984) has suggested that athletics teaching should focus on understanding and intelligent performance as well as technique. This will require more than didactic methods of teaching that inevitably dominate when there is a heavy emphasis on achieving a textbook-type technique (O'Neill, 1992). Guided discovery may be appropriate for the exploration of movement: which types of jump take you furthest? Can you find ways of running faster by changing an aspect of your running style? The technical aspects of athletics mean that there is always plenty of material for productive reciprocal partner work: is your partner transferring their weight appropriately during the throw? (see Chapter 4).

Teachers should try to use language that really illustrates the action which pupils are expected to perform, and this strengthens the subject's cross-curricular dimension too. Thus, in throwing events teachers can use terms like 'explode', 'thrust', 'drive' and 'punch'. Analogies work very effectively across all the physical education activities, and athletics is no exception. Pupils can try to 'leap like salmon' in the high jump or 'sprint as if they are running on hot coals!'

THE ATHLETICS LESSON

Ideally, pupils should be given the opportunity to run, jump and throw during each lesson. If facilities or time do not permit this, the teacher should aim for two elements. It may be that one aspect is incorporated only as part of the warm-up and acts to cement good practice from last week's lesson. Young children generally have short attention spans, so by working on a combination of the different elements pupils are unlikely to become bored. Furthermore, as children's bodies are not well adapted to sustained intensity or repeated actions, they are better suited to a variety of challenges that stress different parts of their bodies (Bailey, 1999). The cool-down section of the lesson is an ideal time to work on developing good habits towards flexibility and a greater understanding of the body's anatomy. Muscles should be more supple as they will be warm from the lesson's activity and pupils can work on learning the names of muscles they are stretching.

KEY POINTS

- The emphasis in the 5–11 age range is on introducing children to a range of athletic activities in a way that is educational, motivational and enjoyable.
- The teacher should focus upon the core elements of running, jumping and throwing.
- Teachers should search for imaginitive ways of challenging children through athletic activities.

Chapter 11

Teaching Dance

ANN DAVIES

INTRODUCTION

This chapter attempts to demystify the teaching of dance. It intends to provide teachers with an understanding of the nature of dance and its specific contribution to children's education. The reader is taken stage by stage through the principles underlying the successful planning and teaching of a dance programme. Obviously, the ideas, content and methods suggested in the chapter should be viewed as examples only. Teachers will need to develop their own material and methods to suit their individual circumstances and needs.

THE IMPORTANCE OF DANCE

Dance makes a distinctive contribution to the education of all pupils, in that it uses the most fundamental mode of human expression – movement. Through its use of non-verbal communication, pupils are able to participate in a way which differs from any other area of learning. It provides aesthetic and cultural education, opportunities for personal expression and it also introduces students to a wealth of traditional, social and theatrical forms. In a broad and balanced curriculum, this important area of human experience should not be neglected. (NDTA, *et al.*, 1990)

Historically, dance in schools was fostered mainly within physical education programmes, as the basis of dance is movement. There are particular similarities between gymnastics and dance since they are both concerned with composing, performing and appreciating sequences of movement. Both provide children with opportunities for inventive and creative responses to stimuli and help to develop versatility in a variety of purposeful situations. There is, however, an essential difference between them. Gymnastics is mainly concerned with the development of skilful body management for its own sake and may be described as being objective in purpose, with any expressive qualities being merely incidental. However, unlike other areas of physical education, in dance the ultimate concern is with the expressive qualities or the meaning of movement, rather than its purely practical function. It is, above all, concerned with the aesthetic and artistic nature of movement.

Dance offers children opportunities to experience life aesthetically: to heighten children's awareness of the qualities of objects and events; to encourage the viewing of things purely for the way they look, sound or feel and enjoying them for what they are, for their qualities of line, pattern, dynamics, colour, texture and shape. Through discussion, children should be encouraged to respond to aesthetic qualities in the dance – to describe what they see and how the dance makes them feel. They should be encouraged to make informed judgements about the dance. It is not enough, however, just to say 'I like it' or 'I don't like it'; instead, children should be encouraged to give the reasons for their judgements through direct reference to the qualities of the dance, which everyone can perceive.

Aesthetic qualities are embodied in many aspects of dance including traditional and folk dances. While these are obviously enjoyed by the dancers themselves for social and kinaesthetic reasons, they are also enjoyed and appreciated by onlookers for the intricacy of pattern, rhythm, line and form. It is only when dance is taught as an artistic activity that aesthetic elements are deliberately used 'to enhance the experience for both performer and audience, to create meaning and communicate through movement' (Arts Council of Great Britain, 1993, p. 17).

For dance to be taught as an artistic activity, three areas must be addressed – those of composition, performance and appreciation. *Composition* entails creating dances with movements being intentionally selected, refined, moulded, shaped and formed into an identifiable whole to communicate an intended idea. The composition is a conscious expression of the composer's comment on the world. The composer will have abstracted the essence from actual feeling or literal movement, which can then be modified and manipulated to be used as a symbol to convey meaning. Therefore, if pupils are working on a dance based on the emotions of anger, sadness and happiness, they would not be asked to be angry, but they would be encouraged to talk about their observations of what people sometimes do and how they move when they feel these emotions. These movements could then be exaggerated by the children and made into movement phrases or motifs. These could then be repeated exactly, or varied, by using different body parts, levels or by making the movements travel instead of remaining on the spot. The ideas could then be refined and shaped, emphasizing highlights and contrasts to give form to the dance.

While composition entails the making of dances, *performance* is concerned with dancing – with the interpretation or re-creation of the composition. To do this successfully the performer must have physical skills, an understanding of the composer's intention and a sensitivity to the accompaniment, other performers and the space in which the dance is to be performed. The dancers will also need to develop skills of projection and interpretive and expressive qualities so that they can successfully convey the composer's idea.

Performance in a learning context does not necessarily mean a full-blown dance performance in a theatre. This may sometimes be relevant, but performance usually means sharing in a class situation. It may begin with a partner when the children evaluate each other's work and offer constructive comments for its improvement. It may then progress to sharing with the rest of the class and then perhaps with another class or the rest of the school in an assembly. Obviously, there will be times when it is appropriate to show the work to parents or a wider audience. The polishing of the performance may be time-consuming, but it is an integral part of the whole process of dance education, and can be a very worthwhile experience for performers and audience alike.

Watching dances provides endless opportunities to develop the pupil's skills of *appreciation*. Through guided questioning, the children can be encouraged to describe and interpret what they have seen, in terms of the performance and composition of the dance. They should also be encouraged to make value judgements concerning the dances and be helped to substantiate their opinions with specific reference to what actually exists within the dance and how well it was performed. In addition to this objective evaluation, children must also be allowed to say how the dance makes them 'feel', since education in the arts should encourage the education of feeling.

Access to the 'literature' of any art-form is invaluable in the understanding of that particular art, and dance is no exception. In order to create dances, good models must be available for the pupils to view. Just as it would be inconceivable to think of a fine art course that did not include access to established two-dimensional and three-dimensional art-works, or a music course that did not encourage pupils to listen to pieces by established composers, similarly, studying dance without reference to the work of professional dance artists and companies would be equally unsatisfactory.

The use of repertoire can also give pupils access to a rich diversity of cultural forms. Dance epitomizes the expression of culture and heritage and can provide a focus for both multicultural and dance education. It is important, however, that pupils are not offered a diluted or Westernized version of what is purported to be the authentic dance of another culture. Instead, pupils should see the real thing either on video or in live performance, and be taught by dance artists with a deep knowledge, understanding, technical expertise and respect for that particular dance form.

CONTENT OF A DANCE PROGRAMME FOR 5–11 YEAR OLDS

Dance is all about communicating ideas through a non-verbal language. In order to do this successfully, children need to know, understand and be able to use a movement vocabulary just as they use words and numbers to solve problems and communicate ideas in other curriculum areas.

Movement vocabulary

Whenever human movement occurs, the body does something, somehow, somewhere, and possibly in relation to somebody or something. Children therefore need to know:

What actions the body can do
It can:

- transfer weight – e.g. kneel, sit, rock or sway;
- travel – e.g. run, walk, skip, slither, slide, creep or gallop;
- turn – e.g. spin, roll, spiral or pivot;
- jump – e.g. leap from one foot to the other, bounce from two feet to two feet, two feet to one foot, from one foot to two feet or hop;
- gesture – this is any movement that does not involve transference of weight – e.g. shrugging the shoulders, clapping, pointing, opening and closing the whole body or parts of the body.

The body can also stop moving to freeze or balance or pause. It can also bend, stretch or twist to make different shapes, e.g. curled, stretched, twisted, flat, tall, thin, pointed or spiky.

How the actions can be done – the dynamics of movement
The dynamic aspects of the action are concerned with the use of energy and time and will colour the action:

- energy – the amount of force used to perform the action;
- time – the speed with which the action is performed.

Words such as 'quickly', 'slowly', 'smoothly', 'jerkily', 'gently' and 'forcefully' describe the dynamics of movement.

Where the actions can be done – the spatial aspects of movement
The body may use:

- personal space – the space immediately surrounding the body;
- general space – the space in the rest of the room;
- levels – high or towards the ceiling, low or near the floor, and medium (in between);
- directions – forwards, backwards, sideways, up and down and on different diagonals;
- size – movements can be big or small, e.g. a leap or a small bounce, a small tap or a large stamp of the foot;
- pathways – the designs that the body makes in space as it moves across the floor and through the air. The pathway may be straight or curved or it may zigzag or spiral.

With whom the actions can be done – the relationship aspect of movement
The action can be performed in relation to:

- parts of the body;
- a prop or piece of apparatus;
- the teacher;
- a partner or a group;
- one group in relation to another group.

    Working with a partner or group may involve:

- doing the same (i.e. matching);
- mirroring;
- using a question and answer;
- making contrasting movements;
- meeting and parting;
- avoiding, passing, going around;
- surrounding;
- going under, over, between or through;
- moving in unison (everyone moves at the same time as each other) or in canon (dancers take it in turns to perform a movement or movement phrase).

The above activities may be performed using different group formations, including:

- a line;
- a circle;
- solid group formations (e.g. a square);
- a wedge;
- a crescent;
- an irregular group formation;
- a scattered group formation.

Children then need to know how to use this movement vocabulary to compose dances.

Composition
To communicate an idea through dance, children should know how to select appropriate movement content, how to shape it and give it form. In order to do this the following processes may be used:

- Responding to the stimulus. This might initially be a verbal response or it might be a movement response, leading to improvisation and movement exploration.

- Selecting and refining appropriate movements to express the idea, e.g. jumping and stamping movements to express anger.
- Creating a simple movement phrase or motif using the movements selected, e.g. jumping and stamping may become a phrase of three stamps on the spot, then three stamps while turning, followed by running and jumping to finish in an angular, strong shape.
- The phrase/motif may then be developed or varied.

Variation of a motif
Some ways in which a motif can be varied include:

- It can be repeated by dancing the phrase exactly the same again.
- The *action* features may be varied by using the opposite side of the body, by using different parts of the body to do the action, or by adding more actions to the original phrase.
- The *dynamics* can be varied by doing the whole or part of the motif very quickly or very slowly, with a great deal of energy or with a light quality, or by changing the rhythmic pattern.
- The *spatial* features of the motif can be varied by dancing the whole or part of the motif using different directions, levels, pathways or sizes of movement.
- The *relationship* features can be varied by reversing the order or subtracting an action from the motif.

How to structure motifs to make dances
Motifs may be made into dances by using simple musical structures as guiding principles, such as:

- *Binary form (AB)*: Section A is followed by Section B.
- *Ternary form (ABA)*: Section A is followed by Section B with Section A repeated.
- *Rondo form (ABACAD)*: this provides a chorus and verse framework, with Section A as the chorus and sections B, C and D as verses.
- *Narrative form*: this is not a musical form but the gradual unfolding of the dance idea to make a story (ABCDE).

Whatever form is used, the dance should have a very clear beginning, middle and end. It should also have the following features:

- climaxes and highlights:
- variation and contrasts;
- smooth transitions between phrases and sections;
- proportion, balance and unity.

PROGRESSION

Progression in dance is concerned with the pupils' abilities to compose, perform and appreciate dances with increasing understanding, complexity, control, depth and independence. The Arts Council of Great Britain (1993) outlines progression as follows:

Pupils generally progress from:

- using given criteria to using their own criteria to evaluate performance;
- simple tasks to more complex ones;
- natural movements to more deliberate and complex performance.

Progression is also cyclical, and pupils generally move between:

- dependence–independence in learning;
- performing given tasks–being able to structure their own as their capacity to deal with more complex tasks develops.

Progression in dance can be seen in:

- range of type of movement and use of parts of the body;
- appropriate use of energy, flow and bodily tension;
- physical ability and confidence;
- clarity of shape, line and form;
- efficiency and fluency in movement;
- developing specific dance vocabulary;
- increasing complexity in use of rhythm;
- linking of the familiar and unfamiliar;
- ability to move from the literal to the abstract;
- ability to move from given tasks to choosing own task and finding own resource material;
- ability to move from describing to comparing, analysing, evaluating;
- ability to identify and record intention and outcome.

DANCE EXPECTATIONS

By age 7, children should be able to:

1. show poise, resilience and control in the basic body actions of travel, turn, jump, gesture, transference of weight and stillness, both singly and in simple combinations;
2. use a range of body parts to lead and support movement;
3. show contrasts of speed and dynamics; reproduce a simple rhythm through clapping, stamping or emphasis on different body parts;
4. move with a degree of fluency;

5. find a space and move safely from one space to another, using different levels, directions, sizes of movements or pathways;
6. respond to a variety of stimuli including music, percussion, words, poetry, story, pictures, sculptures, natural objects, through improvisation and through structured tasks directed by the teacher;
7. make a dance phrase or short dance showing a clear beginning, middle and end within a given framework provided by the teacher;
8. show some compositional possibilities of working with a partner;
9. comment constructively on their own and other people's short dances or dance phrases describing the movement content, and begin to recognize the appropriateness of material to convey the intended dance idea.

By age 11, children should be able to:

1. perform more complex combinations of simultaneous actions, e.g. turning while jumping and travelling;
2. reproduce step patterns created by themselves or others;
3. show expressiveness in performance to convey the intended idea;
4. show an increased clarity of body shape in stillness and in motion;
5. show straight and curved air and floor pathways;
6. perform a short rhythmic phrase with clarity;
7. show increased fluency in performance;
8. explore, select and refine appropriate movement content for a dance idea;
9. create movement motifs; show simple variation of motifs; use motifs to create short dances;
10. show increased compositional possibilities of working with a partner and some possibilities of working in threes and small groups;
11. describe dances, commenting on the action, dynamics, spatial features and the relationship of dancers to each other;
12. show some understanding of the relationship of accompaniment and design, i.e. costume, set, make-up, props and lighting to the total dance image; describe the mood or feelings conveyed by the dance; identify and describe simple compositional devices, e.g. repetition and variation of motifs; give some simple justifications why children like or dislike a dance.

STIMULI

It is vital that the stimulus or starting point for the dance motivates the children to want to dance. It must excite you as a teacher and be meaningful to the children. Jacqueline Smith (1976, p. 28) defines a stimulus as 'something that arouses the mind or spirits or incites activity'. She categorizes the various stimuli as auditory, visual, kinaesthetic, tactile and ideational.

Auditory stimuli

Music is often the first thought of many people when choosing a stimulus for a dance. It is possible to work very closely with the music, structuring a dance according to the overall musical form, or to be inspired by other aspects of the music, such as the mood or atmosphere that it creates. Sometimes the music may be used as a springboard for the dance idea, but it may not necessarily be used for the final accompaniment of the dance.

There are many kinds of musical stimuli and teachers should try to introduce their pupils to as many styles as possible, broadening children's musical, as well as dance, experience. Children respond readily to music from a variety of cultures, particularly if the pieces of music are short with rhythmic vitality and clarity of phrasing. Very young children enjoy using nursery rhymes and action songs, both as a stimulus and as an accompaniment for their dance.

Percussion instruments often provide an auditory stimulus, being used either rhythmically or for the quality of movement that different instruments inspire. The human voice, percussive body sounds such as clapping, clicking or stamping, or sounds in nature or the environment can also be used effectively, both as stimuli and to accompany dance. The sound of a cat purring or a police siren will stimulate very different actions and movement qualities or dynamics. In addition, poetry can be used as an accompaniment for dance and as an auditory stimulus when the rhythm of the words or the qualitative manner in which they are said excites the movement.

Visual stimuli

Pattern, shape, colour, line are all sources of inspiration for dance and can be found in the world about us as well as in pictures and sculptures. The twisted roots of a tree, the spiral pattern of a shell or the shape of doors and windows in the dance space itself can all spark off dance ideas. Abstract patterns, with the emphasis on colour and shape, may stimulate a dance based on dynamics and a variety of air and floor pathways.

Kinaesthetic stimuli

Dances are often made about movement itself, leading from the exploration and manipulation of contrasting movement ideas. A dance may evolve from a movement that the composer enjoys doing, such as turning or jumping, or it may evolve from a movement phrase, such as 'explode, travel, turn and sink'.

Watching the way other creatures move can also inspire the creation of dances. Look at birds hovering, swooping and gliding or fish that dart, glide and undulate. The gracefulness and power of lions, pumas and cheetahs seen in slow motion may also stimulate children to create dances. Inanimate objects, such as balloons, dandelion clocks, bubbles and machinery, also have specific movement qualities which encourage children to respond with their own movements.

Tactile stimuli

Different materials or objects with different textures will also suggest different ways of moving. The spiky nature of the casing of a horse chestnut might suggest sharp, sudden movements, while smooth, sustained, curving movements might be suggested after the horse chestnut has lost its outer coating. Some tactile stimuli, such as fabric, can become an accompanying prop, manipulated by the dancers to form an integral part of the dance.

Ideational stimuli

The list here is almost endless, ranging from literature to recipes; from myths and legends to scientific or mathematical concepts. Television and comic book characters, emotions, feelings, the natural world and the technological world are all rich sources of inspiration.

DEVELOPING THE DANCE IDEA

While it is possible to make a dance about almost anything, some ideas lend themselves more easily to dance than others. It might be useful to ask the following questions relating to the stimulus in order to assess its dance potential:

1. What does it look like?
2. What does it do?
3. How does it move?
4. Where does it move?

Decide if there are movement possibilities in the list and whether or not these possibilities will enable the aims and desired learning outcomes of the unit to be met. What actions are inherent within the words? Let us take the theme of fireworks as an example. Actions like rise and sink, soar and fly are quite obvious. Some, such as explode, also have dynamic connotations suggesting strong, sudden movements, while sparkle and shimmer may suggest much lighter ones. Inherent within the idea are the shapes of the fireworks – tall and thin for rockets and sparklers and round for Catherine wheels. The main spatial features suggested by the idea may be the use of different levels and a variety of air and floor patterns or pathways.

The next stage is to select the most important movement ideas for your class. The teacher will not usually prescribe every movement as he will also be using suggestions from the children. He will, however, need to give clear guidelines within which the children can explore the movement ideas and make them their own.

The ideas will also need to be organized into a dance-like form or framework. A framework is a structure for a dance that determines the type of movement to be used and the order of phrases that link to create a whole dance. It forms the skeleton and the children fill in the detail. Through creating dances employing the teacher's well-made structure, children will gradually learn how to structure their own dances.

ACCOMPANIMENT

Once the planning of a unit of work and individual lessons is completed you will need to decide on suitable accompaniment for the lessons. You will probably find it easiest to use percussion instruments and your voice during the movement exploration and development part of the lesson. Possibly the most useful percussion instrument is the tambourine, as you can play so many different sounds on it.

The voice is also a valuable instrument. By using the voice expressively, the teacher may indicate what the children are to do, and also how they might do it. The voice can stimulate different qualities of movement or it can be the rhythmic accompaniment to the action. Onomatopoeic words ('plop', 'whiz', 'pitter-patter') are particularly effective with young children, as are vocal sounds. Young children enjoy using their own voices while they dance, causing their movements to come alive.

The teacher will also need to decide on the best way of accompanying the dance itself. If music has been used as the stimulus for the dance idea there should be little problem, as the stimulus will probably become the accompaniment. Music will not always be the stimulus and it is essential to use a variety of different stimuli for making dances.

It is possible to plan a dance and then find a piece of music which is suitable as an accompaniment. It is very unlikely, however, that a piece of music will be found without considerably modifying the dance idea. It is tempting to select short extracts from various pieces of music and join them together, but this should be avoided at all costs. Children should be encouraged to appreciate and value music for its own sake and not merely as an accompaniment for dance. It should be listened to as the composer intended and not chopped up and reassembled.

Ideally, dance and music should grow together, each stimulating and enlivening the other. This is possible, particularly if you work with a teacher who is especially interested in music, with the children creating both the music and the dance around a given theme. Pupils may make their own music using percussion instruments interspersed with words and sounds. They may play it live for other children in the class to dance to, or the music may be recorded so that everyone can dance at the same time.

AN EXAMPLE OF A FRAMEWORK BASED ON FIREWORKS

1. Turning movements on different parts of the body, e.g. feet, seat, etc. (Catherine wheels).
2. Starting low, run and jump into a tall, thin shape. Sink gently to settle on the floor (rocket).
3. Curving air patterns, using turning and jumping (sparklers). In groups of three, make a dance using any of the above material.

SAMPLE MEDIUM-TERM PLAN – UNIT OF WORK FOR 7–8 YEAR OLDS INCORPORATING THE FIREWORKS FRAMEWORK

Aim

To develop the child's knowledge, understanding and use of:

- jumping and turning actions;
- quick and slow movements;
- strong and light movements;
- working in a small group to include matching and mirroring.

Learning outcomes

By the end of the unit of work, the children will have:

- composed and performed dances with clear beginnings, middles and ends based on fireworks and snow;
- observed, described and made value judgements about elements of the dances;
- enriched their movement vocabulary by varying the speed, dynamics, levels and pathways of their actions;
- improved their knowledge, understanding and performance of jumping and turning actions;
- developed their knowledge of some possibilities of working in a pair or small group to include matching and mirroring, canon and unison.

Lessons 1 to 4 – Fireworks dance

Main learning activities:

- exploring different actions for different fireworks, e.g. rockets exploding, Catherine wheels spinning on different parts of the body and travelling with jumps and turns for the sparklers;
- exploring different dynamic qualities and speeds according to the firework, e.g. sudden strong jumps for the rocket, light hand gestures as the stars from the rocket drift to the ground, and acceleration and deceleration for the Catherine wheel;

- exploring different spatial features, e.g. low and high levels for the rocket and the use of different air pathways for the sparklers;
- making phrases of movement for each firework;
- exploring ways of working in threes to include the use of canon and unison and different formations;
- observing, describing and making value judgements on the effectiveness of dance phrases.

Lessons 5 to 6 – Snow dance

Main learning activities:

- exploring travelling, turning and jumping actions;
- mirroring a partner's movements as if snowflakes are sliding down a window-pane;
- exploring making combined shapes with a partner as if the snow has melted on a window-sill;
- exploring different speeds and dynamic qualities, e.g. the strength and speed with which the snow is blown against the window; the slow, soft qualities as if the snow is melting and sliding down the window-pane;
- observing, describing and making value judgements on the effectiveness of elements of the dance.

AN EXAMPLE OF A DANCE FRAMEWORK FOR 5–6 YEAR OLDS BASED ON RAIN

1. Rhythmic pattern beating fingers on the floor, finishing with a jump into the air.
2. Run and curl up close to the floor. Run and stretch high. Repeat.
3. Gradual sinking to the floor with staccato movements.
4. Own ending, e.g. flat shape or roll and stop.

Lesson 1

Objectives
- To increase the child's awareness of body shape, dynamics and levels;
- To introduce the concept of linear and curved floor pathways.

Learning outcomes
By the end of the lesson the children will have:

- improvised within the teacher's dance framework to create and perform part of a dance;
- explored the actions of rising and sinking, freezing movements, the use of high and low levels and curled and stretched shapes;

- created rhythmic patterns;
- used appropriate vocabulary to describe movement.

(The original stimulus for this dance was *Rain* by K. Taniuchi and P. Blakeley. However, it is not essential to have read the book in order to use the idea of rain as a starting point for this dance.)

Introduction
Show me how tall you can be. Stretch as high as you can. Now curl up very small. Remember to tuck your head in, but keep your weight on your feet. Repeat several times.

Movement exploration and development
1. Run into a space and stop when I hit the tambourine. Give coaching points for stopping suddenly, e.g. ask the children to pull in their stomachs and grip the floor with their feet.
2. This time, when you stop, freeze in your curled shape. Practise this.
3. Run and stop in your tall shape.
4. This time we will play a game. If you have to finish in a tall shape I will hit the tambourine twice. If you have to finish in a curled shape I will only hit it once. By making this a game-like activity you will be able to practise these movements for a longer period of time to improve the quality of the sudden stopping and of the curled and tall shapes.
5. The children will already have listened to the story in the classroom, but show them again the pictures of children running through the rain. Ask the children how the boys ran for cover in the story and remind them of the curled shapes they might have to make to shelter from the rain. Remind them how they might stretch up tall to see if it is still raining.

   (If you have not read the book with the children, ask them to imagine sheltering from the rain – curled shapes – and then stretching up tall to check if it is still raining.)

6. Put together the phrase of running and curling up small and running and stretching tall. Repeat the phrase several times, then slowly sink to the floor.
7. Discuss the noise the rain makes on the pavement or on a roof. Tap your fingers on the floor so that they sound like rain. Discuss words which describe the sound of the rain, e.g. pitter-patter, split, splat, splot, drip, drop, plip, plop.

   (Use voices to create rhythmic patterns, e.g. pitter, patter, pit; split, splat, splot. You could beat these one at a time on the floor while the children listen. They then beat the same pattern back. Decide on one simple pattern (e.g. pitter, patter, pit), perhaps repeated three times.)

8. Remind the children how the rain sometimes falls so heavily that it rebounds from the pavement. Practise tapping the rhythm with fingers on the floor and then jumping up suddenly into the air.
9. Practise the rhythm of:
    * Pitter, patter, pit.
    * Pitter, patter, pit.
    * Pitter, patter, PIT (explode into the air with a jump on the final 'pit'.

Dance
Dance parts 1 and 2 of the rain framework.

Conclusion
1. Look at some of the dances and discuss their effectiveness with the children.
2. Curl up very small. When I touch you on the shoulder, tiptoe quietly to the door.

AN EXAMPLE OF A DANCE FRAMEWORK FOR 10 TO 11 YEAR OLDS ENTITLED 'ORIENTAL ADVENTURE'

1. Solo fan section based on symmetric and asymmetric opening and closing movements linked by spinning and turning movements on different levels.
2. Karate section in pairs using mainly asymmetric movements. 'A's dance their phrase of run, jump, roll and freeze. 'B's dance their phrase of run, jump, roll and freeze. Repeat with 'B's finishing next to their partners.
3. Partner sumo section based on slow-motion wrestling movements, using mainly symmetric movements.
4. Each pair travels to meet another pair to dance their group fan dance based on the movement of the spokes of a fan using canon and unison.

Lesson 1

Objectives

* To introduce the concept of symmetric and asymmetric movement;
* To improve the child's dynamic range.

Learning outcomes
By the end of the lesson the children will have:

* used symmetric and asymmetric movements on different body parts and at different levels;
* created a dance phrase by linking together at least four of these movements, using rolls and spins;
* used appropriate vocabulary to describe their movements;
* observed, described and commented on the appropriateness of a partner's phrase.

Introduction

1. Stretch as high as possible and curl up as small as possible. Repeat several times.
2. Stretch as high as possible, then spread both arms out to the side and spin down into a curled shape again.
3. Run smoothly into a space, stretch up tall, spread both arms out and spin gently down. Repeat several times.

Movement exploration and development

Using a fan as a stimulus, show how it opens and closes. Does it open symmetrically or asymmetrically? Is it in an asymmetric or symmetric shape when it is closed?

What happens if one side of the fan is opened first, followed by the other side? The opening is asymmetric, but the final position is symmetric.

1. Let us play with some of these ideas of opening and closing using the movements of the fan to help us. Starting in a tall position, show me how you can spread your arms to finish in an open fan shape and close back in again to hold your tall shape. Emphasize that one arm may open out first followed by the other, and similarly they may close one after the other. Encourage the children to open into the forwards and backwards dimension as well as the sideways one. Ensure that the movements are performed as smoothly as possible.

   (Show some examples, asking the children to pick out some symmetric shapes and some asymmetric ones.)

2. Lie on the floor in a long thin shape as if the fan is closed. Show me how you can spread your arms and legs to open symmetrically. Let's try it now, opening asymmetrically.
3. Show me how you can spread into your fan shape while supporting your weight on different parts of the body. Perhaps you could try sitting or kneeling. Perhaps you could make your fan shape by using an arm and a leg at the same time. Remind children of the two-dimensional movement of the fan as it is opened and closed.

Dance

Choose at least four opening and closing movements and see if you can join them together using gentle spins and rolls. You should include the use of:

- both symmetric and asymmetric opening and closing movements;
- different levels;
- weight supported on different body parts.

Conclusion
Show your phrase to a partner who will check that you have included the use of both symmetric and asymmetric movements as you move into your fan shapes.

CONCLUSION
This chapter has suggested that dance should be an integral part of any physical education curriculum. This is due to its distinctive contribution to movement, artistic and aesthetic education.

KEY POINTS
- Be knowledgeable. Ensure that you know the language of movement, how to make and vary movement phrases and how to structure dances.
- Provide good role models. Children should have opportunities to view professional dance works in order to inspire them in making and performing their own dances.
- Be enthusiastic. Show this in your voice and body language. Enthusiasm is infectious. Respond to the children and their ideas. Even if you do not physically join in the activities, look as if you could.
- Be sensitive. Treat children's ideas with care. Through dance, children are expressing their ideas and innermost feelings about the world. This makes them very vulnerable.

Chapter 12

Teaching Games

TONY MACFADYEN AND MIKE OSBORNE

INTRODUCTION

Games and athletics are often considered to be the basis of sport. Evidence for this can be seen every day in the media. Although public awareness of other activities increases at various times, such as the surge of interest in gymnastics during the Olympics, the fundamental position of these activities in most people's concept of sport is clear. Children also place a high value on games, as Evans and Roberts (cited in Roberts and Treasure, 1993, p. 5) report:

> It is clear that children with above average physical skills are accepted more, and have more status than do under-achieving youngsters. Children with better motor skills are likely to have positive peer relations, while children with low motor skills are disadvantaged when trying to establish friends with peers.

The way in which children are introduced to these activities is very important, both physically and culturally. Indeed, the teaching of team games in particular has been discussed in terms of political, social and moral significance. Furthermore, it is often teachers of physical education who are held responsible for the nation's social and moral decline (Penney and Evans, 1994). After many of the recent failures of our national teams, the education system has also been held responsible for the problems of elite sport. Since it appears that a government's popularity can be affected by the success or failure of its national teams, it is no wonder that recent governments have treated the teaching of games in our schools as a political football! The pre-eminence of games in the Physical Education National Curriculum for England and Wales (DFE, 1995) is a case in point. The fact that it was the only activity within physical education which needed to be taught at all ages is of some significance. As Penney (1995, p. 7) comments, 'Government ministers' . . .

paramount concern is the development of future national team players, and instilling in children "traditional values" inherent, they argue, in team sports such as soccer, rugby and cricket.' Similarly, *Sport: Raising the Game* (DNH, 1995) aimed to put traditional sports like cricket, hockey, rugby and football back at the centre of school life.

Such initiatives put great pressure on generalist primary teachers who often find the teaching of physical education difficult. Thomas (cited in Thorpe, 1990, p. 83) has highlighted that '(many) teachers lack confidence in their ability to teach PE properly. They often express feelings of inadequacy in this area of the curriculum, they may be excellent teachers in other respects.' Yet many of the key skills of classroom practice are applicable to physical education lessons, such as setting children tasks that enable them to get on with some work quickly and then introducing modifications to individual or small-group tasks.

Games, as part of a balanced curriculum, can contribute to children's cognitive, affective and psycho-motor development (Wuest and Bucher, 1995). Games represent many opportunities to help a child's education in terms of her personal and social skills, attitudes and understanding. In addition to problem-solving and communication skills, the acceptance of disappointments and establishment of team work and trust illustrate some of the aspects involved.

The aim of this chapter is to provide an overview of the teaching of games in the primary school. It is not intended to provide detailed content and a lesson-by-lesson guide to the teaching of games; this has been done effectively elsewhere (cf. Bunker *et al.*, 1998; Cooper, 1993; Read and Edwards, 1992). The chapter is presented in three main parts. After a rationale for the inclusion of games within physical education, the first section challenges some of the received conventions associated with the teaching of games and emphasizes the importance of the teacher's attitude. The second part explores some of the expectations and content issues involved in effective games teaching. The final section includes practical examples to illustrate the preceding principles.

ATTITUDES TOWARDS THE TEACHING OF GAMES

The effective teaching of games is analogous to effective strategies employed in other areas of the curriculum. That is, to provide pupils with the opportunities to *have a go* at something, *assess* how well they are doing it and then to *intervene* appropriately to help develop the skills, understandings and strategies involved still further. One would not expect to see queues of pupils lining up to show their teacher how they hold a paintbrush before being told how to execute a stroke, and then eventually being allowed access to the paper on which to try out their new techniques. Regimental stroking of the brush upwards, downwards or sideways (probably nowhere near any paper or canvas) followed by evaluation of how well one's partner has executed her particularly 'wafting' would seem inappropriate in terms of effective teaching and learning. Why is it, then, that it is possible to see such decontextualized situations on games fields and courts?

Effective games teaching permits children to consider the whole picture, often with only their own concept of what is involved, and to construct it as they see fit. If children make fundamental mistakes in that construction, then good practice would necessitate intervention to rectify those errors, or perhaps discussion of what is trying to be achieved, and how best that objective might be addressed. In this way children develop their learning in context.

The convention under question is that technique is a *prerequisite* for participation, enjoyment and development in or through games. The important aspect of 'having a go' at the activity should not be lost in worrying about technical details of exactly how to hold the bat/stick, how to kick the ball or how to pass it before 'having a go', especially during the primary years. Aspects of technical improvement should be encouraged and developed as part of the processes involved in participation, not separated from it. Cooper (1990, p. 3) has suggested that lessons should be based on the principle of 'explore, guide, refine and apply'.

Whitehead (1993, p. 114) points out that:

> Young children are more concerned with mastering their own environment and developing their own skills than with beating others – at least until someone else tells them that it is important to win!

It therefore seems appropriate to create activities that focus on personal achievement, and to offer children frequent opportunities to improve upon their results. In this way the teacher can help provide an environment in which children become agents of their own improvement. The key is to structure the 'play' appropriately as part of a developmental curriculum, thus avoiding unsystematic arrangements where children are merely active, happy and well behaved. The approach being advocated relates to Graham's (1992) 'Play-Teach-Play' model. Primary-aged children would rather be active than listen to long explanations and dry drills. Moreover, they rarely see the long-term benefits of practising a skill (*ibid.*, p. 73); they would rather play a game. There are numerous virtues of the 'Play-Teach-Play' approach, but two are particularly important:

1. Children's interest is heightened if instruction is related to and enveloped within games play.
2. Children practise tasks in the actual context in which they will be used, and so skills become more meaningful.

Activities should be *contextualized*, in that they simulate the main ingredients of the 'identifiable' model of the game. Lines of children passing a ball to and fro between them, involving no progress towards a goal area, lacks authenticity. This is why activities for children need to relate intelligently to the 'game' model. Diagnosis of problems and difficulties should similarly be in context. There is little point in becoming good at a practice which cannot translate to the purposes of the activity. If the child is achieving the important aspects of the task, it may not be necessary for the teacher to interrupt and change so-called 'technical' features unless the individual's response is impaired by some fundamental disadvantage in the way she is addressing the task or holding the stick. Indeed it is the management of this intervention which is the crucial element of successful teaching. Sometimes it is wise to say nothing!

The 'Teaching Games for Understanding' (TGFU) approach (Bunker and Thorpe, 1982) has been fundamental in challenging the domination of a skills-based approach. Advocates of TGFU identified large numbers of children achieving little success due, they claimed, to an over-emphasis on perfor-mance of techniques (Thorpe, 1990). A games-for-understanding approach, however,

> is characterized by a focus on the development of tactical awareness and decision-making within the framework of an appropriate game, the use of modified games and the teaching of skills when appropriate and always at the individual's level. (Allison and Thorpe, 1997, p. 10)

Establishing modified games that enable children to learn through play is central to teaching games in the primary school. Sleap (1984) emphasizes the need to avoid adult versions of games and dogmas about technique so that children have realistic opportunities to participate, and develop an under-standing of games. It is the development of criterion-referenced games teaching, where personal improvement and adaptability are emphasized, that is being advocated, not a normative-referenced approach where rivalry with others is the focus. The criteria are based on dealing with situations rather than 'an early emphasis on mastery of technical efficiency and teaching technique in isolated drills, which bear no resemblance to the context of the game [and] can each have a detrimental effect on the child's knowledge and understanding of the game' (Alexander-Hall, 1986, p. 163).

The adoption of modified games is further supported by the recognition that an over-emphasis on attempts to facilitate automated skills by isolating and focusing on specific components of the skills often results in a decline in performance (Masters, 1992). Earls (cited in Rink, 1993) studied the content development of lessons and reported that the process where skills are practised and then reintroduced to complex games situations, and through which teachers lead the learner to accomplish an objective, not only fail to ensure progress in the psychomotor outcome in many cases, but it is evident that much of what teachers ask students to do as lessons progress 'causes a regression in the level of movement patterns exhibited by the students' (*ibid.*, p. 51). That is, the difference between many traditional skill practices and the context of the game presents problems of understanding and application for these pupils. If Rink (1993, p. 51) is correct in her assertion that 'breaking down complex skills into more manageable parts facilitates learning', over-analysis of component parts impairs effective learning. The solution seems to lie in setting games activities that integrate and contextualize skills, but do not initially involve young children in overly complex skills. Furthermore, Cornwall (1999, p. 102) has pointed out that

> Children (particularly very young children) derive great security from predictable routines – regular events that cannot be anticipated will heighten stress levels . . . [and] celebrating mastery experiences . . . encouraging and working from strengths is a good technique for building up a child's personal resource kit to apply to the next difficult or challenging situation.

These issues highlight the importance of setting appropriate targets for pupils, so that they are encouraged and their skill levels are extended, while at the same time their self-image and self-esteem remain buoyant. Once children can repeat a 'pattern' of manipulation, or master a static skill, it is time to see if they can develop a more complex pattern or apply the skill in a more dynamic situation that adds to their repertoire of movement and movement memory.

To summarize, there are no special barriers preventing the effective teaching of games. Good practice is based on the principles of:

- let pupils 'have a go';
- teach in context;
- choose the time and place for analysis and intervention.

Making these principles work requires intelligent decisions about initial activities which will affect motivation, confidence, development and learning. Listing numerous rules and regulations before any activity takes place is likely to confuse and overwhelm children. Indeed, the very process of children seeking clarification and information about how the game is played *is* learning. Negotiation and understanding rules and strategy structures is part of effective teaching and learning.

Appreciation of resource implications is also important. As in other subjects, all pupils do not have to do the same thing at the same time, therefore they do not require the same equipment. Differentiation of tasks may require different types of equipment which reflect pupils' capabilities and experience. Where small-group activities use relatively little equipment, more resources are available for individual tasks. Such 'split group' teaching is a strategy that is underemployed in physical education at all ages.

GAMES FOR 5 TO 7 YEAR OLDS

The way in which young children approach learning games suggests that motivation is rarely a problem. However, the teacher needs to harness this natural enthusiasm most effectively. Children of this age group are rarely interested in the progress of other children when they are performing tasks, and they are often not even aware of other participants (Bailey, 1999). These observations point to a fundamental principle for effective teaching, which is the *individualization* of tasks for younger children. From 5 to 7 years of age, most infant games activities should focus on what sports psychologists often call 'closed-loop processing: motor skills' (cf. Schmidt, 1988), performed in predictable, unchanging situations such as striking or rolling an object towards a static target, or negotiating one's way through static obstacles. Teachers should therefore attempt to provide situations where pupils can perform these self-feedback tasks modifying the degree of difficulty for the individual child. Smaller targets and 'tighter' manoeuvres challenge the more able child, while larger targets with more room for error, and arrangements that allow more time for skill execution as well as decision-making permit the inclusion of less able pupils. Indeed, the absorbing nature of the 'mastery perspective' or task orientation exhibited when children are focusing on achieving their own personal goals illustrates the self-improvement or self-comparison factor of child development (see Chapter 7).

Whitehead (1993) reports that pupils who focus upon self-improvement rather than winning are more likely to respond flexibly to challenges. Performers who can react to changing circumstances and solve problems for themselves are likely to be more successful games players than those who are merely operatives carrying out a coach's instructions – certainly they represent better physically educated individuals.

The provision of a variety of tasks is another important aspect of teaching this age range. Schmidt (1988) has suggested that practising generic movements under a variety of conditions increases subsequent ability to learn new movements and sports skills. In other words, a wide base of movement experiences helps children retrieve and combine learned movement patterns. Providing a variety of equipment to send, travel with, retrieve and so on in a variety of situations and spaces is part of this wide experience. Utilizing different equipment, targets, sizes of playing areas and groups helps to make tasks appropriate to children's various stages of development. Modification of task variables in this way is fundamental in addressing the issue of effective progression.

The professional skill of the teacher is to give children the best chance of achieving mastery of a variety of skills (and later, the concepts) of games. Diagnosis of problems and the wisdom to reassure and calmly try remedies or regimes of improvement is not a simple list of dos and don'ts. Indeed, it is thoughtful experimentation that enables progress to be made. Teachers must not be hamstrung by the notion that there is one correct way to teach games to children of any particular age. Curriculum development occurs when teachers try new ideas and approaches. Some 'mistakes' may occur, but without them it is unlikely that 'progress' and fresh approaches will develop. Games innovation should be included in this. However, there are themes that need to be considered in planning games lessons for 5 to 7 year olds.

Games to warm up

These are relatively gentle, simply organized, and relate to the type of game skills emphasized in the intended learning outcome (for example, 'Everyone collect a ball each, roll it and scoop it up').

Games to develop competence

These include manipulating, sending objects, moving in relation to static environments or 'dynamic' situations for the most able (for example, throwing a bean bag into a hoop, rolling a ball into a large hoop or bouncing a ball into a wastepaper basket, 'slaloming' around some skittles using a stick and a puck).

Modification of games to challenge

These are used to extend or remediate work for responses to the tasks set (such as increasing or decreasing the target size and/or distance, increasing or decreasing the size of the implement and/or the object being manipulated).

Cooling down/consolidation tasks

These are used to calm down and to reiterate key aspects for the whole class (such as 'See if you can practise the skill quietly or slowly' – while offering reminders of important features, like 'Where are our hands when we try to catch the ball?' or 'Where are our eyes looking?').

General considerations

Locomotor actions such as walking, running, stopping, changing direction, jumping, skipping, hopping and dodging may be part of whole-class activities and will therefore include aspects of spatial awareness and moving in relation to others. Manipulative skills that involve hand–eye co-ordination, foot–eye co-ordination and dexterity with implements can be practised at different levels, at different speeds and include changes of direction.

The emphasis should be on the development of control and confidence and there is a wealth of time-proven activities like 'Follow my Leader', 'Simon Says' and 'What's the Time, Mr Wolf?', as well as more recent and invented games, each of which illustrates the fun aspect of whole-class activities. The requirement to listen to instructions and to respond intelligently often justifies this type of initial feature of lessons. Capitalizing on such a start should enable the setting up of clearly identified tasks, with children undertaking collection and deployment of equipment accordingly. For younger pupils the tasks will be largely individual, though some sharing of items may be necessary and even desirable. Working with others may be part of the intended outcomes of a lesson.

Within the framework for developing units of work, it is also worth remembering that:

- sending tasks relate to games in which attackers move towards a goal or target (invasion games), where an object is projected into space, away from fielders (striking and fielding games) and where an object is hit over a net or a mark on a wall (net and wall games);
- dodging games (which are useful in whole-class parts of a lesson) relate to invasion games;
- travelling with (dribbling) tasks relate to invasion games;
- throwing and catching activities relate to most games.

All these activities can be developed initially through individual tasks, which are the basis of working with younger pupils. Partner and opponent situations can further develop these aspects of games but need to be introduced carefully as children mature and grow in confidence, and are more able to handle social situations.

Units of work should provide an appropriate range of motor tasks firmly based on self-improvement. They may represent relatively short-term goals which are quickly assessed to help inform longer-term alternative routes towards mastery. Children should be given sufficient time to achieve the intended learning outcomes, rather than trying to cover too many activities too quickly (Clay, 1997).

Games units of work should allow for extension as well as remediation activities and could include the following for each type of game (invasion, net/wall and striking/fielding).

Warm-up activities – usually whole-class tasks
Individual tasks:

- Sending
- Receiving
- Travelling with } objects to a form of 'target'.
- Moving in relation to an object.
- Moving in relation to others.

Partner or small group tasks
- Sending to
- Receiving from } objects to other pupils.
- Travelling with

GAMES FOR 7 TO 11 YEAR OLDS

This period represents an extremely important phase in the learning and understanding of games. The attitude to teaching this age group remains fundamentally the same as for earlier years: warm-up, set simple tasks, get pupils working in context, modify tasks appropriately. The model is generally easier to employ because of the increasing maturity and independence of most pupils (Graham, 1992). The versions of the activities are often nearer the adult versions of a game, but it is still the child's movement development which is important. This principle has been clearly recognized in the National Curriculum for England and Wales (DFE, 1995), which identifies greater emphasis on the playing and understanding of small-sided games than individual practices.

During this phase of development children become more aware of others and begin to make comparisons with their peers as well as other models (cf. Bailey, 1999). Buchan and Roberts (cited in Roberts and Treasure, 1993 p. 10) emphasize that 'the cues and feedback given by significant adults is critical in determining the achievement goal children will hold, particularly for children under 12 for whom social approval is very important'. These cues are conveyed by factors such as how tasks are organized and defined, how children are grouped and how they are recognized and evaluated by others.

The importance of appreciating the cues a teacher is sending out is significant in terms of the labels which children may attach to their own progress as well as to that of their peers. The power of the self-fulfilling prophecy is particularly relevant in motor skill learning, and appropriate goal setting and reassurance to help pupils persevere with tasks are all part of effective teaching.

It is important that teachers continue to present games in ways that are appropriate and accessible to children, rather than some form of the adult version. It is the child-centredness of activities and not the 'properness' of the 'real' game that remains paramount. Contextualized activities with this age group are more relevant because the basic movement patterns developed earlier may now be utilized in a wider range of situations: 1v1 situations can become 2v1, 2v2, 3v2, 4v4, and so on, to develop and 'test' the resilience of the skills so far developed.

Good teaching involves monitoring individual as well as whole-group progress, and when a good 'model' is demonstrated by a pupil it can be 'shown' as a peer demonstration to good effect. Using peer demonstrations in this way highlights the fundamental approach of 'getting children playing', followed by the monitoring of opportunities to celebrate and increase good 'behaviours' and the incorporation of those behaviours into wider, more effective use.

The emphasis with this age group is still on the development of motor skills across a range of situations, but the 'medium' for this development is increasingly 'social' in context. Children are more aware of others and are performing in environments explicitly involving others. The skilful teacher will plan and organize activities which include all pupils (rather than 'exclude' those who aren't batting or bowling, or who cannot catch a hard ball). He will try to ensure that the tasks selected match pupils' abilities, so that they participate with a sense of competence rather than being made aware of what they cannot do. Games teaching where pupils are allowed to 'have a go' and are helped to participate with children of similar ability is important in preventing children of this age group from suffering stress and anxiety. In net games, small paired games should not be allowed to reach very high scores, where one pupil wins easily: a greater rotation of partners should be used. More opportunities to play more opponents means that not only will children learn about others and how they master an activity, but importantly more children will experience a range of challenges and degrees of success.

Buchan and colleagues (cited in Roberts and Treasure, 1993) report that 9 to 10 year olds still predominantly focus on mastery goals, and that boys are more competitive than girls. As games are often taught to mixed-sex groups at this age, it is essential that teachers select situations that encourage appropriate goals and behaviours, and do not permit any one group to dominate games. Rotation of roles within games is also important at this age. Tall girls being stereotyped as netball goalkeepers often deny such children access to the full range of experiences required to develop balanced skills and understanding. Children need to be offered the chance to attack and defend, to officiate and score; only by doing so will they develop a complete understanding of games principles and play.

The generalization of skills to a range of games is a key indication of progression. For example, the 'cushioning' or 'softness' required in catching an object needs to be transferred to the 'trapping' of a ball with foot or stick. The transference of weight involved in successfully throwing an object needs to be generalized to more powerful striking, kicking or sending; this in turn involves the adoption of a side-on approach, rather than a frontal approach to sending.

Diagnosis of a pupil's technical errors can be helped by observing three key phases of the skill execution, for example, in sending an object.

The preparatory phase

- Is the child positioned appropriately?
- Is the implement held adequately?
- Is the child watching the important cues?
- Is the angle of approach helpful?
- Is the equipment suitable?

The impact phase

- Are the hands used appropriately at the point of sending, stopping, receiving?
- Is the right part of the object being focused on?
- Is the object being struck in front or alongside the body?
- Is the object being released at the right time?

The post-impact phase

- Is there a follow-through to the action required?
- Is the weight on the correct foot?
- Is balance regained/maintained?

The skills of sending can be seen to represent perhaps the 'easier' aspect of sending and receiving because they are more controllable and modifiable. The receiving aspect is usually more difficult because it often involves moving into a position to receive the object, as well as the skill of computing the difference between the perceived trajectory/path of the object and the actual one. It is very important that children come to interpret and react to stimuli: 'it is useless to know how to hold your hands if you cannot predict where the ball will arrive' (Cooper, 1990, p. 2). Children who find this aspect of games difficult may benefit from using larger, more distinguishable objects to catch or trap, as well as developing these skills in relation to the easiest trajectories at first (e.g. rolling).

PLANNING FOR GAMES TEACHING 7–11

Plans for invasion games could include decisions about the following:

Individual aspects

- Technical execution of skills.
- Strategic decision-making.

In sending and receiving, teaching points to help technique might include kicking the 'equator' of a football to send it on a low trajectory or keeping the ball 'on a lead' for dribbling skills. Situations may be created where pupils have to make decisions about whether to shoot, pass or dribble a ball in a variety of situations.

Team aspects

- Attacking principles such as width and penetration (using different shaped pitches to encourage appropriate play, e.g. seven-point zones in the corners of small rugby areas).
- Defending the 'danger' areas – 'funnelling' formation (again, use of asymmetric areas can help develop understanding of these principles).
- What to do during a 'transition' in play: reacting to the loss or gain of possession.
- Investigating the main requirements of players in key 'zones' of the playing area.
- How to maximize the rules of a game to your advantage, e.g. in cricket, hitting the ball into the spaces created by only allowing a certain number of players within the in-field.

For net and wall games plans could include decisions about the following:

Individual aspects

- Grip of implement
- Footwork: moving into position to hit the ball
- Striking the ball: contact point 'out in front' for tennis
- Follow through: what are the consequences for trajectory

Decision aspects

- Should I hit a high (long) or low (short) shot?
- Should I hit a wide or straight shot? (Use of long and narrow, or short and wide areas can help development understanding.)

Team roles (doubles formation)

- How and why do attacking and defending formations differ?

For striking and fielding games, plans could include decisions about the following:

Individual aspects

- Body position for hitting, position of striking implement in relation to body, flight of ball
- Weight transference in bowling
- Catcher's movement to a flighted ball and cushioning of the catch

Team aspects

- Setting appropriate field placements
- Different fielders' roles in responding to an outfield hit
- 'Staggering' attacking hitters with 'safe' players

CONCLUSION

Games represent a key part of the physical education curriculum, which should be taught in ways similar to most other parts of it. This chapter has emphasized that while improving children's technical ability and understanding in games is very important, avoidance of a long list of prerequisites in these respects facilitates good, effective teaching by allowing children to test their initial responses to situations and adapt them, sometimes intuitively, at other times as a direct consequence of teacher intervention. Teachers should not be intimidated by old-fashioned conceptions of what is required to be a 'sportsman', particularly as those stereotypes focus on a narrow, elitist view of sporting expertise. The essential role of teachers of games in the primary years is to nurture the enthusiasm and application of their pupils by letting them have a go.

KEY POINTS

- Get children to play child-centred activities that replicate the context in which the skills are to be used.
- Modify the tasks to set appropriate challenges.
- Units of work for games should be based on a broad repertoire of skills. For younger children tasks should focus on the individual learner. As children mature they can be introduced to more activities involving small-group work.

Chapter 13

Teaching Gymnastics

TONY REYNOLDS

INTRODUCTION

Gymnastics has always had a central place in the physical education curriculum, but has not usually been far from controversy. There has been much discussion, for example, concerning the nature of gymnastics and issues over teaching methods. For many teachers, confusion may still persist over what actually constitutes the make-up of the various approaches to gymnastics such as educational gymnastics, the thematic approach and the Olympic style. Perhaps as a consequence of these factors the quality of teaching in gymnastics has been variable (Benn and Benn, 1992).

This chapter explores the content and delivery of a gymnastics curriculum but includes a realistic acceptance of the constraints which limit and frame the current primary curriculum of our schools. It intends to set out a rationale for teaching gymnastics in primary schools which reflects the importance placed upon this vital activity for children's development. The first section defines gymnastics within the wider context of primary physical education. In the second and third parts the chapter explores the key features of gymnastics in the infant (5–7 years) and junior years (7–11 years). The fourth section examines some of the different approaches to the effective teaching of primary gymnastics. The final section discusses the use of apparatus.

DEFINING GYMNASTICS IN THE CONTEXT OF PRIMARY PHYSICAL EDUCATION

According to the DES (1991, p. 5):

- Physical education aims to develop physical competence so that children are able to move efficiently, effectively and safely and understand what they are doing.
- Physical education is achieved through the combination of physical

activity with the mental processes of making decisions, selecting, refining, judging, shaping, adjusting and adapting.

These statements highlight the need for fundamental physical education experiences through which movement confidence and competence is effectively fostered in young children. Gymnastic activity is a core element of the physical education curriculum for primary children. It plays a key role in developing a child's confidence in using the body in a skilful and controlled way. Gymnastics enables problem-solving, individuality and creativity in selecting one's own actions, in refining those actions and applying them in different contexts and relationships. Other physical activities will enable similar responses, but it is through gymnastics that so many different aspects of the education process come together. Gymnastics is thus an activity that should be taught regularly in each year of the primary curriculum.

Formal and informal gymnastic teaching is evident in our schools, and teachers employ different teaching and learning approaches relevant to their experience, training and the needs of the activity and their children. The form of gymnastics employed by teachers should vary according to the age, background experience and specific needs of the children in the class. However, the essential aims of gymnastics remain consistent:

- the development of skilled body management;
- the development of confidence in and through movement;
- the development of quality in performance and an understanding of how it is achieved.

Bruce Long (1982, p. 5) suggests that in educational gymnastics,

Children are set action tasks which are concerned with natural activities such as running, jumping, twisting, turning, hanging, rolling and spinning, balancing, transferring weight from one part or set of parts to another ... they may also be set quality tasks which are concerned with how these activities are performed, e.g. at high level or low level, quickly, slowly, with acceleration, heavily, lightly.

KEY FEATURES OF A GYMNASTIC PROGRAMME IN THE 5–7 YEARS

In general, the gymnastic activities scheme of work should be cyclical in nature. Thus, each year group could experience:

- travelling activity;
- jumping (and landing);
- balancing and stillness;
- use of space;
- key actions such as rolling and turning and climbing (when appropriate).

Table 13.1: Some of the material and ideas teachers may wish to draw upon in planning their gymnastic curriculum

Infant years	*Junior years*

In each phase, gymnastic learning activities might enable children to develop different ways of performing the basic gymnastic actions:

• travelling using hands and feet	• turning
• turning	• rolling
• rolling	• swinging
• jumping	• jumping
• balancing	• climbing
• climbing	• balancing
	• travelling on hands and feet

Children will:	Children will:
• develop these actions both on the floor and using apparatus;	• adapt, practise and refine these actions, both on the floor and using apparatus;
• be guided to link a series of actions;	• emphasize changes of shape, speed and direction through gymnastic actions;
• perform both on the floor and using apparatus, and be able to remember how to repeat them;	• practise, refine and repeat a longer series of actions, making increasingly complex movement sequences;
• be guided to explore the basic gymnastic actions in changing contexts – low and high level, at different speeds, in changing relationships (own or sharing with a partner).	• be guided to explore and refine the basic gymnastic actions in varying contexts – at different levels, in changing relationships – individually, in pairs or in a group.

In addressing these basic gymnastic actions, each year group should:

- develop their gymnastic responses on the floor and on the apparatus;
- be guided to find and use space safely;
- be expected to develop sequences by linking simple gymnastic movements together – the complexity of remembering being enhanced as children progress through the years (Table 13.1 summarizes some of the salient material and ideas that can be utilized in planning primary gymnastics).

A gymnastic sequence may be developed in many different ways, and teachers need to consider the demands they might make on different age groups as they ask children to plan and perform linking actions. A suggestion for progressive tasks might include opportunities for children to:

- remember and repeat a single action;
- repeat a single action in two places on the floor or using the apparatus;
- repeat the same action in two places with travelling link;
- repeat the same action in two places with a start and finish and travelling links.

This final task might be the ultimate expectation for children of 5 or 6 years of age, though the more able performer may be encouraged to work through a similar series of progressions using more than one gymnastic action, for example:

- Two actions in different places with start and finish and good linking movement.
- Three or more actions with flowing links and good quality in start and finish.

In developing an understanding of their own and others' performance, children can be asked to observe, copy and describe the gymnastic actions they and others have performed. They can be encouraged to use the information of their observation to improve the control of their individual gymnastic actions and the 'flow' of their linked actions. It is suggested that children experience working individually and in pairs or in small groups when ready.

In completing the infant focus it is important for teachers to plan and implement an induction into safe apparatus use. It is recommended from the earliest opportunity that children are 'trained' how to lift and carry gymnastic equipment, as they learn how to organize, move and place their own apparatus. The degree of 'independence' in this aspect of the child's learning may vary as children mature in the infant phase of their education (see Chapter 9).

Figure 13.1 presents an outline scheme of work for gymnastics in the infant years. This long-term plan suggests a regular gymnastic experience in each infant year. It is based on four modules of work in each year group, though the opportunity for this level of activity has been significantly reduced in recent years under the pressure of other educational initiatives. Each unit of work has a theme and additional support material that will enable a teacher to develop that theme over a series of lessons.

A useful description of a scheme of work is put forward by Val Sabin (1990, p. 18):

In each school there should be a fairly detailed scheme of work for gymnastic lessons – a scheme which outlines the themes to be covered throughout the duration of each year. This will ensure that the children will all have had a similar physical experience by the time they leave school, and also that they progress through the themes and do not repeat work unnecessarily.

The two examples of schemes of work for infants and juniors in the next section follow this advice, albeit on a single side of text for simplicity and clarity. It is strongly recommended that the gymnastic programme should not drop below a minimum of two gymnastic units or modules for any one age group. This plan is based on a *minimum entitlement* of two physical education lessons each week throughout the year (cf. DNH, 1995).

Early years	Reception	Year 1	Year 2
Physical areas of experience: run, jump, climb, balance	*Travelling* – with emphasis on use of space whole body hands, feet hands and feet	*Travelling* using different body parts with turning	*Travelling* using hands and feet with an apparatus focus for climbing and swinging
Use small apparatus with confidence: bean bags, quoits, ropes, hoops, etc.	*Travelling* + stillness using balancing with a focus on: shape body orientation	*Travelling* – a partner theme of meeting and parting on feet, hands and feet, with rolling	*Jumping* – variety of take-off degrees of turning with an emphasis on good landings
Use of other equipment: bikes, trikes, outdoor equipment	*Travelling* – on feet with an emphasis on jumping with good landing – explore: feet together feet apart	*Balancing* – movement and stillness using floor and apparatus: into and out of balances on small body parts	*Turning and rolling* transferring weight from body part to body part with control
	Travelling – emphasis on climbing, going up and coming down, including: pulling and pushing actions with arms and feet	*Jumping* – foot patterns shape with an emphasis on good landing	*Balancing* – using small body parts: high and low partner – linked balances
	Revision theme from the above	Revision theme – using any or all of the material from the above units	*Developing a revision unit* or composite theme using gymnastic material from each of the above units
		Focus to be addressed	
	Linking actions Watch others' work	Linking and repeating actions	Linking and repeating a series of actions
		Talk about their own and each other's work	Evaluate their own and others' work
		Basic skills to be addressed	
Work together	Control	Increased control	Increased control
Play together	Bunny hop	Rolling log tucked	Remember + repeat
Listen attentively	Basic shapes	Turning actions	Climbing rope
Use a range of tools			Rolling – fwds/swds

Figure 13.1: An outline scheme of work for gymnastics in an infant school

In the examples given in Figure 13.1, the top box on the plan is the theme for the scheme of work (for example, *travelling* in Year 1). Additional information can be drawn upon by the teacher in planning: travelling on *different body parts* with an emphasis emerging during the work on *turning.*

This level of planning forms an outline scheme of work: it identifies a number of themes to be covered during the year for each of the age bands. An opportunity to introduce a revision theme is planned for any one year group.

In addition, the content is extended with progressing references to sequence development from year to year and a degree of differentiation related to pupil evaluation. Basic skills, which may be addressed during the infant phase, are identified on the outline scheme, again with a recommendation of year-to-year progression.

THE KEY FEATURES OF THE GYMNASTIC PROGRAMME IN THE 7–11 YEARS

The recommendations for appropriate content and expectations need to be cross-referenced carefully with the gymnastic curriculum entitlement outlined above.

As with the infant years, the gymnastic activities scheme of work for this age group remains cyclical in nature. Each year group might experience:

- travelling activity;
- jumping (and landing);
- balancing and stillness;
- variations of speed level and direction;
- key actions such as swinging and climbing.

As children address any one theme, they should be encouraged to design sequences by linking gymnastic actions together. Improvements in the accuracy, fluency and complexity of remembering should be evident as children mature. The following suggestions give an example of increasing demand in a task focusing on sequence development:

- remember and repeat a gymnastic action in different places;
- repeat one or more gymnastic actions in two places on the floor or using the apparatus;
- repeat one or more actions in different places with flowing, travelling links;
- repeat and refine more than one action in two places with a start and finish and smooth travelling links;
- remember and repeat two actions in different places with start and finish and good linking movement;
- remember and repeat three or more actions with flowing links and good quality in start and finish.

As children develop their gymnastic response, they should be encouraged to transfer their floor activity to gymnastic apparatus, and the tasks set by the teacher should reflect a need to guide children to apply, refine and adapt their floor movements to use on the apparatus. At the same time pupils in each year group could experience working individually, in pairs or in small groups, with the group focus more likely towards the end of the junior phase.

As they move from infant to junior age groups, children may experience a change in hall layout and be required to lift and carry different sizes and weights of gymnastic equipment. The process of training and an understanding of safe practice in apparatus use established with infant pupils should continue throughout the junior years; greater levels of independence can be developed as children are able to deal with increasingly *more* complex safety principles.

In each of the schemes of work (see Figures 13.1 and 13.2) a progression of gymnastic skills and themes is suggested that follow three key areas of experience:

- travelling;
- balancing (and stillness);
- jumping and landing (flight).

Over time, teachers need to focus on identifying learning activities that address these overall themes, and consider what the theme title means to children.

Other gymnastic activity such as climbing and swinging; varying body orientation including inversion (hanging upside-down); changing level, speed and direction, are all additional quality tasks which enhance the three key areas. Additional variation may be achieved by the teacher changing the context of the activity through work at floor level, using floor and apparatus and by transferring the activity to apparatus. This inter-relationship of actions and movement qualities is evident in the example of a topic web analysis for 'balance' (Figure 13.3). This format of brainstorming content ideas for developing a theme such as balancing is a well-used and well-trusted method of initial planning in primary gymnastics.

APPROACHES TO TEACHING GYMNASTICS IN THE PRIMARY YEARS

In making recommendations for the teaching of gymnastics, arguments can be made for the inclusion of different forms of gymnastics. Four types of gymnastic teaching are generally evident in schools:

- educational or informal gymnastics;
- formal/general gymnastics;
- rhythmic gymnastics/sports acrobatics/tumbling;
- artistic gymnastics.

Year 3	Year 4	Year 5	Year 6
Travelling and turning feet and hands/feet in travelling movements. – rolling – levels – directions – speeds	*Travelling:* – speeds/directions – jumping – rolling and linking a series of actions. Lifting body parts high linking a series of actions in a travel + stillness sequence	*Balancing:* – large + small parts – an emphasis on linking a series of actions in continuous movements. An apparatus focus on swinging, climbing + shape	*Travelling* with a focus on sequence work in small groups. Emphasis on: – meeting and parting – use of levels, shape and speed variation
Basic shape in travelling on feet and hands/feet. An apparatus focus on: – shape in swinging – working with a partner	*Balancing and rolling* Exploring balancing and over-balancing to initiate movement into and out of balances. Emphasis: – shape – turning/twisting with partner matching	*Jumping* – landing revision – take-off revision linking a series of jumps with shape variation and turning movements	*Balancing in sequence* – using large and small parts – from jumping and landing – emphasis on linking. Apparatus focus on climbing
Jumping and landing – shape in the jumps – exploring take-off pattern and its affect on the shape – two foot and one foot take off	*Jumping* on to, off and over. Take-off variations: to include hands and feet to initiate take-off	*Shape* as the focus: symmetry + asymmetry working with a partner in matching a series of actions. Transferring body weight in – rocking + rolling – pushing + pulling	*Shape* in travel, in balancing and in a sequence with a partner. Linking + contrasting symmetrical and asymmetrical movements
Balance + use of *turning* to move into and out of balance. Developing a series of actions into a sequence with a partner	*Travelling* individually with a focus on: – stopping and stillness – *speed* variations – *directions* and pathways. Linking a series of movements to create a sequence with a partner	*Turning* in a travelling context: – on different body parts – varying the levels – with a change of direction – including the different elements in a composite sequence	*Turning* – into and out of balance – on to and from different body parts – *in linking a series of balance/travel and turns*
Developing a revision unit or composite theme using gymnastic material from each of the above units	Composite theme	Composite theme	Composite theme
Focus to be addressed			
Practise and repeat a series of actions	Adapt, practise and refine actions Practice, refine and repeat longer series of actions		Adapt, refine, practise and repeat increasingly complex movement sequences
Basic skills to be addressed			
Revise all the basic skills from Key Stage 1 Rope climb Swinging on a bar, on the wall bars and/or on a rope Taking weight on hands and lifting feet high in cartwheeling and handstanding movements			

Figure 13.2: A gymnastic programme for the four junior years

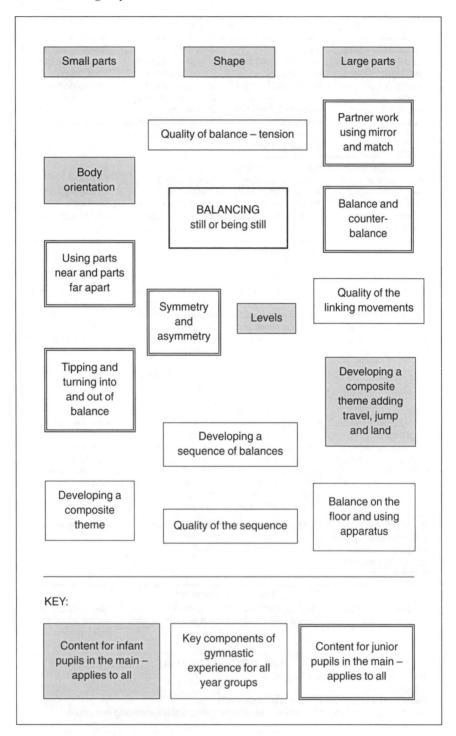

Figure 13.3: Approaches to teaching balancing in primary gymnastics

Educational or informal gymnastics

This is the most popular form of gymnastics taught in primary schools. In using the educational gymnastics forum, there is an intention that the pupil works at her own level within the framework of the task set by the teacher. The wide range of interpretation that can ensue makes it impracticable, and even undesirable, for the teacher to support the pupil's movement. This does not preclude physical contact designed to give moral support, however (for example, holding a young child's hand or simple manual guidance when a child first attempts a rolling movement).

The most important aspect of accepted, safe practice in this informal teaching approach, is the good judgement of the teacher in selecting suitable and appropriate tasks for the pupils. While maintaining the physical challenge within a safe framework, the teacher should provide opportunities for spontaneous and inventive responses. It is important that the demands of the task made upon pupils present the prospect of success.

The aim of educational gymnastics is to develop and refine a range of controlled gymnastic movements/actions within a flexible frame, as movements may be performed singly, in a combination of movements or in a gymnastic sequence, with pupils working individually or with others on the floor and apparatus. A range of teaching styles can be employed in this form of gymnastics, drawing on both direct and indirect methods, depending on individual circumstances and lesson aims. Further advice on these styles of teaching can be found in BAALPE (1995, p. 175, and 1999, p. 199).

Other forms of gymnastics

There is a general acceptance that the primary generalist teacher tends to work within the context of educational gymnastics unless by virtue of additional training (and hence qualification) they are able to teach the other forms of gymnastics:

- In *formal/general gymnastics*, the performer will be required to perform stylized vaults and other gymnastic agilities.
- *Rhythmic gymnastics, sports acrobatics and tumbling* are an extension of the formal gymnastics programme, providing more specialized aspects of the sport for the purpose of competition and display.
- *Artistic gymnastics* is the coaching of female gymnasts using four pieces of equipment (floor, beam, vault and asymmetrical bars) and male gymnasts using six pieces of equipment (floor, vault, parallel bars, rings, high bar and pommel).

A teacher would be prudent to check that his training, qualifications and/or experience have prepared him to undertake the form of gymnastic activity he wishes to teach. This applies to those running a post-school gymnastic club as well.

Over time, teachers, lecturers and advisers have worked closely to develop models of good practice. The teaching of gymnastics in the primary school maintains a high focus of development in most education authorities, not least because the teaching of gymnastics, and particularly the safe use of large apparatus and its movement, fixing, etc., can cause continuous anxiety for some teachers.

The models provided on the following pages (see Figures 13.4 and 13.5) provide a framework for a teacher setting out to develop a unit of work in gymnastics. In addition, each provides an indication of progression in children's ability to plan, perform and evaluate, which are key aspects of children's participation in curriculum gymnastics. The aims of gymnastics demand more of children than simply performance. An understanding of how to develop patterns of activity and how to improve performance through observation and refining is enhanced by giving children the opportunity to plan their responses and to judge the effectiveness of their planning.

THE USE OF APPARATUS IN PRIMARY GYMNASTICS

A useful progression in gymnastics is for teachers to ask children to transfer the movement they have been rehearsing at floor level to different apparatus at some stage in the lesson. Consequently, the effective use of apparatus to extend children's learning should be an important part of a teacher's planning.

The range of equipment available to the teacher of gymnastics includes:

* nesting tables;
* bar box or movement table;
* benches and planks;
* wall bars – double-hinged frame;
* mats;
* horizontal ladder and pole;
* ropes with/without ladder.

Infant alternatives include smaller and lighter benches, planks and mats. Combination/blend mats which use a soft (chipfoam layer) and a firm (expanded polyethylene layer) are recommended for ease of movement and for their increased lightness.

Teachers need to consider a number of issues when deciding how to lay out equipment which facilitates access for the whole class:

* to ideally attempt to create five or even six islands of equipment – catering for five or six groups of children;
* to use equipment in combinations – table + plank + bench + mats to create L- or T-shaped layouts with more than one way 'in and out/on and off';
* to use the mats to *extend* the layout – NB: mats are apparatus;

Week	Teaching and learning focus	Emphasis
1	**Phase I** Introduce and explore the theme/topic using tasks which develop: • a range of ideas • control of the actions • use of the floor and apparatus	Children work: • alone • with a partner
↓	**Phase II** Select from these exploratory ideas, limit the range of actions: • Practise and improve the quality and control of the selected actions • Children remember their actions and are able to repeat them • Children use both floor and apparatus	Children choose ideas they have tried on the floor and learn how to 'adapt' them as they work on the apparatus
↓	**Phase III** • Children start to link the actions together and begin to repeat a series of actions • Children use both floor and apparatus	Emphasize quality in the way they link actions together – flow, continuity, making it look 'gymnastic'

5–7 year olds will be encouraged to respond to tasks by:

- *planning*   – exploring, remembering and choosing actions to repeat
- *performing* – practising, repeating and improving their actions
                     – practising, repeating and improving how they link actions together
                     – showing their actions to others
- *evaluating*   – observing and talking about their own and others' work

This process will be continuous throughout the unit of work

Figure 13.4: A model for developing a unit of work in the infant years

Week	Teaching and learning focus	Emphasis
1	Plan and perform a range of actions with increased efficiency and control: • a range of ideas • control in the movement • use the floor and the apparatus	Children work: • alone • with a partner • in a small group
↓	Select from these exploratory ideas, limit the range of movements: • Improve the accuracy and consistency of their actions through practice • Increase the number of actions in a sequence, developing their control and understanding • Use both floor and apparatus in refining and improving their control of different actions	Children choose ideas they have tried on the floor and learn how to adapt/apply them as they work on the apparatus
↓	Children link actions together and build a sequence of actions with increasing complexity	Emphasize particular qualities in linking actions including changes in shape, speed, and direction
↓	• Practise and refine their sequences to develop clarity and efficiency, control and accuracy • Children use both floor and apparatus in developing their sequences	Emphasize quality in the separate actions and the way they link the actions.
6	• Perform, repeat and 'show' the sequence – using strategies which promote a sense of 'performance'	

8 to 9 year olds will be encouraged to respond to tasks by:
* *planning*   – exploring, selecting and analysing movements
* *performing* – practising, repeating and refining their movements
               – demonstrating/showing their movements
* *evaluating* – observing, describing and analysing in order to improve their own performance

10 to 11 year olds will be encouraged to respond to tasks by:
* *planning*   – exploring, selecting and applying a longer series of actions in making an increasingly complex movement sequence
* *performing* – practising, refining and repeating a longer series of actions
               – demonstrating/showing their movements
* *evaluating* – making simple judgements about their own and others' performance to improve the accuracy, quality and variety of their own response

This process will be continuous throughout the unit of work

Figure 13.5: A model for planning a unit of work in the junior years

- to establish a layout for the unit of work – same group puts equipment out and stores it away for the six weeks of the unit;
- to ensure use is not unduly restricted by too many rules – numbers in places, etc.;
- to use wall bars and ropes but to maintain the apparatus response in line with the theme.

A teacher can further vary the equipment layout by adopting different styles of apparatus use. The two styles suggested here act as examples and deploy very similar equipment; however, the task, which frames the children's response, varies the context. *Free use* allows for considerable variety of movement in that it can be used to encourage purposeful use of the floor space as children travel from one part of the hall to another. Free use of the whole floor space allows children to work continuously and individually. At the same time this enhances a teacher's focus on good use of space and raises children's awareness of others moving in and through each other's spaces. Free use of apparatus can create a more varied context for the pupil to address the task. For example, in developing a sequence of linked balances, the pupil can be encouraged to plan a route which takes her to two or three different places in the hall. The teacher can emphasize the quality of the balance and at the same time encourage a more varied 'travelling' pattern as the pupil links the balances. In doing so the teacher is helping the pupil to begin to move into and out of a balance in varying ways to initiate the travel links.

An alternative approach is that of *grouped use,* where the apparatus is set out in designated areas and a group of children (ideally five or six) work on each area/island of apparatus. Grouped use provides a good opportunity for repetition and rehearsal of gymnastic actions in a limited space. This format will help in developing the quality of a pattern of movement. It allows children to see a 'route' more easily than in the context of free apparatus use.

Grouped apparatus is easier to control and it allows for slightly different tasks to be set in the one lesson, thus helping with differentiation. It allows the teacher to focus on a particular group or individual for observation of performance and can be a useful strategy for assessment. The use of a 'home' base approach allows for a safe initial movement from floor to apparatus at each stage of the unit. The home base is the equipment a group of pupils lay out and work on before moving on to another space to adapt and develop their response in a new context. One move per lesson is generally about right in allowing pupils enough time to develop quality moves through repetition and rehearsal.

Whichever form of apparatus use applies, teachers have a responsibility to guide children in the movement, fixing and adjustment of apparatus to meet the needs of the hall space. The teacher has a responsibility to check all of the equipment fixings and fastenings and this responsibility should be seen in action. By making this action overt the teacher can help children develop an understanding of being safe.

It can be very helpful for the teacher (and the children where appropriate) to use an *apparatus plan* – a simple diagram of the hall with the islands of apparatus identified. Such a plan promotes speedy and consistent apparatus layout each week of the unit. A large plan, possibly A3 size, can be displayed in the classroom/hall, and a series of A4 or A5 cards can be used to help each group 'build' its apparatus.

CONCLUSION

This chapter has highlighted the key role of gymnastics in the primary curriculum. Gymnastics provides children with the opportunity to develop greater confidence in using their bodies in a fluent and precise manner.

KEY POINTS

- Primary gymnastics involves not only the performance of movements, but an understanding and integration of the elements of planning and reflection to produce a holistic learning experience.
- The three main areas of experience – travelling, balancing, and jumping and landing – can be used to develop a variety of progressive and thoughtful schemes of work using both floor and apparatus work.
- The good judgement of the teacher is important in selecting suitable and appropriate tasks for pupils, who should be allowed to work at tasks that are challenging yet achievable for their stage of development and ability.

Chapter 14

Health-related Exercise

JO HARRIS

INTRODUCTION

Physical education has always had a close relationship with health. Being physically active forms part of a healthy lifestyle, and physical education programmes in schools should teach children the necessary skills and understanding to encourage and allow them to be active in their own time, and to help them to appreciate and experience the benefits of being active. In recent years, this particular component of the physical education programme has come to be more clearly defined and described, and is commonly referred to as 'health-related exercise' (Harris, forthcoming).

This chapter justifies the rationale for health-related exercise within a physical education programme. It details appropriate content and expectations for children aged 5–11 and provides guidance on the assessment of pupil achievement in this area. A range of approaches to delivering health-related exercise is described and units of work and lesson plans are presented to exemplify how the content can be integrated within the physical education programme. A number of key resources are recommended to assist teachers in their practical delivery of health-related exercise within a balanced and comprehensive physical education programme.

RATIONALE OF HRE AND ITS PLACE WITHIN PHYSICAL EDUCATION

Health-related exercise (HRE) embraces the teaching of knowledge, understanding, skills, attitudes and confidence associated with the promotion of current and future involvement in health-enhancing physical activity. HRE is a core component of physical and health education for the following reasons:

- Physical activity has a beneficial effect on the physical and mental health of children.
- Many children possess at least one modifiable risk factor for coronary heart disease, childhood obesity is increasing, and many young people have symptoms of psychological distress.
- Many children are relatively inactive and activity levels decline as children get older.
- Physical activity behaviours are often established during childhood.
- Schools reach virtually all children and have the potential to improve children's health by providing programmes and services that promote enjoyable, lifelong physical activity.
- There is evidence that school programmes have successfully promoted children's physical activity-related knowledge and understanding, attitudes, activity and fitness levels.

(Almond and Harris, 1998; Armstrong and Welsman, 1997; Harris and Cale, 1997; HEA, 1997).

A structured HRE programme aims to provide:

- a knowledge base about the effects and benefits of exercise;
- practically applied understanding of exercise ('learning through doing');
- experience of a wide range of physical activities;
- behavioural skills associated with activity promotion (e.g. knowing how to go about being more active);
- enhanced attitudes, self-esteem and self-confidence through physical activity.

In terms of health-related outcomes, a 'physically educated' child is one who has learned the skills necessary to perform a range of physical activities, chooses to be active on a regular basis, understands the benefits and implications of being active, and values physical activity's contribution to a healthy lifestyle (Harris, forthcoming).

APPROPRIATE CONTENT AND EXPECTATIONS FOR 5–11 YEAR OLDS

A quality physical education programme should promote physical activity and healthy lifestyles, develop positive attitudes and ensure safe practice. In particular, children aged 5–11 should learn to recognize, describe and come to understand what happens to their bodies during exercise and how this relates to good health. The knowledge, understanding and skills associated with this learning are given in Tables 14.1 and 14.2 in the form of specific learning outcomes relating to safety, exercise effects, health benefits and promoting activity.

Table 14.1: Appropriate content and expectations for health-related exercise issues in physical education: 5–7 year olds. *Source:* Adapted from Harris (forthcoming)

Health-related exercise issues	5–7-year-old pupils should:
Safety	• know and adhere to simple safety rules and practices (e.g. no contact; no skipping with a rope in bare feet unless on a mat; no running to touch walls) • know that activity starts with a warm-up and finishes with a cool-down

Exercise effects	• experience, recognize and be able to describe changes to their bodies during exercise:
	  – breathing (e.g. breathe faster)
	  – heart rate (e.g. heart pumps faster)
	  – temperature (e.g. feel warmer)
	  – appearance (e.g. flushed face)
	  – feelings (e.g. feel tired/energetic)
	  – body parts (e.g. arm/leg muscles are working)
	• know that exercise uses energy which comes from food and drink

Health benefits	• know that regular exercise improves your health • know that regular exercise can make you feel good • know that exercise helps body parts (e.g. arms and legs) to work well
Promoting activity	• know when, where and how they can be active at school (in and out of lessons) • use opportunities to be active, including at playtime

APPROACHES TO TEACHING HRE

In addition to the delivery of specific learning outcomes within the curriculum, primary schools are encouraged to promote physical activity by:

- establishing a whole-school approach to the promotion of enjoyable, lifelong physical activity;
- providing physical and social environments that encourage and enable safe and enjoyable physical activity;
- making a commitment to teaching HRE involving the implementation of programmes of study which emphasize enjoyable participation in physical activity and help pupils develop the knowledge and understanding, skills, attitudes and confidence needed to adopt and maintain physically active lifestyles;
- providing curricular and extra-curricular physical activity programmes

Table 14.2: Appropriate content and expectations for health-related exercise issues in physical education: 7–11 year olds. *Source:* Adapted from Harris (forthcming)

Health-related exercise issues	7–11-year-old pupils should:
Safety	• demonstrate their understanding of safe practices (e.g safe lifting; wearing appropriate footwear) • know the purpose of a warm-up and cool-down • recognize and be able to describe parts of a warm-up and cool-down, i.e. exercises for the joints (e.g. arm circles), whole-body activities (e.g. running) and stretches for the whole body or parts of the body
Exercise effects	• know that large muscles (e.g. in the legs and arms) are working during exercise and need a supply of oxygen to continue exercising • experience and understand the changes that happen to their bodies during exercise: – the rate and depth of breathing increases in order to provide more oxygen to the working muscles – the heart increases to pump oxygen to the working muscles – the temperature increases because working muscles produce energy as heat – the skin can become warm and sticky because the body sweats when it is very warm in order to cool down and avoid overheating – the appearance can become flushed due to blood vessels becoming wider and closer to the surface of the skin – know that the body needs a certain amount of energy every day in the form of food and drink to function properly • know that body fat increases if energy intake (food and drink) is greater than energy expenditure (all activity which uses energy, e.g. moving, growing, exercising, breathing, sleeping, eating)
Health benefits	• know that exercise strengthens bones and muscles (including the heart) and helps to keep joints flexible • know that exercise can help you to feel good about yourself and about being with others • know that exercise can be sociable (e.g. involves sharing and co-operating) and can be fun and enjoyable • know that being active can help to maintain a healthy body weight
Promoting activity	• perform and understand how moderate-to-vigorous activity feels (e.g. brisk walking, skipping, jogging, cycling, swimming, dancing, playing games) • know their current levels of activity (e.g. daily, once a week) and be able to describe the energy demands of those activities (e.g. light, moderate, vigorous) • know that people have different feelings about the types and amount of exercise they do and enjoy • be able to make decisions about which physical activities they enjoy • know when, where and how they can be active outside of school • use opportunities to be moderately to vigorously active for 30 minutes to 60 minutes (with rest periods as necessary) every day including lessons, playtimes and clubs

that meet the needs and interests of all pupils including those who are physically less able and those with special educational needs;

- contributing to the provision of support and training for individuals involved in imparting the knowledge and skills needed to effectively promote enjoyable, lifelong physical activity;
- collaborating with families and community organizations to develop, implement and evaluate physical activity programmes.

Adopting a whole-school approach to the promotion of physical activity is desirable, as the subtle messages which pupils receive about health from the daily life of a school are as important as those given during lessons. A whole-school approach entails exploring the potential of every aspect of the school environment to promote physical activity. An 'active school' aims to increase the physical activity levels of the whole-school population in a way that is likely to have a positive and sustained impact on their physical activity habits. Clearly, in order to do this effectively, teachers need to inform children and their parents about how much physical activity primary school-aged children should be doing (Table 14.3).

Table 14.3: Physical activity recommendations for children

Physical activity recommendations for children

Children should participate in physical activity of at least moderate intensity for *one hour per day* (i.e. 60 minutes accumulated over the course of a day) (moderate intensity is equivalent to brisk walking, and vigorous intensity exercise is equivalent to at least slow jogging) (HEA, 1998).

Children who currently do little activity should participate in physical activity of at least moderate intensity for *at least half an hour per day* (i.e. 30 minutes accumulated over the course of a day) (HEA, 1998).

At least twice a week, some of these activities should help to enhance and maintain muscular strength and flexibility, and bone health (HEA, 1998).

In particular, weight-bearing activities are recommended. These include activities in which the body has to support (1) all or part of its own weight (e.g. running, jumping, dance, gymnastics) or (2) the weight of additional objects (e.g. a throwing or striking implement such as a bat, ball, bean bag, quoit). Primary schoolchildren should be involved in a wide range of weight-bearing activities for both the upper body (e.g. throwing, catching, striking) and the lower body (e.g. running, jumping, skipping).

Older primary schoolchildren can be involved in low-level exercises involving their own body weight such as 'easy' curl-ups (with legs bent and hands along floor) and 'easy' push-ups (against a wall or in a box position). These exercises can be performed four to six times, progressing over time to eight to ten repeats. Controlled lifting and lowering is important, and the emphasis should be on safety and quality.

Simple stretching exercises are recommended for primary schoolchildren. All stretches should be held still for up to ten seconds.

HRE IN THE CURRICULUM

With specific reference to the curriculum, there are several ways in which the teaching of HRE can be approached, and each of these has specific strengths and limitations. Curriculum leaders in physical education need to make appropriate decisions concerning the approach(es) adopted, taking into consideration factors such as curriculum content, time and resources.

Permeation

HRE is taught through the physical education activity areas. The potential strengths of this approach are that HRE knowledge, understanding and skills are seen as integral to all physical education experiences; children learn that all physical activities (e.g. games, dance, gymnastics, swimming) can contribute towards good health and can become part of an active lifestyle. However, the possible limitations are that HRE knowledge, understanding and skills may become 'lost' or marginalized among other information relating to skills and performance; there may be an overload of information for pupils; the approach may be somewhat haphazard and piecemeal.

Focused

HRE is taught through specific focused lessons or units of work. The potential strengths of this approach are that it can help to ensure that HRE does not become lost or take second place to other information; there is less likelihood of HRE being regarded as an assumed 'by-product' of physical education lessons; HRE is perceived as important through having its own time slot and identity; and the value and status of the associated knowledge, understanding and skills is raised. However, the possible limitations are that HRE may be seen in isolation and not closely linked to the physical education activity areas; the HRE knowledge, understanding and skills may be delivered over a period of time with long gaps in between, which is problematic in terms of cohesion and progression (e.g. one short block of work per year); the knowledge base may be delivered in such a way as to reduce lesson activity levels (e.g. through 'sitting down' lessons with too much talk).

Topic

HRE is taught through a series of lessons following a specific topic or theme in physical education and classroom-based lessons. The potential strengths of this approach are that HRE may be delivered in a more holistic manner with closer links to other health behaviours (such as taking care of oneself and eating well) and aspects of other subjects; the area can be covered in more depth and be closely related to pupils' personal experiences; the amount of time spent engaged in physical activity in physical education lessons might be increased if introductory and follow-up work is conducted in the classroom setting. However, the possible limitations are that it may be more time-consuming with respect to planning, and could be less practically orientated than other approaches (if it incorporates a high degree of classroom-based work).

Combined

HRE is taught through any combination of the above approaches. The potential strengths of this approach are that it can build on the strengths of the different approaches and, at the same time, minimize their individual limitations; it can ensure that value is placed on HRE and that the area of work is closely linked to all physical education experiences and other health behaviours. However, the possible limitation is that it may be more time-consuming initially to plan, structure, implement and co-ordinate within the curriculum.

DELIVERING HRE

Educating children about exercise and promoting lifelong participation cannot be left to chance. Children do not automatically develop the knowledge, understanding, skills, attitudes and behaviours that lead to regular participation in physical activity. These need to be taught and this teaching must be planned, effectively delivered and evaluated. The teaching of HRE involves more than just passing on information. Many children know that exercise is good for them but they do not do enough exercise to gain health benefits. They need to be motivated to be active and to feel good about being active. Clearly, the way in which health-related information and experiences are taught to children is critical. The delivery of HRE should embrace the following guiding principles:

- exercise can be a positive experience which is enjoyable;
- exercise is for all;
- everyone can benefit from exercise;
- everyone can be good at exercise;
- everyone can find the right kind of exercise for themselves;
- exercise is for life;
- excellence in health-related exercise is maintaining an active way of life.

Positive experiences of physical activity are critical to the promotion of active lifestyles. Pupils should gain pleasure, enjoyment and satisfaction from being active and should be presented with opportunities to make progress, succeed and feel confident about activity. Exercise experiences should be offered that meet individual needs, demands and preferences, including the less able and those with specific disabilities and health conditions. Teachers need to select teaching approaches which ensure inclusion and permit every child to be actively involved. Further, in order to promote participation effectively, teachers must value and reward effort, commitment and personal progress.

ASSESSING PUPIL PROGRESS IN HRE

Achievement in HRE relates to improvements in knowledge and understanding, physical competence, behavioural skills, and attitudes and confidence. These improvements can be monitored through:

- responses to focused questions (e.g. What happens to your breathing when you exercise? How do you feel when you are active? Why does your heart rate change when you exercise? Which parts of your body are working hard when you run?);
- teacher observation of pupil performance in practical tasks (e.g. Show me an exercise that makes your heart pump quicker. Show me a stretch for the whole body);
- pupil records of involvement in physical activity (e.g. pupil entries in activity diaries such as keeping a record for a number of days or weeks of all the activity performed at home and at school);
- pupils' attendance records, and participation in and commitment to physical education lessons and the extra-curricular programme (e.g. the proportion of physical education lessons missed and/or not participated in by a pupil; the degree of interest shown and effort put into the lesson activities; pupil involvement in school clubs, practices, events);
- participation in physical activity outside of school (e.g. pupil involvement in out-of-school clubs, activities and events).

Another monitoring method in health-related programmes is fitness testing. However, there has been much debate about the educational value of fitness testing in the physical education curriculum (see Armstrong and Welsman, 1997). Indeed, formal fitness testing of primary schoolchildren is not recommended as it is neither necessary nor appropriate due to the early maturational age of pupils and the limited evidence that younger children readily show fitness gains following exercise programmes (see Harris, 1998). Not every child can reach a high level of fitness because the latter is constrained by genetic limitations, maturational status and trainability, and even if they train hard over a period of time, some children's fitness levels may show only small improvements. The majority of children will never be able to run a mile in a set time or perform a specific number of pull-ups even if they train hard and do their best. However, they can increase the length of time they are active, and the number of times they do this. Most importantly, being active for up to an hour a day is an attainable target for every child. While formal fitness testing is not recommended for the above reasons, primary school pupils can be involved in simple monitoring methods such as keeping activity diaries and recording the effects of exercise on their bodies (e.g. heart rate, breathing rate). Any practical monitoring procedures should be presented in a positive individualized manner which promotes learning and provides pupils with personalized baselines from which to improve.

Unit: Invasion games   Duration: 8 hours

Year 2

Objectives   Links to statutory guidance

To enable pupils to: Pupils plan and perform simple skills safely,
• play simple competitive games as individu- and show control in linking actions together.
  als, in pairs and in small groups   They improve their performance through prac-
• perform a variety of ways of sending,   tising their skills, working alone and with a
  receiving and travelling with a ball   partner. They talk about what they and others
• experience elements of invasion games   have done, and are able to make simple judge-
  that include running and chasing   ments.
• *recognize and describe the short-term*   *They recognize and describe changes that*
  effects on the body of playing invasion *happen to their bodies during exercise.*
  games.

Learning outcomes	*Learning activities*	*Assessment*	*Resources*
Pupils should be able to:	*Opportunities for pupils to:*		
1. roll, kick and travel with a ball in a con-trolled manner	send a ball by rolling	1	balls, cones/lines on playground (optional)
	send a ball by kicking	1	
2. stop/control a ball that has been kicked or rolled to them while they are stationary	travel with a ball using the feet or holding the ball	1	
	receive a ball that has been rolled or kicked	2	balls, cones/lines on playground (optional),
3. understand how to play simple competi-tive invasion games	play simple competitive games in pairs and small groups which incorporate kicking or rolling, receiving, travelling with the ball and running and chasing (e.g. How many passes in 30 seconds?, How many people can you tag in 1 minute?)	3	bibs or bands (optional) breathing and heart rate charts (e.g.: a scale ranging from very slow to very fast) (optional)
4. *recognize and describe the effects of playing invasion games on their breathing and heart rate*	experience and describe how playing invasion games makes their heart pump quicker and makes them breathe faster and deeper	4	

Figure 14.1: Example of unit of work for permeating HRE through games for children aged 5–7. *Source:* Adapted from Harris (forthcoming)

Unit: Topic 'My body'	Duration: 12 hours
Year 6	
Objectives	Links to statutory guidance

To enable pupils to:
- know the structure of the heart and how it acts as a pump
- know how blood circulates around the body through main arteries and veins
- experience and understand the short-term effects of exercise on the body.

Physical education: Pupils demonstrate that they understand what is happening to their bodies during exercise.
Science: Pupils use scientific names for the circulatory system and identify the position of organs in the body. Pupils describe the functions of the heart and explain how it is essential to the organism.

Learning outcomes	Learning activities	Assessment	Resources
Pupils should be able to:	Opportunities for pupils to:		
1. demonstrate knowledge of the circulatory system	Locate and recognize the different parts of the circulatory system (heart, lungs and blood vessels) (classroom)	1	diagrams, posters, books
2. demonstrate knowledge of the heart's structure and function	Find out and discuss the function of the different parts of the circulatory system (classroom)	1, 2	diagrams, posters, books
3. understand the effect of exercise on the pulse rate	Find out and discuss how oxygen travels in the blood from the muscles to the heart, into the lungs, back to the heart, and to the muscles again (physical education: e.g. 'circulatory circuit' involving continuous travel from the 'muscles' to the 'lungs', back through the 'heart' and to the 'muscles' again – the circuit can be walked then jogged and different actions can be performed at various parts of the system)	1, 2	equipment for selected activity (e.g. cones, task cards, posters)
4. understand the short-term effects of exercise on the body	Measure and record what happens to their pulse rate and breathing rate when they are involved in an energetic activity (physical education: e.g. a series of skipping activities (without and with a rope) progressing from single rope work to pairs work)	3, 4	equipment for selected activity (e.g. ropes)
	Explain why their heart rate and breathing rate increase when they exercise (physical education: e.g. 'Card Game' activity which involves selecting a playing card and performing one of four exercises determined by the suit and number on the card, e.g. 4 of 'hearts' means jogging around the area four times)	3, 4	equipment for selected activity
	Find out and discuss the effects of everyday activities on the heart rate and breathing rate (e.g. climbing stairs, walking to school, sitting, playing sport) (classroom)	4	

Figure 14.2: Example of unit of work for delivering HRE within a topic approach for children aged 7–11. *Source:* Adapted from Harris (forthcoming)

Objectives	Resources
HRE: to explore the changes that occur to body temperature and appearance when playing games. *Games:* to develop and practise a variety of ways of sending, receiving and travelling with a ball. *Cross-curricular links:* to think about what is expected to happen, to make observations, and to communicate what happened (science); to understand the language of comparatives (mathematics).	One ball between two; Two marker cones for each pair of pupils; Charts/posters/worksheets with prompt words/illustrations to describe body temperature and appearance (optional)

Phase	Tasks	Teaching points
Introduction	Describe your body temperature (how hot or cold you feel). What do you think will happen to your body temperature when you play games? Describe what you think it will be like after playing games. Do you think you will look any different?	Provide prompt words as necessary, e.g. hot, cold, freezing, warm.
Warm-up	In pairs, 1s jog in space and 2s follow – swap on instruction; march on spot lifting knees high and clap hands under each knee; repeat 'follow my leader' but this time the leader holds a ball – on instruction, 1s hand ball to 2s who become the leaders; standing back-to-back, pass ball over heads and beneath legs; repeat 'follow my leader' with ball but gently throw ball when changing leaders; perform a whole body stretch (e.g. reaching tall) holding it still for a count of ten.	Controlled actions and sensible use of space, avoiding collisions with others; when passing ball, look where partner is beforehand and pass it carefully into their hands; when receiving, watch the ball and have hands ready to receive it; holding stretches as still as possible.
Developing accuracy in rolling a ball along the ground and receiving it	Pupils stand a short distance apart. 1s run around 2s and back to their places, holding a ball. When they have returned, they roll the ball accurately along the ground to 2s who receive the ball with feet/hands and then pick it up. 2s then run around 1s and repeat the activity.	To pass ball: bend your knees; look where you want to send the ball; let your hands swing back and follow the direction of the ball after you have let it go. To receive ball: watch the ball carefully; position yourself behind the ball; get hands/feet ready to receive the ball.

Figure 14.3: Example lesson plan of teaching HRE through games: 5–7 year olds.
Source: Adapted from Harris and Elbourn (1997)

Phase	Tasks	Teaching points
Developing accuracy in dribbling and rolling a ball and receiving a ball that has been rolled along the ground	1s dribble ball using feet/hands around 2s and back to place. 1s then pass ball accurately to 2s using feet/hands (along the ground) and 2s receive ball using feet/hands and the activity continues. On completion of the activity, the pupils are asked: What has happened to your body temperature as a result of playing games? Can you think of words to describe your body temperature now? Has your appearance changed in any way?	Keep ball close to your foot and under close control; kick with inside of foot; swing foot backwards to prepare for kick; look where you want to send the ball; when you have kicked, let your foot follow the ball in the direction you want to send it; keep your eyes on the ball when receiving; be prepared to move quickly to get behind the ball; get your hands/feet ready to receive the ball.
Developing accuracy in kicking at a target (shooting) and in receiving a kicked ball	Two cones as a mini-goal, about 3–5 metres from a starting line. 1s kick ball towards goal and 2s receive ball with feet/hands after it has crossed the goal line. 2s dribble ball back to line while 1 jogs to goal ready to receive 2's shot. Every shot that passes between the cones scores one point and every successful receipt of the ball after it has crossed the goal line scores one point. Developments: (1) pairs score as many points as possible in one minute and are given the chance to improve on their combined score, (2) the goal is moved one pace further away from the line, after both players have performed successful shots and receipts at the shorter distance. Questions about effects on body temperature and appearance are repeated.	Kick with inside of your foot; swing foot backwards to prepare for your kick; look where you want to send the ball; when you have kicked, let your foot follow the ball in the direction you want to send it. Keep your eyes on the ball when receiving; be prepared to move quickly to get behind the ball; get your hands/feet ready to receive the ball.

Figure 14.3 *continued*

Phase	Tasks	Teaching points
Cool down	Walk or jog to collect one piece of equipment until all equipment is in; perform two 'whole body' stretches, holding each one still for a count of ten.	Controlled actions and sensible use of space; reaching tall or wide in the stretches, holding stretches as still as possible.
Conclusion	Describe your body temperature and appearance while you were playing games. In what ways did it differ from before? Were you able to accurately guess what would happen to your body temperature and appearance when you played games?	Develop vocabulary of prompt words, e.g. hot, cold, freezing, warm, tired, flushed.

Figure 14.3 *continued*

Objectives	Resources
HRE: to understand that muscles need a supply of oxygen to keep working and that the heart rate increases to pump oxygen to the working muscles.	Cones; 'Heart' circuit notices; stop-watch or watch with second hand;
Health education: to understand that exercise strengthens the heart.	skipping ropes; paper and pencils/pens;
Cross-curricular links: to understand a simple model of the structure of the heart and how it acts as a pump, how blood circulates in the body, and the effect of exercise on pulse rate; to use simple equipment to make careful observations and measurements and to use the results of observations to draw and explain conclusions (science).	pupil worksheet (optional); whistle/music (optional).

Phase	Tasks	Teaching points
Introduction	What happens to the heart when we exercise? How can we measure what happens to our heart rate when we exercise? Pupils are shown how to locate and count the pulse at the wrist, neck or heart for ten seconds. This is recorded on paper or on a prepared worksheet.	Prompts and/or visual stimuli are provided as necessary.
Warm-up	The group is walked clockwise around a simple 'heart' circuit (made using cones with notices – 'lungs' at one end, 'muscles' at the other, 'heart' in the middle), explaining what each part represents; pupils repeat the circuit, walking then jogging; pupils perform stretches for the back of the lower leg (calf) and the front of the upper leg (quadriceps), holding each stretch still for a count of ten.	All pupils travelling in the same direction around the circuit. Holding stretches as still as possible.

Figure 14.4: Example lesson plan of teaching HRE through a focused lesson: 7–11 year olds. *Source:* Adapted from Harris and Elbourn (1997)

Phase	Tasks	Teaching points
Travelling around the body as a blood cell	Pupils exercise the 'muscles' (e.g. jog; march); Which parts of your body are working hard? Where do muscles get energy from? How does food and oxygen get to the muscles? Our blood is now low in oxygen, so we must collect more and bring it back to the muscles. The blue cones/notices indicate that the blood is short of oxygen. What pumps the blood around the body? The pupils are led to the 'heart'. The top parts of the heart collect the blood and the bottom parts pump it out. We need to go to the bottom part of the heart to be pumped out. The blood is still short of oxygen – where is it going to get oxygen? From the lungs. The pupils are led to the 'lungs'. This is where the blood receives oxygen. How does the oxygen get into the lungs? Pupils perform large, slow arm circles, taking a big breath with each circle. Now the blood has lots of oxygen and it is going back to the heart. The heart will pump it back to the muscles. The cones/notices are now red because the blood is carrying lots of oxygen. The heart collects the blood and pumps it out to the muscles. In pairs, pupils start at different points on the circuit and complete continuous laps, discussing with their partner where they are in the heart and what is happening.	Controlled exercises performed with good technique at the 'muscles' and the 'lungs'. Tall backs and high knee lifts when marching. Large and steady arm circles, with arms brushing ears. All pupils travelling in the same direction around the circuit.
Exploring the effects of different activities on the pulse rate	Pupils are divided into four groups and asked to complete two minutes of each of the following activities: jogging; walking; marching; skipping. After each activity, pupils count their pulse for ten seconds and record it on paper or on a worksheet.	Tall backs and high knee lifts when marching. Feet close to ground and heels down when skipping.

Figure 14.4 *continued*

Phase	Tasks	Teaching points
Cool-down	Pupils walk quickly around the 'heart' circuit and collect the cones; pupils perform stretches for the back of the lower leg (calf) and the front of the upper leg (quadriceps), holding each stretch still for a count of ten.	Controlled movements and sensible use of space. Holding stretches as still as possible.
Conclusion	The pupils can discuss their recordings. Why did your pulse rate change during the lesson? Which activity raised your pulse the least? Why do you think this was? Which activity raised your pulse the most? Why do you think this was?	Pupils should find that their pulse rate is higher in the activities which feel more demanding. They should understand that working muscles need oxygen to keep working, and that the heart rate increases during exercise in order to pump oxygen to the working muscles.

Figure 14.4 *continued*

CONCLUSION

Health-related exercise is an important component of an effective physical education programme as it focuses on teaching children why they should be active and provides them with the basic know-how and encouragement to help them make activity part of their everyday lives. This chapter has hopefully provided primary schoolteachers with information and ideas to assist them in meeting the health-related exercise expectations for children aged 5–11. By delivering this aspect of the physical education programme effectively, primary schoolteachers will be making a major contribution to children's health.

Chapter 15

Teaching Outdoor and Adventurous Activities

BRIN MARTIN

INTRODUCTION

In this chapter I hope to set out a rationale for teaching outdoor and adventurous activities (OAA) in primary schools. I will attempt to argue that the activity has continued to survive rather than to thrive in the face of the many pressures facing schools. This strength, I will suggest, emanates from the distinctive nature of the activity, being an essentially process-based aspect of the primary physical education curriculum, dealing explicitly with perceived adventure. This will be explored by examining the key principles of teaching the activity, concluding with a practical teaching model for schools.

A DEFINITION OF OUTDOOR AND ADVENTUROUS ACTIVITIES

It would be useful first to state how I intend to use the term OAA: a personal definition, based upon experience of primary classroom practice and realism. Thus, for the purposes of this chapter, OAA refers to those activities which are taught as part of the normal school curriculum; using the existing facilities and campus of the primary school; by the generalist class teacher, without the need for additional qualifications, and to the whole class at the same time. This differentiates it from those other activities: outdoor pursuits and outdoor education. The former will normally require additional qualifications, and usually employ a small number of pupils in extra-curricular time and off the school site, while the latter may well involve other aspects of environmental or field study, but again require similar organizational management. I recognize that this differential may cause debate or concern from those anxious to preserve the pure sport form of the activity. As I will argue later, I see that the sport/craft forms, in the context of this chapter, define the same attributes as OAA, through adopting progressive principles at the appropriate developmental stage.

THE DISTINCTIVE NATURE OF OAA

Irrespective of the context of the work, I am committed to the belief that OAA delivers similar, if developmentally simpler, experiences, attributes and characters as outdoor pursuits. I know this holds good, but I cannot substantiate that claim, except through experience. It is recognized that to undertake risky activities, such as rock climbing and fell running, inherently develops attributes such as challenge, leadership, catharsis and personal insight. My experience, and that of primary children, would suggest that they develop equal, if developmentally simpler, attributes through participation in OAA. These processes indeed form the basis of the content of the teaching in a planned and controlled learning environment. This comprises the essence of the subject, and the basic thesis for this chapter.

OAA is a methodology. The reason to teach OAA is process based. This differentiates OAA from other activities, such as games, gymnastics or dance. The reason to teach games, such as cricket, is primarily focused on content: to learn the skills of cricket. I fully accept and agree that in learning cricket, pupils might also develop team-work, respect, leadership. But this is not the primary purpose of the activity. Conversely the primary focus of OAA is to teach problem-solving skills, to focus on process, to learn to co-operate and to learn from group mistakes while participating. In a significant majority of OAA activities, the skills, knowledge and understanding are almost immaterial to the primary focus, and do not significantly feature even as a secondary focus.

THE CONTINUED SURVIVAL OF OAA

The fact that OAA continues to survive is remarkable, and is testament to the strength of the nature of the activity. It can only be as a result of the contribution that OAA makes to the primary curriculum, even at an unconscious level, both inside and outside of physical education. I suggest that good OAA exemplifies the best in primary practice. Good primary teaching is about skilful craft, and it is about delivering content through process. It is about clarity of purpose, about challenge through expectations, about effective management of pupils and resources to best achieve the purposes, and it is about letting pupils know how well they are doing in relation to that purpose. The purpose in the case of OAA is the process rather than the content. I will suggest below that where OAA is taught most successfully, teachers are using the activity as a vehicle to deliver the processes involved, as does good drama, and good personal and social education. This is and must remain the central purpose of OAA lessons.

In my enthusiasm for the activity and the enjoyment in participating in OAA I sometimes lose that clarity of focus. I enjoy playing the 'game', and forget that the purpose of the game is to focus on the processes involved, the vehicle and the context behind the activity. When I do not forget, I am constantly trying to consider, to review, to refine or construct alternative situations that will best allow the pupils to learn from the purpose behind the activity. It is a danger that in our enthusiasm for the activity we lose sight of that central feature of the work. We cannot afford to lose sight of the strength of this tool, and must continue to ensure that teachers' planning should clearly indicate and prioritize these process elements in their work.

THE CONTRIBUTION OF OAA TO THE (PHYSICAL EDUCATION) CURRICULUM

For OAA to have survived, it therefore must make a very significant yet focused contribution to the school's aims and aspirations. Its home is not necessarily within physical education, but it clearly does have a well-respected and sustained home in the primary school. There are many examples of the long-standing contribution that OAA has made to the curriculum within and outside of school, which should remain an entitlement for all pupils. Good practice is not recognized only in orienteering skills, but also in the pupils' confidence and genuine involvement in personal and social education. In one outstanding example during an inspection, pupils' clear and unembarrassed sharing of spiritual aspects of their work was deeply moving. It was also planned for by the teacher. I have never seen a more complete example of spiritual, moral, social and cultural excellence in my many inspections of physical education.

Thus the central thesis of this chapter lies with the significance of delivering the processes. Within the curriculum, it is within the remit of the teacher to plan for these experiences, and to manage their delivery. To return to the spiral nature of the progression identified above, it is perhaps another central difference between OAA and outdoor pursuits that, while recognizing the process elements in the latter, they exist as a result of activity rather than as a planned purpose. Someone cycles off-road for a number of reasons: exercise, leisure, enjoyment of the environment, company, etc. They also gain a number of experiences – catharsis, exhilaration, a sense of achievement or failure, understanding of others' strengths and weaknesses, etc. – but do not plan these as a purpose of the activity.

Explicitly, OAA and outdoor pursuits can be seen to deliver a range of attributes, among them adventure, technique and process skills. A useful summary of these attributes can be seen in Figure 15.1, which proportions the contributions each make at particular phases of education. The proportions represent the primary focus behind the intended activity. Adventure refers to how participants perceive their participation, the challenge, and will be discussed further later in the chapter; technique includes the skills, knowledge and understanding required to successfully participate in the activity, with the remaining proportion resting on the contribution of the process elements discussed earlier.

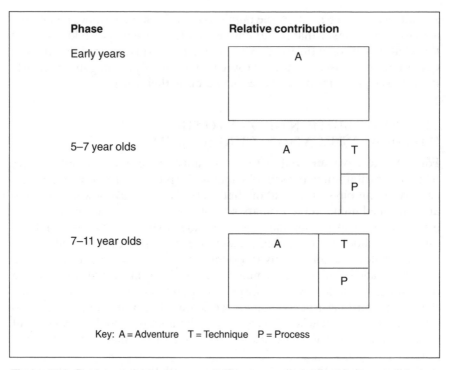

Figure 15.1: Outdoor and adventurous activities, a progressive model. *Source:* Adapted from one originally devised by the Dudley Advisory Team (Dudley, n.d.)

PROGRESSION IN OUTDOOR AND ADVENTUROUS ACTIVITIES

Figure 15.1 shows that the obvious and unique feature of OAA is adventure, from early years to upper primary pupils, where the 'outdoorness' is not as crucial as the adventure. A number of aspects of OAA can successfully be taught indoors, although most would agree that the range of opportunities increases markedly out of doors. Again in the primary context, the component of adventure is that which is perceived as adventurous by the pupils. Adventure is variously defined as the degree of 'danger', uncertainty of outcome or risk involved. In the primary context, the degree of adventure is significant in the respect that it is the degree to which the pupils perceive that they are undertaking an adventurous activity. In glorious terms, it is the threshold of perceived danger in which the pupils find themselves as a result of participating in an activity which will determine their attitude to the adventure. This threshold will be different for each pupil. What may seem a simple, non-threatening activity to the teacher, can be regarded very differently by pupils. Teachers must be skilful in recognizing when individuals approach or cross this threshold, and respect the fact that, to the pupil, the component of adventure is unbearable. Situations arise where pupils have been unable to complete a simple activity as, for them, the activity crossed that threshold. The skill of the teacher is to control and manage these variables to challenge pupils at the appropriate level. Many of the activities suggested in the growing number of texts are in no way inherently dangerous or involve risk, but the context and management of the activity may well appear so to the pupil. Some pupils will thrive on adventure, others will balk at it.

If the adventure is perceived, and the degree of technique is limited in the primary phase, the processes involved become all the more important. Progress in gymnastics can be debated but is structured and, for example, can be seen as the development of sequencing, or group relationships, or application to apparatus. Progression in OAA appears in different realms of experience, related to the degree of adventure, and in the limited range of techniques involved (strength and agility also play a part, as does conceptual understanding of some aspects of map work). Progression is most apparent in the developmental ability of the pupils to communicate, co-operate, listen, share, work as a group, solve problems, etc.

KEY PRINCIPLES OF DELIVERY

Best practice in teaching OAA is the same as best practice in any other area. It would be useful to briefly examine what contributes to high quality provision. Clarity of purpose must be central, more so at this phase than detailed subject knowledge. A restricted range of activities, skilfully managed, is far more powerful as a learning tool than a wide range of activities where the purpose and intention of each is misunderstood. Teachers therefore need to be clear about the purpose underlying the lesson and the activities that support it, and be able to pursue that purpose in flexible ways.

Teachers should endeavour to develop a clear understanding of the principles involved, such as the interplay of group dynamics on the outcome of the activity; of how best to challenge process skills; where to adapt tasks to best match them to the abilities of the pupils, and how best to enable the pupils to reflect and refine their initial responses. Teachers need to be able to select and prepare resources and facilities to best meet the purpose of the activity. A barren site, used imaginatively, sometimes supported through appropriate scenarios, can be equally successful as the most inspiring of school grounds.

It is crucial to understand the pedagogy behind the process skills, especially related to pupil learning. To manage activities that, for example, challenge independence, responsibility, reflection, the ability to co-operate, is the key to successful learning. Overtly, the same activities can be used with early-years pupils as with 11 year olds. The purpose behind the activity will be entirely different, and it is this which forms the central focus of that purpose. Equally, exactly the same activity can be used in subsequent weeks with the same group, through manipulation of the context and the dynamics of the work. Unfortunately, using progression as a learning tool is a skill that cannot be acquired from the text. It comes through experience of trialling activities, context and variables with pupils, and determining what works and how it works. High-quality provision, therefore, can only be reflected in effective learning, and out of necessity reflected in the range of approaches adopted by the teachers. Teachers should therefore be encouraged to hone the skills of teaching that exist at classroom level into the teaching of OAA.

CONCLUSION

I have a vision of skilful, independent learners, using their OAA competences flexibly to meet the demands of the whole curriculum; learners who are confident enough to enjoy their learning, and convinced enough to anticipate the progression through to outdoor pursuits.

KEY POINTS

- Plan for pupil learning rather than activity.
- Relate the content to the needs of the learner.
- Manage the teaching to extend and challenge pupils.
- Employ strategies that will match this purpose.
- Be excited by the opportunities available to the pupils.
- Take 'risks' in your teaching: experiment.

But above all:

- be clear about the purpose behind the activity.

Title of the unit: We're Going on a Bear Hunt

YEAR 1/2

About the unit

In this unit children will use the story of the 'Bear Hunt' to explore two areas related to outdoor and adventurous activities, the introduction of early map work orientation skills and basic group activities using the school hall and grounds. Specifically the pupils will develop their ability to co-operate to solve simple problems.

Where the unit fits in

This unit builds on the work in earlier units, which explored the use of simple maps and map symbols to locate objects in the school grounds. This made particular use of the environmental area, linking it to other curriculum units, in particular minibeasts.

Adapting the units for a different age group

Early-years children could:

- Undertake the orientation skills without the use of a map
- Use trails to develop the idea of following a route
- Use a restricted area
- Undertake simple individual physical challenges rather than group challenges
- Adapt the tasks to meet their physical capabilities

Prior learning

It is helpful if the children have:

Done some introductory work on the use of simple maps;
Learned about trails;
Worked in gymnastics using apparatus.

Vocabulary

In this unit, children will have opportunities to use:

Words associated with maps, e.g. symbol, key, control, plan, view.
Words and concepts associated with co-operating with others, e.g. listening, sharing, taking turns, helping others.

Resources

Simple maps, e.g. map 1, the school hall, and map 2, the environmental area.
The bear hunt control markers and work cards.
The outside play apparatus.
The bear hunt resource pack of equipment including the rope and elastic.

Expectations

At the end of this unit:

Most children will: be able to use a map to locate markers in the school grounds; be able to navigate around simple courses and trails; give reasons why they have undertaken particular actions; have co-operated in small groups to overcome simple physical challenges.

Some children will not have made so much progress and will: be able to undertake trails with the help of a partner; be able to recognize simple picture maps of the hall; undertake simple physical challenges.

Some children will have progressed further and will: be able to follow more complex routes using the map; be able to set simple trails for a partner; begin to be able to help others by making suggestions to solve group physical challenges.

Figure 15.2: Example unit of work

Bear Hunt
Lesson notes
(NB This is for reference only, you do not need to plan in this amount of detail)

Short-term planning, within the lesson

Subject	Physical education
	Outdoor and adventurous activities, physical challenges
Unit of work	Bear Hunt
Year group	One/two
Phase in unit	Week one out of three
Previous	Covered other aspects of orientation skills
Next	Building on the challenges in this lesson
Learning Objective:	By the end of this lesson pupils will be able to begin to co-operate in small groups to overcome physical challenges.

Introduction/warm-up
- Actions in relation to Bear Hunt story from previous weeks, stumble, swish, etc.
- Follow-my-leader actions.
- Setting up the equipment.
- Teacher will group children based on friendship groups. Five groups of six children, mixed gender.

Main theme
- Groups allocated to one set of apparatus.
- Teacher quickly runs over safety and rules of each activity. Ask for points of clarification.
- Allow pupils to explore possible ways of solving the following tasks (full details in Hunting the Griz, in staffroom)

- Narrow dark cave, use the 'tunnel'
- Forest, use the 'lattice'
- Mud, use the 'stepping stones'
- River, use the 'rope swing'
- Up the stairs, use the 'climbing'.

Teacher circulates, extending activities to challenge further, modifying tasks if pupils have found a solution, listening and questioning individuals and groups.
Depending on the pupils' progress in their task, the teacher may rotate groups around to a second task, or choose to extend the original task further.
When appropriate, pull the group together and explore a particular theme in relation to the learning objective, such as the pupils' listening skills, how they take turns, keeping to the rules, etc.

Concluding activity
Put away equipment.
Relaxation activities using breathing and listening to sounds in the hall.

Extension activities
By the end of this lesson:
(All) pupils will be able to undertake the physical challenges with some degree of success, and understand that to be successful they will need to work as a team.
(Most) pupils will successfully overcome the problems, and be able to listen to the suggestions of others to improve their own attempts.
(Some) pupils will begin to take a leading role within their group, and recognize that others will need additional help, and begin to make suggestions as to how to help them.

Figure 15.3: Example lesson plan

Learning objectives	Possible teaching activities	Learning outcomes	Points to note
Children should learn:		**Children:**	
To use simple symbols on a map	Finding photocopies of pictures from the bear hunt hidden around the field. Ask them how they went about locating the picture, how did they split up the task. Introduce the idea of following a route to find the pictures in a particular order, extend the activity to colour in a copy of the picture using crayons located around the field. Begin to use the map to mark on the map the location of where each marker was found. Use a map with the location of the controls marked on it to find markers hidden prior to the lesson. Begin to ask pupils to plan their routes prior to the activity by telling them to visit the markers in a particular order.	Understand map symbols	The majority of children will be able to use and understand simple maps. However, much of the work can be taught by using plan views of desks, the classroom, etc. Use the controls in the staffroom from *Hunting the Griz*, and photocopy the masters needed.
To use a simple map to follow routes and trails		Locate pictures using simple maps	You might want to pair children in different ways and for different activities, such as more able pupils with ones who have difficulties, or boy/girl, or by physical attributes.
To use maps to navigate around simple courses to locate markers		Follow routes to locate markers using maps	
To use maps to navigate in pairs around simple courses	Develop the variety of courses in the school hall, make them longer, more complex, use a code to challenge pupils' understanding, use two different courses running at the same time. Set up a 'score' course by putting out a number of markers, and giving the pairs a certain amount of time to find as many as possible. Get the children to hide a bean bag in the hall, mark it on a simple map and let others try and locate the bean bag. Extend this out of doors. Use four bean bags, find them in a particular order. Pairs set up a four-bag course for another pair and race them to find each other's course.	Co-operate to navigate round simple courses	For this section, link the teaching in with work in geography on the route to school. Setting up more permanent courses that children could use at lunchtimes could extend the work further.
To set simple courses for others to follow		Navigate round more complex courses	With each of the units, continue to challenge children through questioning that will deepen their understanding, and will make them reflect upon how successful they were in specific tasks.
		Set up their own courses for others to follow	
To undertake physical challenges outside and in the hall	Set up and carry out a carousel of physical challenges in the school hall using simple gymnastics apparatus (see resource pack in staffroom from *Hunting the Griz*). Base challenges on bear hunt story, swishy swashy grass, stumble trip, narrow, gloomy cave, etc. Adapt and refine the challenges to extend the activities further by making them more difficult, complex, involving more variables, etc. Get pupils to talk about how they and others have done, focusing on co-operation, listening skills, taking turns, sharing, etc. Allow them additional attempts to see if their ideas worked, were more effective, etc.	Negotiate around obstacles	Photocopy pictures from bear hunt to add to the scenario of the activities; for example, the tunnel could be the narrow, dark cave, the lattice would be the stumble trip wood, etc.
To begin to co-operate in small groups to overcome physical challenges		Keep within rules set	All activities are described in detail in the book in the staffroom, including how to challenge or enable pupils to succeed further.
To evaluate their own and others' attempts		Discuss how they and others negotiated obstacles	It is important to spend time reviewing the outcomes of the tasks, by asking questions such as how groups listened to each other, who broke the rules, who had a good idea but no one else would listen, etc.
To learn how to make subsequent attempts more effective			

Figure 15.4: Possible teaching activities and learning outcomes from the unit of work: We're Going on a Bear Hunt

Chapter 16

Teaching Swimming

COLIN A. HARDY

INTRODUCTION

In the late nineteenth and early twentieth centuries there was a lobby mounted in the United Kingdom by representatives of swimming and life-saving bodies, schools' swimming associations and education authorities to establish swimming as an activity within the 'physical training' syllabus (Hardy, 1991a, 1991b). The arguments for including swimming in the school curriculum revolved around the issues of health and safety. With the success of the Baths and Wash-houses Movement to build swimming facilities, partic-ularly in urban areas, swimming became a reality for many schoolchildren. In fact, the experiences of Edith and Hilda Cossey suggest that swimming was being developed as a well-organized activity for the upper elementary classes in the County Borough of West Ham in these early years:

> When we went to the local baths once a week with our teacher, it was something we looked forward to (average age of girls 10 to 11). We lined up in pairs and off we went with our teacher at the side of us. Arriving at the baths we were allowed two girls in one cubicle – once we were in our costumes we would wait at the side of the pool for our teacher's instructions. There were two pools at the baths, one 2nd class and the other 1st class. Our teacher taught us in a group. The children were encouraged by merit stripes for the width and for the length. One headmistress (Miss Collins) encouraged children by giving them a silver 3d piece when they swam the length, which was well sought after. (Cossey, 1988; age: 85)

> There was no swimming in the lower classes. I started at the age of 10 and went swimming every year until I left school. In my later years I was made Captain of the Girls' Swimming Team. Our teacher would assemble the girls and escort them to the baths about half a mile away.

It was a happy walk, with our towels and costumes tucked under our arms, most girls had their own costume and towel – but these could be borrowed for a small fee. There was no fee for the school lesson, but 1½d was charged out of school hours. I was responsible for selling these 1½d yellow tickets. Our school team had competitions with other schools, and these were very exciting, with children shouting for their team to win. There was an instructor at the baths who coached us in the over-arm stroke, the breaststroke, life-saving and diving. (Cossey, 1988; age: 80)

However, nearly a century later concerns for swimming as a primary school activity were being expressed in national surveys (CCPR and NAHT, 1992) and by researchers (Bass and Hardy, 1996a, 1996b). It was noted that, although swimming is included as a National Curriculum activity (DFE, 1995), the problems of pool availability, teaching expertise, time, cost and the demands of other school subjects have marginalized swimming in many primary schools. Furthermore, and more specifically relevant to this chapter, the emphasis placed on children completing the 25-metre requirement has narrowed the swimming programme in many schools and excluded children from swimming lessons once the target has been achieved.

A recent government document (QCA, 1999), reiterating a point made by researchers over the years (Barter and Firth, 1994; Bass and Hardy, 1996a, 1996b; Langley and Silva, 1986; Langley *et al.*, 1981), noted that the ability to swim 25 metres is not always sufficient to ensure safety in water environments, as it takes time to develop the basic skills and understanding necessary for effective and safe swimming. If it is accepted that swimming is basically about confidence, propulsion and water safety, teachers will need the knowledge and skills to develop and monitor these attributes with their pupils. Confidence in water provides the base for development, propulsion gives pupils the ability to move around in water, and water safety ensures that the pupils gain the understanding and learn the appropriate skills to develop some control over the aquatic environment.

SWIMMING PROGRAMME

Teaching

In structuring the swimming programme there will need to be both teacher and pupil objectives. Teacher objectives will emphasize what teachers hope to achieve in their lessons, and pupil objectives will clarify the behaviours expected of pupils during and at the end of a particular phase of the programme. In achieving their objectives teachers must not only instruct and demonstrate effectively but they must also have the ability to observe and analyse accurately, and to be able to respond to the varying demands and ability levels of groups of pupils. The way teachers communicate to pupils and present and organize the activity can all have differing effects on pupils. As pupils mediate the teacher's methods it is essential that teachers use both visual and verbal communication and present and organize material in both part and whole practices, so that pupils' varying cognitive style combinations (Luke, 1998; Luke and Hardy, 1996) and motor abilities are addressed.

In teaching swimming to their pupils, teachers will need continually to ask questions about the strategies they use:

- *Communication:*
  Do I need a simple cue (e.g. 'Point the toes') or a more detailed explanation?
  Is the cue understood by all pupils?
  Is the cue timely for the pupils' stage of development?
  Do I need to reinforce the verbal cue in a visual way?
  Do I need to spend more time praising some pupils?
  Do I need a different tone of voice with some pupils?

- *Presentation and organization of the activity:*
  Do I need to break the skill into part practices?
  Is the practice suitable for all pupils?
  Do some pupils need swimming aids?
  Is enough time being spent on the practice?
  How should I group the pupils for the practice?
  Is the group too large for effective instruction?

If teachers are to encourage pupils to become active in the learning process they must ensure that their teaching strategies 'reach' all pupils. They must continually ask questions about their own strategies in relation to the pupils they are teaching, and be prepared to modify and refine their communication, presentation and organization of an activity. The process of helping pupils move from dependent to independent learners will rely very much on teachers showing this awareness of their own practices.

Content

The content will be developed under the three sections of *confidence, propulsion* and *water safety*. Confidence in water can be divided into the two stages of 'water familiarization' and 'water orientation'. With the former, pupils will need to have a knowledge of the swimming pool, know how swimming lessons are conducted and have experience of simple practices and game forms and, with the latter, they will need to have control of the body position in water, be able to keep afloat, glide, and perform some elementary arm and leg movements in water. Propulsion is about swimming efficiency in such basic strokes as breast-stroke, front crawl and back crawl, and water safety is concerned with making rational judgements in order to play safely in aquatic environments.

Teacher and pupil objectives have to be stated to give direction to the content, and examples of lesson ideas and ways of developing the material have to be provided. Front crawl and breast-stroke have been used to illustrate how a stroke can be developed and monitored (see References for more detailed texts).

Gaining confidence
Water familiarization
Teacher objectives:

- Pupils should be able to carry out changing room and pool procedures, understand the behaviours expected in swimming lessons and become familiar with the water environment by safely performing simple entry, walking and game form practices.

Pupil objectives:

- Arrange clothing tidily and go through a hygiene routine; walk along the poolside and assemble where indicated; enter the pool on the teacher's instruction and in the designated part of the pool.
- Understand that inattentive behaviour can disrupt individual and class activities; obey instructions and signals to maintain a safe environment.
- Stay within the boundaries laid down by the teacher; encourage others to stay within the set boundaries; know the reasons for staying within the set boundaries.
- Use the equipment as it is supposed to be used; ensure that the equipment being used does not disrupt others; place and store equipment in designated areas.
- Enter the water in a controlled way using the poolside steps; maintain contact with the poolside; slide the feet along the bottom of the pool; keep the shoulders beneath the water surface; slide forwards, backwards and sideways; form such patterns as a zig-zag, a square and a circle.
- Use such equipment as floats, hoops and softballs and practise individual, partner and group activities.

The following examples are ways teachers can develop walking and simple game activities. These practices are crucial in pupils' progress as they gradually move the focus of attention from themselves to playing with equipment and with others.

WALKING
Individual practices – can you:

- imagine you are ice-skating?
- lead with one foot all the time?
- walk with your feet turned outwards?
- walk with your feet turned inwards?

Pair practices – can you:

- walk hand in hand with your partner?
- walk holding with two hands?
- walk forwards, sideways and backwards?
- move in a circle?

PLAYING WITH A SOFTBALL
Individual practices – can you:

- push the ball along with your hands?
- push the ball along with your body?
- push the ball along with your nose, chin or forehead?
- move the ball along without touching it?

Pair practices – can you:

- catch the ball from your partner's throw?
- make more than ten throws without the ball hitting the water?
- throw with your right hand?
- throw with your left hand?

HOOP ACTIVITIES
Individual practices – can you:

- get into and out of a floating hoop?
- push the hoop under water and step out of it?
- hold the hoop and walk along inside it?
- push the hoop along with your body?

Water orientation
Teacher objectives:

- Pupils should be able to orientate themselves in water, show breath control and floating skills, and demonstrate some elementary propulsive arm and leg movements.

Pupil objectives:

- Hold the side of the pool or a piece of equipment (e.g. a float) and practise moving from the horizontal to regaining the feet from prone and supine positions; concentrate on moving from a stretched to a semi-tucked position.
- With or without aids, practise controlled floating using different body positions and shapes; demonstrate any stationary float for five seconds; hold the breath during the float.

- Push towards and away from the side and regain the standing position; keep the head and shoulders down and glide along the water surface in a stretched horizontal position; hold the breath during the glide.
- Holding the side of the pool or a float, practise kicking using symmetrical and asymmetrical leg kicks.
- Standing or walking, practise symmetrical or asymmetrical arm actions with breath control.
- Keeping the chin on the water surface, push towards and away from the side, glide and continue with any arm and leg movements for several metres.
- With a partner plan a sequence over a set distance involving a series of glides and different leg and arm movements.
- Push towards and away from the side and continue with a recognized stroke for several metres; concentrate on keeping the body in a horizontal position; practise holding the breath and also try out a breathing rhythm.

Water orientation through such skills as floating, gliding and early stroke actions is probably the most crucial stage in pupils' swimming development. As pupils' feet come off the bottom of the pool and as they adapt to the horizontal position and the buoyancy forces, they begin to learn in and about a new medium.

It is important at this stage that teachers provide practices that encourage pupils to take their feet off the bottom of the pool but in a safe way. Thus, many of these practices will involve the use of the side of the pool and supportive equipment interspersed with opportunities to experiment without help. At the same time teachers should continue to reinforce the early familiarization work to ensure that pupil confidence is maintained.

As pupils will develop at different rates, teachers will need to ensure that the practices provide enough scope for each pupil to be able to perform successfully. In other words, it is better to have a range of practices for a specific activity rather than one practice for all.

Putting the head under the water
As long as the pupils have gained confidence it may now be time to suggest some 'head under' practices. However, do remember that the pupils who appear to do the early practices with ease but lose their smiles immediately water goes into the face should not be forced to place their heads under the water. Observe these pupils carefully and wait until they show very little reaction to water splashing into their face.

Can you hold the side of the pool and:

- blow bubbles on the water surface?
- blow bubbles under water?
- open your eyes under water?
- crouch down under water?

Floating
Can you:

- float on your back with an aid between your legs?
- float on your back holding an aid on your hips or chest?
- remain motionless for five seconds?
- float by gently holding the side of the pool in an upright position?

Gliding
Can you:

- stretch your toes before touching the side?
- pull your legs up and together before touching the side?
- drive away from the side to a partner?
- push to the side holding a float?

Elementary propulsion
Can you hold the side of the pool and:

- circle your legs?
- circle your legs with your feet turned outwards?
- kick your feet up and down with bent legs?
- kick your feet up and down with straight legs?

Can you walk around the pool and:

- pull with bent arms?
- pull with straight arms?
- recover your arms alternately?
- recover your arms together?

Can you:

- swim far wearing a supportive aid?
- go further on your back or front when wearing a supportive aid?
- hold a float and move by kicking only?
- glide to the side of the pool and kick before touching?

Propulsion
Teacher objectives:

- Pupils should be able to propel themselves through water using a variety of recognized strokes and should be able to understand the reasons for efficient propulsion.

Pupil objectives:

- Swim a minimum of 25 metres using a recognized stroke in a direct, continuous and controlled way from shallow to deep water.
- Swim a minimum of 25 metres using a recognized stroke in a circular, continuous and controlled way in shallow and deep water.
- Swim a minimum of 10 metres using a second recognized stroke.
- Be able to demonstrate breast-stroke and crawl-type stroke actions.
- Be able to enter shallow and deep water safely by slipping or jumping into the pool.
- Be able to answer questions on the reasons for efficient propulsion.

If pupils are going to develop the skills to become competent in water they will need to learn different stroke patterns. The ability to perform both crawl-type and breast-stroke movements gives the pupils the versatility to become proficient in a variety of aquatic activities (e.g. life-saving, water polo, synchronized swimming) (Hardy, 1989). In structuring the lessons teachers should focus more on the type of stroke movements than on specific strokes. In other words, front crawl and back crawl should be taught together and breast-stroke should be combined with life-saving movements. In addition, pupils should be encouraged to experiment with stroke patterns rather than concentrate solely on the competitive strokes. For example, can you perform:

- an alternating crawl leg kick with a breast-stroke arm action?
- a breast-stroke leg kick with a butterfly arm action? (i.e. butterfly breast-stroke)
- a life-saving kick with a double arm recovery out of the water and a sideways pull to the body? (i.e. 'Old English' backstroke)
- a double front crawl leg kick with a front crawl arm action?
- a life-saving kick with an alternating back crawl arm action?
- a side-stroke leg kick with a front crawl arm action (i.e. trudgeon)?

Developing front crawl
In the early stages, practise the full stroke and leg activities regularly. Once the swimmer is travelling far enough to need a breath, introduce arm and breathing practices in the shallow water (i.e. standing and walking). Continue with full stroke and leg practices but encourage some breathing when performing the full stroke. As the breathing becomes more proficient, longer distances can be swum and arm practices can be added. As the correct breathing movement is essential for maintaining a good body position, it may be necessary to keep checking the technique and going back to the standing and walking practices.

Developing breast-stroke
In the early stages, practise regaining the feet from a prone glide and attempt the full stroke. Once the swimmers have some idea of the stroke, establish an

efficient leg action. The breathing can then be developed through full stroke and arm practices and, as the arm and leg actions become more effective, the timing of the stroke can be improved.

Water safety

Teacher objectives:

- Pupils should gain an understanding of the principles of water safety and act in a way that reflects these principles.

Pupil objectives:

- To understand the practical dangers related to the home environment.
- To understand the practical dangers related to closed and open water environments.
- To understand the practical dangers related to the performance of aquatic activities in closed and open water environments.
- To understand the health risks of swimming in polluted water.
- To be able to recognize an emergency situation in water and show the ability to take action.
- To be able to perform basic survival skills.
- To be able to act safely in a water environment.

The following questions, practical skills and observations are ways that teachers can develop this understanding of water safety.

Questions
- Why should children be supervised near paddling pools and fish-ponds?
- What protective measures can you take to ensure safety?
- Can you name two pieces of safety equipment in a swimming pool?
- What behaviours are banned in a swimming pool?
- Can you find a notice that tells you of these dangerous behaviours?
- Do you know the dangers related to cold water?
- How do you know whether it is safe to swim at the seaside?
- What precautions should you take if you go boating?
- Why should you never swim alone?
- Do you know what action to take in the event of a swimming emergency?

Skills
Can you:

- float holding a piece of equipment?
- find different ways of holding the equipment?
- find different pieces of equipment to use?
- tread water while you are holding a piece of equipment?
- tread water and scull with the hands without a supportive aid?

- tread water using different types of kick?
- scull with the hands close to the body?
- feel the lift as you move your hands in and out with the palms leading?
- keep afloat by sculling only?
- scull forwards and backwards in a horizontal position?

Observations
Can you:

- spot any dangerous behaviour in the swimming pool?
- spot any dangerous behaviour at the seaside?
- spot any swimming activities that are being performed dangerously?
- talk to anyone about what you have seen?

CONCLUSION

To be able to swim not only provides pupils with the excitement and opportunity to move and exercise in a new medium, but it opens the door to other related activities. However, swimming ability is more than swimming a set distance; it is about confidence and body control in water, swimming efficiency and performing safely in a variety of aquatic environments. 'Good practice' in schools is therefore about structuring a programme that is both developmental and comprehensive and which is taught in a way that matches pupils' practical abilities and cognitive styles.

Table 16.1: Developing and monitoring the front crawl using appropriate practices

Development	Practices	Monitoring
1. Regain feet from a prone position	Push away from the poolside, glide with the arms extended beyond the head and then regain the feet. *Variations:* Push towards a partner who helps with regaining the standing position Push away holding a float flat on the water surface and keeping the arms extended	*Can you:* regain your feet without help? regain your feet quickly and effectively?
2. Glide and kick	Push away from the poolside holding a float, glide and then kick vigorously *Variations:* Holding a float, glide and kick to the poolside Glide with extended arms towards a partner and kick as the partner pulls	Breathing technique is at the discretion of the swimmer
3. Leg action	Practise kicking *Variations:* Hold on to the poolside Hold a float and kick over various distances With or without a float, kick while in the supine position Use a float as resistance Kick with the arms extended beyond the head or down by the sides	*Can you:* keep the legs up? keep the legs going continuously? check that the leg kick is shallow and vigorous
4. Glide, kick and pull	Push away from the poolside, glide with the arms extended beyond the head, kick and pull simultaneously	Practise this movement over short distances. Breathing technique is at the discretion of the swimmer
5.a. Glide and breathe	Push away from the poolside, glide with the arms extended beyond the head and breathe out	Check for bubbles under water
b. Arm action and breathing	Standing in a bent position, practise the arm action and breathing *Variations:* Practise the breathing movement with the breathing side arm only Practise the arm action and breathing while walking	Make sure that the air has been blown out before inhaling *Can you:* get a good breath? breathe on both sides?
c. Full stroke and breathing	Practise swimming short distances and breathe when the need arises	Check that the swimmer is getting rid of the air

Table 16.1 *continued*

Development	Practices	Monitoring
6. Arm action	Practise pulling over various distances (float or pull-buoy between the upper legs) *Variations:* Practise pulling with one arm Practise a catch-up stroke (the pulling arm starts only when the recovery arm is placed next to it) Practise the full stroke but concentrate upon the arms	Breathing technique is at the discretion of the swimmer *Can you:* keep the arms moving continuously? pull beneath the body?
7. Arm action and breathing	Practise the arm action with a regular breathing rhythm	Check that the head is being turned smoothly
8. Co-ordination	Practise the full stroke over various distances and at different speeds	*Can you:* kick the legs continuously? pull and recover without stopping? breathe regularly? Check that the swimmer is looking forwards and downwards Check that the swimmer is developing a rhythmic action

Table 16.2: Developing and monitoring the breast stroke using appropriate practices

Development	Practices	Monitoring
1. Regain feet from a prone position	Push away from the poolside, glide with the arms extended beyond the head and then regain the feet. *Variations:* Push to a partner who helps with regaining the standing position Push away holding a float flat on the water surface and keeping the arms extended	*Can you:* regain your feet without help? regain your feet quickly and effectively?
2. Glide and full stroke	Push away from the poolside, glide, pull and kick, stand up *Variations:* Push and glide from a crouch position in the water, pull and kick, stand up Continue the sequence across the width of the pool Try two or three full strokes after the initial glide	Check that the near-horizontal position is obtained before the pull and kick is made *Can you:* get the arms nearly straight before you kick? glide after the kick? Check that the legs are kept close to the water surface
3. Glide and kick	Push away from the poolside holding a float with the arms extended, glide, kick once and then stand up *Variations:* Push and glide from a crouch position in water, kick once and then stand up Continue the sequence across the width of the pool (with float) Try three or four leg kicks (with float) Push away from the poolside and glide in a supine position, holding the float flat on the water surface and above the hips, kick once and then stand up Try three or four leg kicks in the supine position	*Can you:* keep the hips up? keep the legs near the water surface? *Can you:* keep your chin close to the water surface? check that one kick is completed before the next leg kick starts
4. Leg action Early practice for correcting technique	1. Kick widths of the pool in prone and supine positions (with float) *Variations:* Try kicking widths of the pool in prone and supine positions with arms placed by the sides or beyond the head Use floats as resistance 2. Holding the poolside practise the leg kick (a partner can sometimes guide the legs through the correct movement) *Variations:* Swimmer practises the leg action while being pulled across the pool by a partner b. Swimmer can be towed in the supine position	Ensure that the legs are brought close to the water surface after each kick *Can you:* keep the hips up? keep your chin on the water surface? Check that the partner stays low in the water and keeps the swimmer in a near-horizontal position

Table 16.2 *continued*

Development	Practices	Monitoring
5. a. Full stroke and breathing b. Arm action and breathing	Practise the full stroke over short distances concentrating upon the breathing Practise the arm action and breathing while standing or walking in shallow end *Variation:* Practise the arm action and breathing	*Can you:* blow out hard as the arms go forwards? take in a full breath? Check that the breathing rhythm fits in with the stroke action
6. Arm action	Practise the arm action with a float or pull-buoy between the upper legs *Variations:* Practise the arm action while kicking with a dolphin movement Practise the arm action while trailing the legs Practise the arm action and breathe once every two arm cycles	*Can you:* keep your hands in sight even though you are looking forwards? *Can you:* keep the hands beneath the water surface? Check that the swimmer moves from the end of the pull to the recovery with a minimal delay
7. Co-ordination	Practise various distances using a regular breathing rhythm *Variations:* Try the full stroke with a continuous arm movement Try the full stroke with a glide at the end of the recovery Try both the straight arm pull and the increasingly bent arm action Try delaying the inhalation until the recovery starts	Look for a rhythmic stroke Check that the swimmer is pushing the chin forwards to breathe and that the near-horizontal body position does not alter greatly

References and Further Reading

CHAPTER 1
References
Almond, L. (1997) *Physical Education in Schools*. London: Kogan Page.
Armstrong, N. and Welsman, J. (1997) *Young People and Physical Activity*. Oxford: Oxford University Press.
Arnold, P. J. (1997) *Sport, Ethics and Education*. London: Cassell.
Carr, D. (1997) 'Physical Education and Value Diversity: A Response to Andrew Reid'. *European Physical Education Review*, **3** (2), 195–205.
HEA (1998) *Young People and Physical Activity: A Literature Review*. London: Health Education Authority.
McNamee, M. J. (1998) 'Philosophy and Physical Education: Analysis, Epistemology and Axiology'. *European Physical Education Review*, **4** (1), 75–91.
Parry, J. (1998) 'Reid on Knowledge and Justification in Physical Education'. *European Physical Education Review,* **4** (1), 70–4.
Reid, A. (1997) 'Value Pluralism and Physical Education'. *European Physical Education Review*, **3** (1), 6–20.
Rowland, T. W. (1991) 'Is There a Scientific Rationale Supporting the Value of Exercise for the Present and Future Cardiovascular Health of Children? The Con Argument'. *Pediatric Exercise Science*, **8**, 303–9.
US Department of Health and Social Services (1996) *Physical Activity and Health: a Report of the Surgeon General*. Atlanta, GA: Centers for Disease Control and Prevention.

CHAPTER 2
References
Benn, T. and Benn, B. (1992) *Primary Gymnastics – A Multi-activity Approach*. Cambridge: Cambridge University Press.
Bott, J. (1997) 'Developing Lessons and Units of Work'. In S. Capel (ed.) *Learning to Teach Physical Education in the Secondary School*. London: Routledge.
Bunker, D. (ed.) (1994) *Primary Physical Education – Implementing the National Curriculum*. Cambridge: Cambridge University Press.
Clark, C. M. and Yinger, R. J. (1987) 'Teacher Planning'. In J. Calderhead (ed.) *Exploring Teachers' Thinking*. London: Cassell.
DFE (1995) *Physical Education in the National Curriculum*. London: HMSO.
Gallahue, D. L. (1993) *Developmental Physical Education for Today's Children (Second Edition)*. Madison, WI: Brown & Benchmark.

Hellison, D. R. and Templin, T. J. (1991) *A Reflective Approach to Teaching Physical Education*. Champaign, IL: Human Kinetics.

Kyriacou, C. (1991) *Essential Teaching Skills*. Hemel Hempstead: Simon & Schuster.

Mawer, M. (1995) *The Effective Teaching of Physical Education*. London: Longman.

NCC (1992) *Physical Education Non-Statutory Guidance*. York: National Curriculum Council.

PEA (1995) *Teaching Physical Education at Key Stages 1 and 2*. London: Physical Education Association of the United Kingdom.

Pye, J. (1988) *Invisible Children*. Oxford: Oxford University Press.

Read, B. and Edwards, P. (1992) *Teaching Children to Play Games*. Leeds: National Coaching Foundation/British Council for Physical Education/Sports Council.

Williams, A. (1996) *Teaching Physical Education – A Guide for Mentors and Students*. London: David Fulton.

Further Reading

Two useful sources of guidance on preparation and planning are:

Mawer, M. (1995) *The Effective Teaching of Physical Education*. London: Longman.

Williams, A. (1996) *Teaching Physical Education – A Guide for Mentors and Students*. London: David Fulton.

An excellent general source of information is:

Kyriacou, C. (1991) *Essential Teaching Skills*. Hemel Hempstead: Simon & Schuster.

CHAPTER 3

References

Cruickshank, D. R., Bainer, D. L. and Metcalf, K. (1995) T*he Art of Teaching*. New York: McGraw-Hill.

Graham, G. (1992) *Teaching Children Physical Education – Becoming a Master Teacher*. Champaign, IL: Human Kinetics.

Kyriacou, C. (1986) *Effective Teaching in Schools*. Oxford: Blackwell.

Kyriacou, C. (1991) *Essential Teaching Skills*. Hemel Hempstead: Simon & Schuster.

Mason, V. (1995) *Young People and Sport in England, 1994*. London: Sports Council.

Mortimore, P., Sammons, P., Stoll, L., Lewis, D. and Ecob, E. (1988) *School Matters: The Junior Years*. Wells: Open Books.

Pye, J. (1988) *Invisible Children*. Oxford: Oxford University Press.

Rink, J. E. (1993) *Teaching Physical Education for Learning*. St Louis, MI: Mosby.

Robertson, J. (1989) *Effective Classroom Control (2nd Edition)*. London: Hodder and Stoughton.

Rutter, M., Maughan, B., Mortimore, P. and Ouston, J. (1979) *Fifteen Thousand Hours*. Wells: Open Books.

Siedentop, D. (1991) *Developing Teaching Skills in Physical Education (Third Edition)*. Mountain View, CA: Mayfield.

Smith, C. L. and Laslett, R. (1993) *Effective Classroom Management: A Teacher's Guide*. London: Routledge.

Wragg, E. (ed.) (1994) *Classroom Teaching Skills*. London: Croom Helm.

CHAPTER 4

References

Allison, S. and Thorpe, R. (1997) 'A Comparison of the Effectiveness of Two Approaches to Teaching Games Within Physical Education: A Skills Approach Versus a Games for Understanding Approach'. *The British Journal of Physical Education*, **28** (3), 9–13.

Anderson, A. (1999) 'The Case for Learning Strategies in Physical Education'. *The Journal of Physical Education, Recreation and Dance*, **70** (1), 45–9.

BAALPE (1989) *Teaching and Learning Strategies in Physical Education*. Leeds: White Line Press.

Brady, F. (1998) 'A Theoretical and Empirical Review of the Contextual Interference Effect and the Learning of Motor Skills'. *QUEST,* **50** (3), 266–93.

Capel, S., Kelly, L. and Whitehead, M. (1997) 'Developing and Maintaining an Effective Learning Environment'. In S. Capel (ed.) *Learning to Teach Physical Education in the Secondary School.* London: Routledge.

Denton, C. and Postlethwaite, K. (1985) *Able Children.* London: NFER-Nelson.

DFE (1995) *Physical Education in the National Curriculum.* London: HMSO.

Fitts, P. M. and Posner, M. I. (1967) *Human Performance.* Belmont, CA: Brooks/Cole.

Galton, M., Simon, B. and Croll, P. (1980) *Inside the Primary Classroom.* London: Routledge & Kegan Paul.

Harrison, P. and Warburton, P. (1998) 'Editorial: Quality and Standards of Physical Education and Sport In Primary Schools In Wales'. *Primary PE Focus,* Winter, p. 3.

Hellison, D. and Templin, T. (1991) *A Reflective Approach to Teaching Physical Education.* Champaign, IL: Human Kinetics.

Housner, L. (1990) 'Selecting Master Teachers: Evidence from the Process–Product Research'. *Journal of Teaching in Physical Education,* **9** (3), 201–26.

Keighley, P. (1993) 'A Consideration of the Appropriate, Learning and Assessment Strategies in the Outdoor Adventurous Activity Element of Outdoor Education as it Relates to the Physical Education National Curriculum'. *British Journal of Physical Education,* **24** (1), 18–22.

Lawson, H. (1998) 'Rejuvenating, Reconstituting and Transforming Physical Education to Meet the Needs of Vulnerable Children, Youth, and Families'. *Journal of Teaching in Physical Education,* **18** (1) 2–25.

Marjoram, T. (1988) *Teaching Able Children.* London: Kogan Page.

Mawer, M. (1995) *The Effective Teaching of Physical Education.* London: Longman.

Mosston, M. (1992) 'Tug-O-War, No More: Meeting Teaching–Learning Objectives Using the Spectrum of Teaching Styles'. *Journal of Physical Education, Recreation and Dance,* **63** (1), 27–31, 56.

Mosston, M. and Ashworth, S. (1986) *Teaching Physical Education.* Columbus, OH: Merrill.

Pieron, M. (1998) 'A Review of the Literature in English on Instruction During the Years 1994–95'. *International Journal of Physical Education,* **35** (1), 5–16.

Rink, J. (1993) *Teaching Physical Education for Learning (Second Edition).* St Louis, MI: Mosby.

Schmidt, R. A. (1975) 'A Schema Theory of Discrete Motor Learning'. *Psychological Review,* **82**, 225–60.

Severs, J. (1997) 'Success for All'. *Primary PE Focus,* Spring, 4–6.

Siedentop, D. (1991) *Developing Teaching Skills in Physical Education (Third Edition).* Palo Alto, CA: Mayfield.

Silverman, S. (1991) 'Research on Teaching in Physical Education'. *Research Quarterly for Exercise and Sport,* **62** (4), 352–64.

Thompson, L. (1998) 'Teaching Strategies to Enhance Motivation to Learn in Elementary Physical Education'. *CAHPERD,* **64** (1), 4–10.

Whitehead, M. (1997) 'Teaching Styles and Teaching Strategies'. In S. Capel (ed.) *Learning to Teach Physical Education in the Secondary School.* London: Routledge.

Williams, A. (1989) 'The Place of Physical Education in Primary Education'. In A. Williams (ed.) *Issues in Physical Education for the Primary Years.* London: Falmer.

Williams, A. (1993) 'Aspects of Teaching and Learning Gymnastics'. *British Journal of Physical Education,* **24** (1), 29–32.

Further Reading

BAALPE (1989) *Teaching and Learning Strategies in Physical Education.* Leeds: White Line Press.

British Journal of Physical Education (1993) Special Edition on Teaching Styles, **28** (1).

Mawer, M. (1995) *The Effective Teaching of Physical Education.* London: Longman.

Mosston, M. and Ashworth, S. (1986) *Teaching Physical Education.* Columbus, OH: Merrill.

CHAPTER 5
References
Bailey, R. P. (1999) 'Physical Education: Action, Play and Movement'. In J. Riley and R. Prentice (eds) *The Curriculum 7–11*. London: Paul Chapman Publishers/Sage.

Carroll, B. (1994) *Assessment in Physical Education*. London: Falmer.

Clay, G. (1997) 'Standards in Primary Physical Education: OFSTED 1995–1996'. *Primary PE Focus*, Autumn, 4–6.

DES (1991) *Assessment in Physical Education. National Curriculum Physical Education for Ages 5–16*. London: HMSO.

DES (1992) *Physical Education in the National Curriculum* (National Curriculum Council, Physical Education Non-Statutory Guidance). London: HMSO.

DfEE/QCA (1999) *Physical Education. The National Curriculum for England*. London: QCA.

Gallahue, D. L. and Ozmun, J. C. (1995) *Understanding Motor Development: Infants, Children, Adolescents, Adults*. Boston, MA: WCB/McGraw-Hill.

Gilbert, R. (1992) 'Recording and Reporting Achievement in Physical Education'. *British Journal of Physical Education*, **23** (2), 12–14.

Latham, A-M. (1990) 'Recording Achievement in Physical Education'. *BAALPE Congress Report*, July, 62–9.

Leah, J., Lockwood, A. and Watson, G. (1997) 'Assessment'. In S. Capel (ed.) *Learning to Teach Physical Education in the Secondary School*. London: Routledge.

Office of Her Majesty's Chief Inspector (OHMCI) (1998) *Standards and Quality in Primary Schools – Good Practice in Physical Education and Sport*. London: HMSO.

Robinson, S. (1995) *Planning the Physical Education Curriculum: Part 3 – Assessment*. Stowmarket: Aspects Publications.

Sabin, V. (1995) *A Practical Guide for: Planning, Assessing, Recording and Reporting in Physical Education*. Northampton: Val Sabin Publications.

Schools Curriculum and Assessment Authority (SCAA) (1996) *Consistency in Teacher Assessment: Exemplification of Standards: Key Stage 3*. Middlesex: SCAA.

Spackman, L. (1998a) 'Assessment and Recording in Physical Education'. *British Journal of Physical Education*, **29** (4), 6–9.

Spackman, L. (1998b) 'Assessment, Recording and Reporting in Physical Education'. *Primary PE Focus*, Winter, 4–8.

Sutton, R. (1990) 'Assessment and the National Curriculum: A Framework for the Future'. In British Association of Advisers and Lecturers in Physical Education (BAALPE) Physical Education *A Foundation for the Future. Report of the 70th Annual Congress and Course*. Leeds: BAALPE, White Line Press.

Wetton, P. (1988) *Physical Education in the Nursery and Infant School*. London: Croom Helm.

Whitehead, M., Hewett, T. and Capel, S. (1997) 'Your wider role as a PE teacher', in S. Capel *Learning to Teach in the Secondary School*. London: Routledge, pp. 218–38.

Williams, A. (1996) 'Physical Education at Key Stage 2'. In N. Armstrong (ed.) *New Directions in Physical Education: Change and Innovation*. London: Cassell, pp. 62–81.

CHAPTER 6
References
Association of Swimming Therapy (1981) *Swimming for the Disabled*. Wakefield: EP Publishing.

Bailey, R. P. (1999a) 'Play, Health and Physical Development'. In T. David (ed.) *Young Children Learning*. London: Paul Chapman.

Bailey, R. P. (1999b) 'Physical Education: Infans Ludens'. In J. Riley and R. Prentice (eds) *The Primary Curriculum 7–11*. London: Paul Chapman.

Barton, L. (1993) 'Disability, Empowerment and Physical Education'. In J. Evans (ed.) *Equality, Education and Physical Education*. London: Falmer.

Bloom, B. (1985) *Developing Talent in Young People*. New York: Ballantine.

Brown, M. and Gordon, W. A. (1987) 'Impact of Impairment on Activity Patterns of Children'.

Archives of Physical Medicine and Rehabilitation, **68**, 828–32.

Bruner, J. (1983) *Child's Talk: Learning to Use Language*. Oxford: Oxford University Press.

Cooper, P. (1996) 'Giving it a Name: The Value of Descriptive Categories in Educational Approaches to Emotional and Behavioural Difficulties'. *Support for Learning*, **11** (4), 146–50.

DES (1978) *Special Educational Needs* (Warnock Report). London: HMSO.

DFE (1994) *The Code of Practice on the Identification and Assessment of Special Educational Needs*. London: Department for Education.

DfEE (1997) *Excellence for all Children: Meeting Special Educational Needs* (Green Paper). London: Stationery Office.

DfEE (1998) *Meeting Special Educational Needs: A Programme of Action*. London: Department for Education and Employment.

Fisher, A. (1988) 'Just One of the Boys?' *Times Educational Supplement*, **3774**, 25.

Gross, J. (1996) *Special Educational Needs in the Primary School (Second Edition)*. Milton Keynes: Open University Press.

Gulliford, R. and Upton, G. (1992) *Special Educational Needs*. London: Routledge.

Haskell, S. and Barrett, E. (1993) *The Education of Children with Physical and Neurological Disabilities (Third Edition)*. London: Chapman and Hall.

Henderson, S. and Sugden, D. (1992) *Movement Assessment Battery for Children*. Sidcup: Psychological Corporation.

Jenkinson, J. C. (1997) *Mainstream or Special: Educating Students with Disabilities*. London: Routledge.

Jowsey, S. (1992) *Can I Play Too? Education for Physically Disabled Children in Mainstream Schools*. London: David Fulton.

Kenward, H. (1997) *Integrating Pupils with Physical Disabilities in Mainstream Schools: Making it Happen*. London: David Fulton.

Malina, R. M. and Bouchard, C. (1991) *Growth, Maturation and Physical Activity*. Champaign, IL: Human Kinetics.

Norwich, B. (1996) 'Special Needs Education or Education for All: Connective Specialisation or Ideological Impurity?' *British Journal of Special Education*, **3**, 100–4.

Norwich, B. (1999) 'Review Article: Special or Inclusive Education?' *European Journal of Special Needs Education*, **14** (1), 90–6.

Oliver, M. (1990) *The Politics of Disablement*. Basingstoke: Macmillan.

Oliver, M. (1996) *Understanding Disability: From Theory to Practice*. Basingstoke: Macmillan.

QCA/DfEE (1999a) *The Review of the National Curriculum in England: The Secretary of State's Proposals*. London: Stationery Office.

QCA/DfEE (1999b) *The Review of the National Curriculum in England: The Consultation Materials*. London: Qualifications and Curriculum Authority.

Ripley, K., Daines, B. and Barrett, J. (1997) *Dyspraxia: A Guide for Teachers and Parents*. London: David Fulton.

Robertson, C. R. (1999) 'Early Intervention: The Education of Young Children with Developmental Co-ordination Disorder (DCD)'. In T. David (ed.) *Young Children Learning*. London: Paul Chapman.

Sugden, D. (1991) 'PE: Movement in the Right Direction'. *British Journal of Special Education*, **4**, 134–6.

Sugden, D. and Henderson, S. (1994) 'Help with Movement'. *Special Children*, **75** (13), 1–8.

Sugden, D. and Wright, H. (1996) 'Curricular Entitlement and Implementation for all Children'. In N. Armstrong (ed.) *New Directions in Physical Education: Change and Innovation*. London: Cassell.

UNESCO (1994) *The Salamanca Statement and Framework for Action*. Paris: UNESCO.

WHO (1980) *International Classification of Impairments, Disabilities and Handicaps*. Geneva: World Health Organisation.

Wright, H. and Sugden, D. (1999) *Physical Education for All*. London: David Fulton.

Further Reading
Two very useful sources of information on physical education for children with special educational needs are:
Jowsey, S. (1992) *Can I Play Too? Education for Physically Disabled Children in Mainstream Schools*. London: David Fulton.
Wright, H. and Sugden, D. (1999) *Physical Education for All*. London: David Fulton.

A clear, practical guide of a more general nature is:
Gross, J. (1996) *Special Educational Needs in the Primary School (Second Edition)*. Milton Keynes: Open University Press.

CHAPTER 7
References
Ames, C. and Archer, J. (1988) 'Achievement Goals in the Classroom: Students' Learning Strategies and Motivation Processes'. *Journal of Educational Psychology*, **80**, 260–7.
Armstrong, N. and Welsman, A. (1997) *Young People and Physical Activity*. Oxford: Oxford University Press.
Bailey, R. P. (1999a) 'Play, Health and Physical Development'. In T. David (ed.) *Young Children Learning*. London: Paul Chapman.
Bailey, R. P. (1999b) 'Physical Education – Action, Play and Movement'. In J. Riley and R. Prentice (eds) *The Primary Curriculum 7–11*. London: Paul Chapman.
Bailey, R. P. and Farrow, S. (1998) 'Play and Problem-solving in a New Light'. *International Journal of Early Years Education*, **6** (1), 165–75.
Birtwistle, G. and Brodie, D. (1991) 'Children's Attitudes Towards Physical Activity and Perceptions of Physical Education'. *Health Education Research*, **6**, 465–78.
Bjorkvold, J. R. (1989) *The Muse Within – Creativity and Communication, Song and Play from Childhood Through Maturity*. New York: HarperCollins.
Bruner, J. (1983) *Child's Talk: Learning to Use Language*. Oxford: Oxford University Press.
Coleman, J. A. (1961) *The Adolescent Society*. New York: Free Press.
Connell, R. (1993) 'Understanding the Learner: Guidelines for the Coach'. In M. Lee (ed.) *Coaching Children in Sport: Principles and Practice*. London: E. & F. N. Spon.
Dishman, R. K. (1986) 'Mental Health'. In V. Seefeldt (ed.) *Physical Activity and Well-being*. Retson, VA: AAHPERD.
Dweck, C. S. (1986) 'Motivational Processes Affecting Learning'. *American Psychologist* **41**, 1040–8.
Evans, J. and Roberts, G. C. (1987) 'Physical Competence and the Development of Children's Peer Relations'. *Quest*, **39**, 23–35.
Gallahue, D. L. (1993) *Developmental Physical Education for Today's Children (Second Edition)*. Madison, WI: Brown & Benchmark.
Gallahue, D. L. and Ozmun, J. C. (1998) *Understanding Motor Development: Infants, Children, Adolescents, Adults*. Boston, MA: WCB/McGraw-Hill.
Gildenhuys, C. A. and Orsmond, C. P. (1996) 'Movement and Second Language Acquisition: The Potential and the Method'. *Sport, Education and Society*, **1** (1), 103–15.
Gruber, J. J. (1986) 'Physical Activity and Self-esteem Development in Children: A Meta-analysis'. In G. A. Stull and H. M. Eckert (eds) *Effects of Physical Activity on Children*. Champaign, IL: Human Kinetics.
Haywood, K. M. (1993) *Life Span Motor Development*. Champaign, IL: Human Kinetics.
HEA (1997) *Young People and Physical Activity: A Literature Review*. London: Health Education Authority.
Lee, M. (1993) 'Growing Up in Sport'. In M. Lee (ed.) *Coaching Children in Sport: Principles and Practice*. London: E. & F. N. Spon.
Macfadyen, T. M. (1999) 'An Analysis of the Influence of Secondary School Physical Education on Young People's Attitudes Towards Physical Activity'. *Bulletin of Physical Education*, **35** (3), 157–71.

Malina, R. M. and Bouchard, C. (1991) *Growth, Maturation and Physical Activity*. Champaign, IL: Human Kinetics.

Mason, V. (1995) *Young People and Sport in England, 1994*. London: Sports Council.

Maude, P. (1996) 'Differentiation in Physical Education'. In E. Bearne (ed.) *Differentiation and Diversity in the Primary School*. London: Routledge.

NCF (1994) *Coaching Children – Course Resource Pack*. Leeds: National Coaching Foundation.

Nicholls, J. (1984) 'Conceptions of Ability and Achievement Motivation'. In K. Ames and C. Ames (eds) *Research on Motivation in Education. Volume 1: Student Motivation*. New York: Academic Press.

QCA (1998) *Maintaining Breadth and Balance at Key Stages 1 and 2*. London: Qualifications and Curriculum Authority.

Roberts, G. (1992) 'Motivation in Sport and Exercise: Conceptual Constraints and Conceptual Convergence'. In G. Roberts (ed.) *Motivation in Sport and Exercise*. Champaign, IL: Human Kinetics.

Roberts, G. and Treasure, D. (1993) 'The Importance of the Study of Children in Sport: An Overview'. In M. Lee (ed.) *Coaching Children in Sport: Principles and Practice*. London: E. & F. N. Spon.

Ross, A. O. (1976) *Psychological Aspects of Learning Disabilities and Reading Disorders*. New York: McGraw-Hill.

Sallis, J. and Patrick, K. (1994) 'Physical Activity Guidelines of Adolescents: Consensus Statement'. *Pediatric Exercise Science*, **6** (4), 302–14.

Sharp, C. (1991) 'The Exercise Physiology of Children'. In V. Grisogono *Children and Sport: Fitness, Injuries and Diet*. London: John Murray.

Shephard, R. J. (1984) 'Physical Activity and "Wellness" of the Child'. In R.A. Boileau (ed.) *Advances in Pediatric Sport Sciences – Volume One – Biological Issues*. Champaign, IL: Human Kinetics.

Shephard, R. J., Volle, M., Lavallee, H., La Barre, R., Jequier, J. C. and Rajic, M. (1984) 'Required Physical Activity and Academic Grades: A Controlled Study'. In J. Ilmarinen and I. Valimaki (eds) *Children and Sport*. Berlin: Springer Verlag.

Smith, R. (1991) 'Exercise Danger in Schools'. *British Journal of Physical Education*, **22** (3), 37–40.

Sports Council (1993) *Young People and Sport*. London: Sports Council.

Sugden, D. A. and Talbot, M. (1998) *Physical Education for Children with Special Needs in Mainstream Education*. Leeds: Carnegie National Sports Development Centre.

Sugden, D. A. and Wright, H. C. (1996) 'Curricular Entitlement and Implementation for all Children'. In N. Armstrong (ed.) *New Directions in Physical Education – Change and Innovation*. London: Cassell.

Walkley, J., Holland, B., Treloar, R. and Probyn-Smith, H. (1993) 'Fundamental Motor Skill Proficiency of Children'. *ACHPER National Journal*, Spring, 11–14.

Weiss, M. and Duncan, S. (1992) 'The Relationship Between Physical Competence and Peer Acceptance in the Context of Children's Sports Participation'. *Journal of Sport and Exercise Psychology*, **14** (2), 177–92.

Williams, A. (1996) *Teaching Physical Education – A Guide to Mentors and Students*. London: David Fulton.

Wright, H. and Sugden, D. (1999) *Physical Education for All: Developing Physical Education in the Curriculum for Pupils with Special Educational Needs*. London: David Fulton.

Further Reading

Two useful and comprehensive textbooks on different aspects of child development relating to physical education are:

Gallahue, D. L. and Ozmun, J. C. (1998) *Understanding Motor Development: Infants, Children, Adolescents, Adults (Fourth Edition)*. Boston, MA: WCB/McGraw-Hill.

Malina, R. M. and Bouchard, C. (1991) *Growth, Maturation and Physical Activity*. Champaign, IL: Human Kinetics.

An excellent general textbook with no concentration upon physical education, but covering a consequently greater range, is:

Smith, P. K. and Cowie, H. (1988) *Understanding Children's Development.* Oxford: Blackwell.

CHAPTER 8
References

Almond, L. (1997) 'The Place of Physical Education in the Curriculum'. In L. Almond *Physical Education in Schools (Second Edition).* London: Kogan Page.

BAALPE (1999) *Achieving Excellence – Subject Leader in Physical Education.* Exmouth: British Association of Advisers and Lecturers in Physical Education.

Blake, B. G. (1998) 'The Role of the Physical Education Co-ordinator in the Primary School'. *The Bulletin of Physical Education,* **34** (2), 109–13.

Casey, C. and Plumb, D. (1988) 'Primary Physical Education: The Way Ahead'. *The Bulletin of Physical Education,* **24** (3), 7–12.

CCW (1994) *A Curriculum Leader's Guide to P.E. in the National Curriculum at KS1 and KS2.* Cardiff: Curriculum Council for Wales.

Chedzoy, S. (1996) *Physical Education for Teachers and Co-ordinators at Key Stages 1 & 2.* London: David Fulton.

Chelladurai, P. (1990) 'Leadership in Sports: A Review'. *International Journal of Sport Psychology,* **21**, 328–54.

Clark, D. (1989) 'Quality Leadership'. *Bulletin of the Federation Internationale d'Education Physique,* **59** (.3), 7–22.

Cox, C. (1987) 'Physical Education in the Primary School: Curriculum Leadership'. *The Bulletin of Physical Education,* **21** (3), 29–32.

Davies, B. and Ellison, L. (1994) *Managing the Effective Primary School.* London: Longman.

Davies, J. (1995) *Developing a Leadership Role in Key Stage 1 Curriculum.* London: Falmer.

Dunn, A. (1998) 'Empowering PE Co-ordinators'. *Primary PE Focus,* Spring, 7–8.

Eastwood, P. and Buswell, J. (1987) 'Education and Training for Leadership in P.E.'. *The Bulletin of Physical Education,* **23** (2), 35–7.

Harrison, S. and Theaker, K. (1989) *Curriculum Leadership and Co-ordination in the Primary School.* Whalley: Guild House.

Jack, S. (1995) 'Improving the Effectiveness of the Physical Education (P.E.) Curriculum Leader, in Primary Schools'. *Primary PE Focus,* Autumn, 4–5.

Kitson, N. and Merry, R. (1997) *Teaching in the Primary School: A Learning Environment.* London: Routledge.

Martens, R. (1987) *Coaches Guide to Sports Psychology.* Champaign, IL: Human Kinetics.

OFSTED (1995) *Physical Education and Sport in Schools – A Survey of Good Practice.* London: HMSO.

Pain, S., Price, L., Forest-Jones, G. and Longhurst, J. (1997) *Find a Space.* London: David Fulton.

Raymond, C. (1998) *Co-ordinating Physical Education Across the Primary School.* London: Falmer.

Robinson, S. (1993) 'Managing a Physical Education Department – A Development Programme'. Devon: BAALPE.

Rowe, F. (1995) 'Effective Observation in P.E.'. *Primary PE Focus,* Summer, 11–12.

SCAA (1996) *Monitoring the School Curriculum: Reporting to Schools 1995/6.* London: Schools Curriculum and Assessment Authority.

Southworth, G. (1998) *Leading Improving Primary Schools – The Work of Head Teachers and Deputy Heads.* London: Falmer.

Sparkes, A. (1991) 'Curriculum Change: On Gaining a Sense of Perspective'. In N. Armstrong and A. Sparkes *Issues in Physical Education.* London: Cassell.

TTA (1998) *National Standards for Subject Leaders.* London: Teaching Training Agency.

Weinberg, R. S. and Gould, D. (1995) *Foundations of Sport and Exercise Psychology.* Champaign, IL: Human Kinetics.

Whitaker, P. (1997) *Primary Schools and the Future – Celebration, Changes and Choices.* Buckingham: Open University Press.

Further Reading
BAALPE (1999) *Achieving Excellence – Subject Leader in Physical Education*. Exmouth: BAALPE.
Raymond, C. (1998) *Co-ordinating Physical Education Across the Primary School*. London: Falmer.
Weinberg, R. S. and Gould, D. (1995) *Foundations of Sport and Exercise Psychology*. Champaign, IL: Human Kinetics.

CHAPTER 9
References
BAALPE (1995) *Safe Practice in Physical Education*. Dudley: LEA.
Benn, T. and Benn, B. (1992) *Primary Gymnastics – A Multi-activities Approach*. Cambridge: Cambridge University Press.
Boucher, C. A. (1977) 'Education and Accident Prevention – The Work of RoSPA'. In R. H. Jackson (ed.) *Children, the Environment and Accidents*. London: Pitman.
Clay, G. (1997) 'Standards in Primary Physical Education: OFSTED 1995–96'. *Primary PE Focus*, Autumn, 4–6.
Cutter, S. L. (1993) *Living with Risk*. London: Edward Arnold.
DFE (1995) *Physical Education in the National Curriculum*. London: HMSO.
DES (1980) *Safety in Physical Education (Safety Series no. 4)*. London: HMSO.
Eve, N. (1997) 'Safe Practice in Physical Education: Some Notes from the Safety Officer'. *Bulletin of Physical Education*, **33** (3), 30–2.
Harrison, P. and Watkins, J. (1996) 'Legal Considerations for Teachers and Instructors'. *British Journal of Physical Education*, **27** (2), 20–2.
Hill, M. S. and Hill, F. W. (1994) *Creating Safe Schools – What Principals Can Do*. California: Corwin Press.
Kelly, L. (1997) 'Safety in PE'. In S. Capel (ed.) *Learning to Teach Physical Education in the Secondary School*. London: Routledge.
NAHT (1999) 'Press Release: The Results of the Survey of PE in Schools'. National Association of Head Teachers.
NCF (1986) *Safety First for Coaches*. Leeds: National Coaching Foundation.
O'Connor, M. (1987) *Out and About – Teachers' Guide to Safe Practice Out of School*. London: Routledge.
Perkins, J. (1997) 'Safety Issues for Pupils with Special Educational Needs in Mainstream Schools'. *Bulletin of Physical Education*, **33** (3), 33–41.
Roberts, H., Smith, S. and Bryce, C. (1995) *Children at Risk? Safety as a Social Value*. Buckingham: Open University.
Warburton, P. (1999) 'Our Sporting Nation – Have We Got the Agenda Right for Our Young People'. *British Journal of Physical Education*, **30** (1), 18–24.
Watkins, J. and Harrison, P. (1996) 'Health and Safety Policy in Schools'. *British Journal of Physical Education*, **28** (1), 9–11.
Welch, A. (1978) *Accidents Happen*. London: Cox & Wyman.

Further Reading
BAALPE (1999) *Safe Practice in Physical Education*. Dudley: Dudley LEA.
Harris, J. and Elbourn, J. (1998) 'Safe and Effective Exercise for Children'. *Primary PE Focus*, Spring, 4–6.
Watkins, J. and Harrison, P. (1997) 'Health and Safety Policy in Schools'. *British Journal of Physical Education*, **28** (1), 9–11.

CHAPTER 10
References
Almond, L. (1984) 'Athletics: A Challenge in Perspective'. *British Journal of Physical Education*, **15** (3), 102–3

Bailey, R. P. (1999) 'Physical Education – Action, Movement and Play'. In J. Riley and R. Prentice (eds) *The Primary Curriculum 7–11*. London: Paul Chapman.

Beaumont, G. (1990) 'Athletics – A Suitable Case for Treatment'. *British Journal of Physical Education*, **21** (2), 295–6.

DES (1989) *Physical Education from 5 to 16*. London: HMSO.

DES (1991) *Physical Education from 5 to 16*. London: HMSO.

DFE (1995) *Key Stages 1 and 2 of the National Curriculum*. London: HMSO.

Dick, F. (1987) *But First – Basic Work for Coaches and Teachers of Beginner Athletes*. London: British Amateur Athletic Board.

Fry, B. (1995) 'Athletics at Key Stage 2'. In PEA, NDTA and BAALPE *Teaching Physical Education at Key Stages One and Two*. London: PEA UK.

Gallahue, D. C. (1976) *Motor Development in Young Children 3–7*. New York: Lea & Feebler.

Harris, J. (1989) 'A Health Focus on Physical Education'. In L. Almond (ed.) *The Place of Physical Education in Schools*. London: Kogan Page.

Littlewood, A. (1998) 'Young People and Athletics'. *British Journal of Physical Education*, **29** (4), 27–30.

McGeorge, S. and Almond, L. (1998) 'Athletic Activities'. In D. Bunker, C. Hardy, B. Smith and L. Almond *Primary Physical Education – Implementing the National Curriculum*. Cambridge: Cambridge University Press.

NCF (1994) *Coaching Children – Course Resource Pack*. Leeds: National Coaching Foundation.

O'Neill, J. (1992) 'Athletics Teaching in Schools – Change at Last? – An Interpretation of Athletic Activities in the PE National Curriculum'. *British Journal of Physical Education*, **23** (1), 12–7.

O'Neill, J. (1998) 'Challenging Athletics at Key Stage 3 and 4'. *British Journal of Physical Education*, **29** (2), 13–7.

QCA (1998) 'Maintaining Breadth and Balance at Key Stages 1 and 2'. London: Qualifications and Curriculum Authority.

Simons-Morton, B., O'Hara, G., Blair, S. and Pate, R. (1988) 'Health Related Physical Fitness in Childhood: Status and Recommendations'. *Annual Review of Public Health*, **9**, 403–25.

Sleap, M. and Warburton, P. (1992) 'Physical Activity Levels of 5 to 11 Year Old Children in England Determined by Continuous Observation'. *Research Quarterly for Exercise and Sport*, **63**, 238–45.

Sugden, D. A. and Talbot, M. (1998) *Physical Education for Chiuldren with Special Needs in Mainstream Education*. Leeds: Carnegie National Sports Development Centre.

Wetton, P. (1992) *Practical Guides: Physical Education*. London: Scholastic.

Wetton P. (1997) *Teaching Physical Education in the Infant School*. London: Routledge.

Further Reading

BAF National Coaches (1996) *Coaching Young Athletes*. Birmingham: British Athletics Federation.

Bunker, D., Hardy, C., Smith , B. and Almond, L. (1998) *Primary Physical Education – Implementing the National Curriculum*. Cambridge: Cambridge University Press.

Fry, B. (1995) 'Athletics at Key Stage 2'. In PEA, NDTA and BAALPE *Teaching Physical Education at Key Stages One and Two*. London: PEA UK.

Murrie, D. (1997/8) 'Athletic Activities in the Primary School' (in three parts). *Primary PE Focus*, Summer and Autumn 1997, Summer 1998.

CHAPTER 11

References

Arts Council of Great Britain (1993) *Dance in Schools*. London: Author.

NDTA, NATFHE, SCODHE, CDET (1990) *Dance in the School Curriculum*. London: Authors.

Smith, J. (1976) *Dance Composition*. Wakefield: Lepus Books.

CHAPTER 12
References
Alexander-Hall, J. (1986) 'A Case for the Retention of Team Games in the Secondary Physical Education Curriculum'. *British Journal of Physical Education*, **17** (5), 163–4.

Allison, S. and Thorpe, R. (1997) 'A Comparison of the Effectiveness of Two Approaches to Teaching Games Within Physical Education: A Skills Approach Versus a Games for Understanding Approach'. *British Journal of Physical Education*, **28** (3), 9–13.

Arnold, P. (1988) *Education, Movement and the Curriculum*. London: Falmer.

Bailey, R. P. (1999) 'Physical Education: Infans Ludens'. In J. Riley and R. Prentice (eds) *The Primary Curriculum 7–11*. London: Paul Chapman.

Bunker, D. and Thorpe, R. (1982) 'A Model for the Teaching of Games in Secondary Schools'. *Bulletin of Physical Education*, **18** (1), 56–8.

Bunker, D., Hardy, C., Smith, B. and Almond, L. (1998) *Primary Physical Education: Implementing the National Curriculum*. Cambridge: Cambridge University Press.

Clay, G. (1997) 'Standards in Primary Physical Education: OFSTED 1995–6'. *Primary PE Focus,* Autumn, 4–6.

Cooper, A. (1990) 'Development of Games Skills in the Primary School: Part One'. *Primary PE Focus,* Summer, 2–3.

Cooper, A. (1993) *The Development of Games and Athletic Skills*. Hemel Hempstead: Simon & Schuster.

Cornwall, J. (1999) 'Pressure, Stress and Children's Behaviour at School'. In T. David (ed.) *Young Children Learning*. London: Paul Chapman.

DFE (1995) *Key Stages 1 and 2 of the National Curriculum*. London: HMSO.

DNH (1995) *Sport: Raising the Game*. London: HMSO.

Graham, G. (1992) *Teaching Children Physical Education – Becoming a Master Teacher*. Champaign, IL: Human Kinetics.

Masters, R. S. W. (1992) *Implicit Knowledge, Stress and Skill Failure*. Ph.D. Thesis, University of York.

Penney, D. (1995) 'A Question of Sport'. *On Track*, Autumn, 4–7.

Penney, D. and Evans, J. (1994) 'It's Just Not (and Not Just) Cricket'. *British Journal of Physical Education*, **25** (3), 9–12.

Read, B. and Edwards, P. (1992) *Teaching Children to Play Games 5 to 11: A Resource for Primary Teachers*. Leeds: NCF/BCPE/Sports Council.

Rink, J. (1993) *Teaching Physical Education for Learning*. St Louis, MI: Mosby.

Roberts, G. and Treasure, D. (1993) 'The Importance of the Study of Children in Sport: An Overview'. In M. Lee *Coaching Children in Sport*. London: E. & F. N. Spon.

Schmidt, R. A. (1988) *Motor Control and Learning: A Behavioural Emphasis*. Champaign, IL: Human Kinetics.

Sleap, M. (1984) *Mini Sport (Second Edition)*. London: Heinemann.

Thorpe, R. (1990) 'New Directions in Games Teaching'. In N. Armstrong (ed.) *New Directions on Physical Education: Volume One*. Champaign, IL: Human Kinetics.

Whitehead, J. (1993) 'Why Children Choose to do Sport'. In M. Lee *Coaching Children in Sport*. London: E. & F. N. Spon.

Wuest, D. and Bucher, C. (1995) *Foundations of Physical Education in Sport*. St Louis, MI: Mosby.

Further Reading
Bunker, D., Hardy, C., Smith, B. and Almond, L. (1998) *Primary Physical Education: Implementing the National Curriculum*. Cambridge: Cambridge University Press.

Cooper, A. (1993) *The Development of Games and Athletic Skills*. Hemel Hempstead: Simon & Schuster.

Read, B. and Edwards, P. (1992) *Teaching Children to Play Games 5 to 11: A Resource for Primary Teachers*. Leeds: NCF/BCPE/Sports Council.

CHAPTER 13
References
BAALPE (1995) *Safe Practice in Physical Education*. Exmouth: BAALPE.
BAALPE (1999) *Safe Practice in Physical Education – Millennium Edition*. Exmouth: BAALPE.
Benn, T. and Benn, B. (1992) *Primary Gymnastics – A Multi-Activities Approach*. Cambridge: Cambridge University Press.
DES (1991) *Physical Education for Ages 5 to 16: Proposals of the Secretary of State for Education and Science and the Secretary of State for Wales. (The Final Report of the NCPE Working Group)*. London: Department of Education and Science.
DNH (1995) *Sport: Raising the Game*. London: Department of National Heritage.
Long, B. (1982) *Educational Gymnastics – Step by Step*. London: Edward Arnold.
Sabin, V. (1990) *Primary School Gymnastics – A Teaching Manual, Volume 1*. Northampton: Val Sabin Publications.

Further Reading
BAALPE (1999) *Safety Practice in Physical Education – Millennium Edition*. Exmouth: BAALPE.
Benn, T. and Benn, B. (1992) *Primary Gymnastics – A Multi-Activities Approach*. Cambridge: Cambridge University Press.
DES (1995) *Physical Education in the National Curriculum*. London: Department of Education and Science.
Hampshire County Council (1984) *The Role of the PE Consultant*. Winchester: Hampshire County Council.
Hampshire County Council (1989) *PE in the Primary Years*. Winchester: Hampshire County Council.
Long, B. (1982) *Educational Gymnastics – Step by Step*. London: Edward Arnold.

CHAPTER 14
References
Almond, L. and Harris, J. (1998) 'Interventions to Promote Health-related Physical Education'. In HEA (ed.) *Young and Active? Young People and Health-enhancing Physical Activity – Evidence and Implications*. London: Health Education Authority.
Armstrong, N. and Welsman, J. (1997) *Young People and Physical Activity*. Oxford: Oxford University Press.
Harris, J. (1998) *Health-Related Exercise Guidance Material (Draft)*. Leicestershire: Loughborough University.
Harris, J. and Cale, L. (1997) 'How Healthy is School PE? A Review of the Effectiveness of Health-related PE Programmes in Schools'. *Health Education Journal*, **56** (1), 84–104.
Harris, J. and Elbourn, J. (1997) *Teaching Health-Related Exercise at Key Stages 1 and 2*. Champaign, IL: Human Kinetics.
HEA (1997) *Young People and Physical Activity: A Literature Review*. London: Health Education Authority.
HEA (1998) *Young and Active? Policy Framework for Young People and Health-enhancing Physical Activity*. London: Health Education Authority.

Further Reading
Harris, J. (forthcoming) *Health Related Exercise Guidance Material*. Loughborough: Department of Physical Education, Sports Science and Recreation Management, Loughborough University.
Harris, J. and Elbourn, J. (1992) *Warming Up and Cooling Down*. Loughborough: Department of Physical Education, Sports Science and Recreation Management, Loughborough University.
Harris, J. and Elbourn, J. (1997) *Teaching Health-related Exercise at Key Stages 1 and 2*. Champaign, IL: Human Kinetics.

CHAPTER 15
Reference
Dudley (n.d.) *Urban Education*. Dudley: Dudley Metropolitan Borough, Physical Education Team.

Further Reading
Martin, B. (1996) *Hunting the Griz*. Nottingham: Davies.
Martin, B. (1997) *Finding the Griz*. Nottingham: Davies.
QCA (1998) *Outdoor and Adventurous Activities in Physical Education at Key Stage 2. Guidance for Teachers*. London: Qualifications and Curriculum Authority.

CHAPTER 16
References
Barter, T. J. and Firth, C. (1994) 'The National Curriculum – Swimming'. *British Journal of Physical Education*, **25** (3), 17–20.
Bass, D. and Hardy, C. A. (1996a) 'Concerns for Swimming in Primary Schools'. *Swimming Times*, **LXXIII** (11), 27–30.
Bass, D. and Hardy, C. A. (1996b) 'Concerns for Swimming in Primary Schools'. *Swimming Times*, **LXXIII** (12), 27–28.
CCPR and NAHT (1992) *National Survey of Physical Education in Primary Schools – A Sporting Chance?* London: Central Council of Physical Recreation.
Cossey, E. (1988) Written Statement on School Swimming, 1912–1916.
Cossey, H. (1989) Written Statement on School Swimming, 1919–1923.
Department for Education (DFE) (1995) *Physical Education in the National Curriculum*. London: HMSO.
Hardy, C. A. (1989) *Let's Go Swimming*. London: Hutchinson.
Hardy, C. A. (1991a) 'Swimming in Schools – Past and Present. Part I: The Fight for Recognition'. *Swimming Times*, **LXVIII** (3), 18–20.
Hardy, C. A. (1991b) 'Swimming in Schools – Past and Present. Part II: The Contemporary Scene'. *Swimming Times*, **LXVIII** (4), 17–20, 31.
Langley, J. D. and Silva, P. A. (1986) 'Swimming Experiences and Abilities of Nine Year Olds'. *British Journal of Sports Medicine*, **20** (1), 39–41.
Langley, J. D., Silva, P. A. and Williams, S. A. (1981) 'Swimming Experiences and Abilities of Seven Year Olds. A Report from the Dunedin Multidisciplinary Child Development Study'. *New Zealand Journal of Health, Physical Education and Recreation*, **14** (2), 45–6.
Luke, I. T. (1998) *An Examination of Pupils' Metacognitive Ability in Physical Education*. Unpublished doctoral thesis, Loughborough University.
Luke, I. T. and Hardy, C. A. (1996) 'Differentiation: A Consideration of Pupils' Learning Preferences in Physical Education Lessons'. *The Bulletin of Physical Education*, **32** (2), 36–44.
QCA (1999) *QCA's Work in Progress to Develop the School Curriculum. Materials for Conferences, Seminars and Meetings, Booklet A*. London: Qualifications and Curriculum Authority.

Further Reading
Bunker, D., Hardy, C. A., Smith, B. and Almond, L. (1994) *Primary Physical Education. Implementing the National Curriculum*. Cambridge: Cambridge University Press.
Langendorfer, S. J. and Bruya, L. D. (1995) *Aquatic Readiness, Developing Water Competence in Young Children*. Champaign, IL: Human Kinetics.

Index